Divine
Signatures

Divine
Signatures

The Confirming
Hand of God

Gerald N. Lund

DESERET
BOOK

Library of Congress Cataloging-in-Publication Data
Lund, Gerald N.
    Divine signatures : the confirming hand of God / Gerald N. Lund.
    p. cm.
    Includes bibliographical references and index.
    Summary: Explanation of the differences between faith and testimony, and introduction of the idea of a "divine signature," blessings or answers given by God in dramatic, unusual, or precisely timed ways that make the answer seem "signed" by God.
    ISBN 978-1-60641-927-4 (hardbound : alk. paper)
    1. Faith. 2. God (Christianity)—Knowableness. 3. Witness bearing (Christianity) 4. The Church of Jesus Christ of Latter-day Saints—Doctrines. I. Title.
    BT771.3.L855 2010
    248'.5—dc22   2010037972

Printed in the United States of America
Publishers Printing, Salt Lake City, Utah

10   9   8   7   6   5   4   3   2   1

To Lynn

My companion of forty-seven years; my partner
in navigating through the reefs and shoals of mortal life;
who frequently receives quiet inspiration and promptings
that bless me and our family; whose faith and testimony have
created divine signatures of her own; and who has greatly
strengthened my faith and deepened my testimony.
My debt to you is an eternal one, as is our relationship.

Thank you.

Contents

Preface

This book is not meant to be a doctrinal exposition. It is more an exploration of how to take a simple gospel principle and actually make it work in our lives.

Much of this book contains my own personal reflections. I suppose there is something in us as we grow older that wants to share with others the lessons we have learned. To do that, I will include some of my own experiences in learning about God. In a way, I hesitate to do so, but these were defining experiences for me because of what they taught me about my Heavenly Father. My hope is that they will clarify the principles I am trying to teach.

I will also share numerous stories that I have either read or heard from individuals, which also became defining experiences for them. I do so to show that such moments are not rare experiences, that they happened to people who are very much like anyone else. They also provide other powerful illustrations of how God helps strengthen our faith and deepen our testimony.

All of the stories in the book are true. They are real-life stories from everyday people. Some come from the lives of early Saints in the Church. Others come from Saints who are alive today. Some of these stories have occurred even as I have been writing this book. I did not get them secondhand. With the exception of those accounts from published sources, I heard them directly from the individuals who experienced them. Wherever possible, I have presented them in their own words.

Some of the experiences I share in this book happened many years ago. It is possible that the person involved has left the Church or turned away from God, though in most cases I know that this is not the case. But if it happens to be so, it in no way lessens the reality of the experience that individual had, nor the feelings that those experiences generated at the time.

It is my deepest hope that these real experiences from the lives of real people will help you either find that testimony you seek, or strengthen and deepen it even more.

This then is what this book is about. It is about strengthening faith and deepening testimony.

We are at a point where it is critical to our eternal salvation that we do so.

A Note from the Author

Here are just a few housekeeping items that may be helpful to the reader.

The inclusion of so many stories and examples in the book necessitated a slightly unusual format. Sometimes a story or example is included within one of the chapters where it illustrates or supports a point of the book. Many, however, are additional examples not tied directly to any particular text. I have therefore included them in additional sections between chapters.

I frequently refer to God throughout the book. I also use the more specific names and titles such as "the Lord," "Heavenly Father," "Jesus" or "Jesus Christ," "the Savior," "the Redeemer," "His Beloved Son," and so on. There are some cases where the use of such titles refers to the individual member of the Godhead. However, in most cases, when I refer to God, what I mean is the Father *and* the Son, with the accompanying influence of the Holy Spirit. It becomes ponderous to specify that plurality again and again, so I do not. But it is important to remember that when we speak of either the Father or the Son, what we say of one almost always applies equally well to the other. They act as one. They are one.

On a more mundane matter: I often emphasize key words or phrases in scriptural passages or quotations with italics. Rather than tediously indicating each time that the emphasis is mine, I have only specified when the emphasis was in the original.

Acknowledgments

While I may be the writer of this book, it will soon be clear that there were many other contributors. I wish to acknowledge my deep appreciation for their part in what you are about to read. In many cases, I am able to give credit by name to the individual whose story I am telling, and I am very pleased to do so. But that isn't always the case. Some of these stories I heard from people who didn't give me their name. Some introduced themselves to me, but at the time, I had no reason to think I would someday want to share their stories, and so I did not write down their names, and thus cannot give them the credit they deserve. But I thank all of the individuals, past and present, whose experiences will, I hope, help others find the strength they need to cope in a perilous world.

In addition, I would also like to acknowledge my debt to my family. Our children are now all grown and have busy lives of their own. I asked them if they would be willing to review the manuscript before I put it into its final form. Some of my children were in the midst of changing occupations or other demanding circumstances and could not, but several of my children did read the entire manuscript in first draft form. The fact that there are numerous differences between the first draft of the manuscript and this finished book is due in part to their insights and their honesty in pointing out places they felt could be improved. A reader of that caliber is a treasure for an author, and I am delighted that I have several of them in my family.

My wife, Lynn, is always my first reader, and my most trusted critic. She is forthright in both her praise and her concerns. I wouldn't have it any other way. Over the years her influence on my writing has been pervasive and profound. In this book, some of the stories are hers, for she has had her own divine signatures in her life.

I appreciate my working relationship with Deseret Book and their staff. So many people contribute to the final product that goes onto the shelves—editing, design, marketing, publishing, and so on. I appreciate their professional competence and their desire to truly fulfill their motto: "Bringing Values Home—Since 1866." There are two individuals at Deseret Book who I must thank by name. My relationship with Cory Maxwell and Jana Erickson goes back nearly twenty years now to the time when they both worked at Bookcraft. Their support is unflagging, our business association has always been professional, and our friendship is both warm and treasured. Thanks to you both.

Introduction

"Heavenly Father, Are You Really There?"

I love the Primary songs of the Church. And I especially love "A Child's Prayer."

Heavenly Father, are you really there?
And do you hear and answer ev'ry child's prayer?
Some say that heaven is far away,
But I feel it close around me as I pray.[1]

The first two lines ask questions that I think virtually every person asks sooner or later in life. Even the Prophet Joseph at one time cried out in utter anguish, "O God, where art thou?" (D&C 121:1).

I think there may be more active, committed Latter-day Saints than we might suppose who sometimes ask themselves those very same questions. And when it comes to the last two lines of the Primary song, there are probably Saints who quietly think, "I am one of those who feels that heaven is far away. When I pray, I do not feel that God is close to me."

The curious thing is that the people I'm talking about are good people. They serve faithfully in the Church. They aren't doubters or skeptics, nor are they sinful and rebellious. It's just that life grinds down on them for so long that they begin to wonder where God is, or what He is doing, and why.

Usually, it is not a question about whether or not God exists. They firmly believe that He does. It's just that something has happened in their lives that makes them feel like the ground has shifted beneath their feet. After years of striving to live the gospel, they begin to grow weary. As one priesthood leader said to me, "I'm still hanging in there, but the joy is gone."

Then the questions become more personalized. It's not just, "Heavenly Father, are you really there?" It's "Are you really there *for me?* Do you really know *me—my* needs, *my* challenges, *my* sorrows, *my* loneliness? When I'm trying so hard, why aren't you doing more to help me?" Such earnest, yearning questions often bring other questions, questions that are riddled with guilt: "What is wrong with me? Why don't I feel about God the same way that others say they feel about Him? Or even as I used to feel? What have I done that makes God seem so far away?"

Tribulation—A Great Dividing Point

Life comes at us with great intensity at times, and such times try the soul—the tragic loss of a spouse or parent; losing one's employment and, in quick succession, one's home, car, and other possessions; a natural disaster that not only wipes out everything we own, but takes loved ones as well; a bitter divorce and child custody battle; the doctor's sobering announcement that what you thought might be stomach ulcers is terminal cancer.

President Harold B. Lee called these things, "the *inevitable* tragedies of life."[2] We don't like the sound of the word *inevitable,* but it is an accurate term. Mortal life is filled with challenges, trials, setbacks, disappointments, misfortune, tragedy, disaster, loss, pain, suffering, and sorrow. This is part of our growth experience, for as God said of our coming to earth, "We will prove them herewith, to see if they will do all things whatsoever the Lord their God shall command them" (Abraham 3:25). Unfortunately, metal is refined best in the "furnace of affliction" (Isaiah 48:10).

Elder Neal A. Maxwell has said:

> God, as a loving Father, will stretch our souls at times. The soul is like a violin string: it makes music only when it is stretched. . . . God will tutor us by trying us *because* He loves us, not because of indifference![3]

President James E. Faust gave this counsel at a time when he was going through his own challenges with his personal health:

> We encounter many bumps, bends, and forks in the road of life that leads to the eternities. There is so much teaching and correction as we travel on that road. . . .
>
> President Brigham Young offered the profound insight that at least some of our suffering has a purpose when he said: "All intelligent beings who are crowned with crowns of glory, immortality, and eternal lives must pass through every ordeal appointed for intelligent beings to pass through, to gain their glory and exaltation. . . . Every trial and experience you have passed through is necessary for your salvation."[4]

The problem is, these personal crises not only drain us physically, emotionally, and spiritually, but they can also create a crisis of faith. The burdens weigh so heavily on us that we grow weary of trying to live with them. It's like we lose our spiritual bearings. In the Old Testament the Lord says, "I have heard thy prayer, I have seen thy tears: behold, I will heal thee" (2 Kings 20:5). But we're not sure anymore that He does see our tears. We're no longer certain that He is hearing our prayers. And we certainly don't feel like we are healed. The answers that once felt so right to us are no longer satisfying. Questions swirl up in our minds like scraps of paper in a windstorm.

Why is it that one individual can understand the purposes behind this testing process and sometimes come through their trials even stronger than before? And why does someone else, perhaps facing lesser trials, falter under the pressure? What makes the difference? Some accept tribulation with equanimity and calm acceptance, while others grow angry, bitter, or disillusioned.

I don't find what I call the "simple answers" to those questions very satisfactory. We sometimes hear people speak of someone who turns away from the Lord and say, "Oh, he just lost his testimony." Or "They just weren't strong enough." Or "She didn't have enough faith." Or "They just didn't have sufficient moral courage to endure."

All of those may be true, of course, but they merely lead to other questions: Why do some people lose their testimonies while others don't? Why is one person's faith weak and another's strong? Where does the courage to endure come from? Is it a gift from God? If so, why didn't He give me more of it?

Jesus closed the Sermon on the Mount with this parable:

> Whosoever heareth these sayings of mine, and doeth them, I will liken him unto a wise man, which built his house upon a rock: And the rain descended, and the floods came, and the winds blew, and beat upon that house; and it fell not: *for it was founded upon a rock.* (Matthew 7:24–25)

I firmly believe that. But what is that rock? What provides the kind of foundation that can help us weather any storm life hurls at us? How do we strengthen our faith and deepen our testimony to the point that we can endure whatever life holds in store for us and come out stronger than before?

That is the central question this book seeks to answer.

"Perilous Times Shall Come"

Trials and difficulties are the common lot of mankind. They have been from the day Adam and Eve were driven from the Garden of Eden and will be until the beginning of the great Millennium. But our day has additional challenges.

The Apostle Paul said, "This know also, that in the last days *perilous times* shall come" (2 Timothy 3:1). And in 1831, two millennia later, the Lord told the Prophet Joseph Smith that the time was "nigh at hand, when *peace shall be taken from the earth,* and *the devil shall have power over his own dominion*" (D&C 1:35).

Every day we see or hear examples of just how perilous our day is—physically, socially, emotionally, morally, financially, politically, and spiritually. If these things were just images and sound bites coming at us through the media, it would be depressing enough. But they have a personal and often devastating impact on individuals and families somewhere, and very often on us.

Living in our day only compounds the likelihood that our faith will be challenged, our strength will be tested, and our testimonies will be tried. So again I ask:

How do we strengthen our faith and deepen our testimony to the point that we can endure whatever life holds in store for us and come out stronger than before?

The Bedrock of Testimony

When we speak of having a testimony, sometimes we make it sound as if it is something you have or you don't have. It may be weak or it may be strong, but we speak as though it's either there or it's not. I don't believe it is that simple.

A testimony is a complex thing with many facets. We can be strong in one area but weaker in another. We can have a testimony that Joseph Smith was a prophet but struggle a little with the importance of tithing. We can have varying degrees of testimony about the Book of Mormon, modern revelation, temple work, priesthood power, and dozens of other things. So saying that a person does or does not have a testimony may not be that helpful in trying to discover why they react the way they do to the challenges of life.

Over the years—and particularly in the past ten years—I have come to realize more and more that there is one particular aspect of the gospel that seems to make this critical difference in individuals. I have listened carefully as people talked about those times when they found great strength to endure the challenges they faced. I have listened carefully to others who bitterly or sadly described why they turned away from the Lord. Again and again I noticed that at the core of their experiences were their feelings and expressions about God—how they felt about Him, what He had or had not done for them, how they perceived Him, and their relationship to Him.

After much thought, I finally tried to put on paper what I had learned.

To strengthen our faith and deepen our testimony to the point that we can successfully endure to the end, we must know for ourselves with a surety that:

- God is our Heavenly Father, and we are His literal children.
- He and His Beloved Son want us to be happy and eventually come to a fulness of joy.

- They know us intimately and love us infinitely.
- They want to bless us, and they actually take great joy in doing so.

I am deeply convinced that this is the bedrock of which Christ spoke. And if we build our house on this rock, we can withstand the rains, the storms, and the floods that may come our way. With this testimony, we will endure. Without it, we are vulnerable.

I have learned an additional truth, and this, too, will be a primary focus of the book:

If we are striving to live our lives in harmony with these concepts, then Heavenly Father and His Beloved Son, will actually help us in the strengthening and deepening process.

So, is it possible to strengthen our faith and deepen our testimony to the point that we can endure whatever life holds in store for us and come out stronger than before?

Yes, it is.

Notes

1. Janice Kapp Perry, "A Child's Prayer," in *Children's Songbook* (Salt Lake City: The Church of Jesus Christ of Latter-day Saints, 1989), 12. Used by permission.

2. Harold B. Lee, *The Teachings of Harold B. Lee,* edited by Clyde J. Williams (Salt Lake City: Bookcraft, 1996), 190.

3. Neal A. Maxwell, *All These Things Shall Give Thee Experience* (Salt Lake City: Deseret Book, 1979), 28.

4. James E. Faust, "Where Do I Make My Stand?" *Ensign,* November 2004, 21.

And this is life eternal, that they might know thee the only true God, and Jesus Christ, whom thou has sent.

JOHN 17:3

CHAPTER ONE

The Relationship of Faith to Our Knowledge of God

Three Things Required in Order to Have Faith

In the introduction I stated that if we are to endure successfully to the end in these troubled and perilous times, we must strengthen our faith and deepen our testimony. Those two concepts—faith and testimony—are so intertwined with each other that we cannot speak of one without at least implying the other. It is not possible to have a deep and abiding testimony without strong and lasting faith. Therefore, let us begin our quest by talking about faith.

In a series of lectures given in the School of the Prophets in Kirtland, Ohio, Joseph Smith outlined some requirements for developing strong faith.* After addressing what faith is, and the object upon which it rests (viz., God), Joseph then outlined three requirements necessary for individuals to have true faith:

---

* Joseph Smith was "substantially involved" in both the preparation and publication of "Lectures on Faith" (see *Encyclopedia of Mormonism,* s.v. "Lectures on Faith"). For simplicity's sake, I have credited Joseph Smith for them, though he may not have actually written all of them.

Let us here observe, that three things are necessary in order that any rational and intelligent being may exercise faith in God unto life and salvation.

First, the idea that he actually exists.

Secondly, a *correct* idea of his character, perfections, and attributes.

Thirdly, an actual knowledge that the course of life which he is pursuing is according to his will. For without an acquaintance with these three important facts, the faith of every rational being must be imperfect and unproductive.[1]

All three requirements involve some form of knowledge about God, and note the progressive nature of that knowledge. We move from an idea, to a correct idea, then to actual knowledge. Clearly, our faith is dependent on a knowledge of God, especially of His character and attributes. Let me say that again: *Our faith is dependent upon our knowledge of God.* If that is true, then we can also say: *Our testimony also rests on our knowledge of God.*

I think it would be safe to say that most members of the Church have already met the first requirement. Even young children have the idea that there is a God.

The Character, Attributes, and Perfections of God

In my younger years, I used to say that I thought the second requirement—having a correct idea of God's character, perfections, and attributes—was also held by most members of the Church. And in a way, that's true. They know that God is loving, kind, all-powerful, all-knowing, and so on. But over the years, I have come to realize why the word "correct" was emphasized in that second requirement. I also have come to better understand why Joseph added the word "perfections" alongside God's attributes and character.

I have come to know that the second requirement can be a major stumbling block, even for those who believe in God as our loving Heavenly Father. It seems oddly contradictory, but there are numerous examples where individuals who believe in God still question the reality of His character and attributes. For example, a person who is deep in sin may believe that God is forgiving and long-suffering, but they can't believe that this attribute would be extended to them. They feel that they have put themselves beyond the reach of God and that there is no hope for them.

Here is another example. Many years ago, a single sister in her mid-thirties was in my office. From the time she was a little girl all she had dreamed about was being a wife and mother. But she was a woman who was large in structure and quite tall. She thought of herself as "homely." She was very intelligent and had a pleasing way with people, but men were not attracted to her. She had not had a date in many years. Now at thirty-five, the possibility that she might never marry and have children of her own left her desolate. Through her tears, she suddenly burst out, "Brother Lund, couldn't God have made me beautiful like other women? And if so, why didn't He?"

Only later did it occur to me that in her pain, she was questioning two of God's attributes. Did He have the power to have put her in a beautiful body? And if His love was perfect, why hadn't He done so?

Here is another example of how trusting in God's attributes can be a source of strength in difficult times. Many years ago, a good friend of our family learned that she was pregnant. This had not been expected and she had been taking a medication that had serious side effects in unborn children. When she told her doctor that she was with child, he immediately recommended an abortion. "If the baby lives at all," he said, "it will be severely handicapped and deformed." She told him that she didn't want an abortion, that she believed it was wrong. He was quite curt with her and told her that, in this case, it was a medical necessity, leaving her no choice.

Deeply troubled, she and her husband fasted and prayed about it. She felt strongly that she was to keep the child. As she explained this experience to my wife and me, she made this remarkable statement: "I believe that God can give us a miracle and let this baby be born healthy and normal. *But,* if He chooses not to do that, I am prepared to accept whatever happens, because I know that Heavenly Father will not ask anything of me that is not for my ultimate good and for the good of my child."

What a remarkable affirmation of her understanding of God's nature. When she announced her decision to the doctor, he was quite disgusted. But about seven months later, she gave birth to a perfectly healthy, normal, and delightful little baby.

Here was a woman of faith, and that faith had come from her understanding and testimony of God's character and attributes.

An Actual Knowledge

The third requirement for faith, according to the Prophet, is that a person have "an actual knowledge that the course of life which he [or she] is pursuing is according to his will." Now that requirement threw me when I first read it. "No," I thought, "that's backward. First you develop faith, and then you put your life in harmony with God's will." But Joseph says true faith depends on our knowing that our life is pleasing to God.

As I pondered that, I remembered an experience my wife and I had when we were first married. I was at BYU doing undergraduate work, and our first child—a little girl—was nine months old. I had to work full time to support myself in college. I was fortunate enough to be hired as a psychiatric attendant at the Utah Mental Hospital. I worked afternoon or evening shifts on a two-week rotating basis for the entire time I was in school.

At the hospital, I was assigned to the maximum-security ward. This was the ward where anyone with a criminal record or a history of violence was placed. We saw the dregs of society: burglars, armed robbers, gang members, rapists, murderers, a cop killer, and about every other kind of criminal you can name.

During those first years of our marriage, my assignment at the hospital, together with working full time, going to school full time, and waking up with the baby when I was home, left me pretty jaded. I was physically, emotionally, and spiritually drained.

I had let my spiritual nourishment slide. I couldn't always make it to Church because of my work schedule. I stopped reading the scriptures entirely, and I prayed only occasionally. I was in a spiritual low.

One night my wife and I had been in bed only a short time when we heard a noise from the other bedroom. Our little girl was crying. When we went in, we found her gasping for breath between her wailing cries. She had a serious case of the croup. She was our first child, and seeing her in such difficulty was terrifying to us. Her whole body would stiffen as she tried to draw in air, and she made a terrible rasping sound I shall never forget.

Lynn immediately called the doctor. The moment she mentioned croup, he stopped her. "Tell your husband to take her into the bathroom," he said. "Have him draw the shower curtain, then turn on the hot water full blast. Let the steam fill the room. This will help her to breathe more easily."

I did so. As I sat in the bathroom, looking down into the face of this precious child, agonizing as I watched her struggle for every breath, a thought came to me: "You're an elder in the Church. Why don't you give her a blessing?" I dropped my head and looked away. The shame was as thick as the steam, for I knew I wasn't worthy to bless her at that time. It was not that I was guilty of some serious sin, it was just that I wasn't doing the things I knew the Lord expected of me.

Now think about that for a moment. Did I question God's power and ability to heal her, or at least relieve her of her struggle? Not in any way. My problem was not with God. My problem was *me*. I knew at that moment that my life was not pleasing to Him. That's what was weakening my faith. Now I understand the third requirement for faith. For a man to have faith he must have an actual knowledge that his life is pleasing to God.

As we begin our search for answers on developing faith and deepening testimony, let us keep this idea in the forefront of our thoughts.

"To Know God Is Life Eternal"

One of the most frequently quoted scriptures in the Church is John 17:3: "And this is life eternal, that they might know thee the only true God, and Jesus Christ, whom thou has sent."

I can remember reading that one day as a young seminary teacher and thinking, "That's all? Could it really be that simple? I believe in God and Jesus. I know about them. So have I now earned eternal life?" As comforting as the idea was, I was never quite comfortable with it. Surely there had to be more to it than that.

As the years passed, I thought about that concept many times, and I began to sense that "to know God" meant much more than to know *of,* or to know *about* God. Going to the temple expanded my understanding considerably.

President Spencer W. Kimball said this about the ordinance of the endowment:

> One of the ordinances performed in the temple is that
> of the endowment, which comprises a course of instruction

relating to *the eternal journey of a man and woman* from the pre-earthly existence through the earthly experience and on to the exaltation each may attain.[2]

As we are taught in the Doctrine and Covenants, the culmination of that journey will be when we "shall pass by the angels, and the gods, which are set there, to [our] exaltation and glory in all things" (D&C 132:19) and enter God's presence. That gives a whole new and deeper meaning to the idea of "knowing God," doesn't it?

But there is another level of knowledge of God. We believe that exaltation is not just to live with God, but to become *like* Him. God has promised the faithful that they shall receive all that the Father has (see D&C 84:38) and become gods. To become like God will be to know Him as we can know Him in no other way. Ultimately then, to know God is indeed life eternal.

To know God on all of these different levels is the key to our happiness and will eventually lead us to a fulness of joy. But, according to Joseph Smith, it begins with faith, and faith depends on three things: The idea that God exists. A *correct* idea of His character, attributes, and perfections. And the actual knowledge that our life is pleasing to God.

Simply put, we must come to know God if we wish to develop the faith and testimony necessary to anchor us onto the bedrock. Otherwise, our foundation is in danger of collapsing when the storms of life descend. Remember, when we build our house upon the sand, everything is fine until the storms come.

Notes

1. Joseph Smith, *Lectures on Faith* (Salt Lake City: Deseret Book, 1985), 38; emphasis in original.

2. Spencer W. Kimball, *The Teachings of Spencer W. Kimball,* edited by Edward L. Kimball (Salt Lake City: Deseret Book, 1982), 535.

*T*hou art angry, O Lord, with this people, because
they will not understand thy mercies which thou
hast bestowed upon them because of thy Son.

ALMA 33:16

CHAPTER TWO

Tender Mercies and Divine Signatures

Tender Mercies

In the Church, we often speak of the tender mercies of the Lord. Elder David A. Bednar, described them in this manner:

> I testify that the tender mercies of the Lord are real and that they do not occur randomly or merely by coincidence. Often, the Lord's timing of his tender mercies helps us to both discern and acknowledge them. . . . The Lord's tender mercies are the very personal and individualized blessings, strength, protection, assurances, guidance, loving-kindnesses, consolation, support, and spiritual gifts which we receive from and because of and through the Lord Jesus Christ. . . . Faithfulness, obedience, and humility invite tender mercies into our lives, and it is often the Lord's timing that enables us to recognize and treasure these important blessings. . . . I testify that the tender mercies of the Lord are available to all of us and that the Redeemer of Israel is eager to bestow such gifts upon us. . . . Each of us can have eyes to see clearly and

ears to hear distinctly the tender mercies of the Lord as they strengthen and assist us in these latter days.[1]

Elder Bednar makes the following points about the tender mercies of God:

- They are real.
- They do not occur randomly or by coincidence.
- Their timing helps us discern them.
- They are very personal and individualized blessings, which can come in the form of strength, protection, assurance, guidance, loving kindness, consolation, support, and spiritual gifts.
- Faithfulness, obedience, and humility bring tender mercies, but they are available to all.
- The Redeemer is *eager* to bestow them upon us.
- The Lord's tender mercies strengthen and assist us in these latter days.

Divine Signatures

Did you notice that Elder Bednar repeats the same point twice? He says that the Lord's *timing* of His tender mercies can help us discern them, acknowledge them, and treasure them. This is a very significant observation. I would add one other aspect. Sometimes, in addition to the timing, the blessings come with such a unique combination of circumstances that it becomes very clear they are from the Lord.

Here is a remarkable example of what I mean. The following story was shared with me by Elder Robert R. Steuer, one of my colleagues in the Second Quorum of the Seventy.

Some years ago, he served as mission president in São Paulo, Brazil. It was his practice with newly arriving missionaries to give them real "missionary experiences" on their very first day as full-time proselyting missionaries. To do this, after their orientation and a dinner at the mission home, they would be sent out that evening with their assigned companions. The seasoned missionary would take the new missionaries out either tracting, street contacting, or giving discussions.

In one of the groups of new missionaries, there was a Brazilian elder who came from the far north of Brazil. It took this missionary about three days travel by bus just to reach the MTC in São Paulo for his initial training. On that first evening, after having a good meal, President Steuer announced that the new missionaries would then go out and do missionary work. This new missionary's companion decided they would go tracting, a frightening experience for this shy new elder. The senior companion said he would take the first door and told his companion to watch closely how it was done as the second door would be his.

The young elder protested, saying he was too frightened, but his companion proceeded to the first door. When this young elder knocked on the second door, the senior companion stepped back and indicated for him to proceed. He shrank back. When the door opened, to the young elder's utter astonishment, the person standing there was his older sister. She had run away from home three or four years earlier. The family had not heard from her since and had no idea where she was, or even if she was still alive. One can imagine the sweetness of that reunion and the tears of joy that were shed that night.

As he concluded this story, Elder Steuer said two things that deeply impressed me and made the point I'm trying to make. He said, "Not only was his sister one of the first nonmembers he contacted in the mission field, but she became his first convert baptism as well." Then he added, "As you think about that, Elder Lund, remember, at that time there were between thirteen and fourteen million people in São Paulo!"

When things like this happen, the world tends to use words like coincidence or good fortune to explain them. "It was an incredible coincidence," they say. "It was really fortunate how everything came together." As a popular saying goes, "Coincidence is God's way of remaining anonymous." But in my experience, it is just the opposite. What we call coincidence is God's way of letting Himself be known. A metaphor used by another author is a better reflection of how I see it: "Coincidence is the word we use when we can't see the levers and the pulleys."[2]

The odds of that missionary finding his sister among fourteen million people during the entire two years of his mission would be astronomical. Yet it happened on his very first night in the mission. Here was not only a stunning example of the Lord's tender mercies, but the timing and the combination of circumstances that brought it about were also amazing. It was almost as though the Lord was signing His name to the event so they would know it was unmistakably His.

There it was. There was the metaphor that captured the essence of what I was feeling about these kinds of stories. They were like a *divine signature,* an autograph from heaven.

Divine Signatures

God loves His children and it pleases Him to bless them, especially when they are striving to do His will. These blessings, also called "tender mercies," come in many different forms and in many different ways.

Sometimes, the Lord sends His blessings in such a highly unusual, dramatic, or precisely timed manner, that it might be likened to a "divine signature." It is as though the Lord "signs" the blessing personally so that we will know with certainty that it comes from Him.

In doing so, God not only gives us the blessing, but at the same time, He also strengthens our faith and deepens our testimony of Him.

A Testimony to Withstand the Storms

While serving as a General Authority, I presided at a stake conference in a nearby western state. I had asked the stake president to invite two sisters in the stake to share their testimonies in the Sunday morning session. As we were seated on the stand waiting for the meeting to start, the stake president pointed out the two sisters he had chosen. He briefly explained that the first woman's husband had been out of the Church for some time, but had recently had his priesthood and temple blessings restored. He said that the other sister had just completed a long but successful battle with leukemia.

What happened in the meeting turned out to be quite notable. My first surprise was that neither woman talked much about their personal situations. The first one said only that their family had undergone some recent challenges, but that they were happier than they had ever been before. The sister with leukemia briefly mentioned "some health problems" she had undergone, but that was all.

The second surprise was how similar their testimonies were. They spoke fervently of how the Lord had blessed them in their lives during their difficult times. In fact, in one case they used almost identical language, saying something like this: "I know without question that my Heavenly Father knows me personally and loves me." The one who had struggled with leukemia immediately added this sentence, "And I know that He *so* wants to bless us."

I was touched and inspired and edified by their words, as was the congregation. Here were two sisters, faithful Latter-day Saints, for whom life had taken a severe downturn. They had faced the kinds of challenges that might cause others to falter or turn away from the Lord. But both sisters testified that their problems had actually drawn them closer to Him. They stood there serenely, yet forcefully bearing witness of how their testimonies had actually been strengthened and fortified by what they experienced. They confirmed Elder Bednar's words: "The simpleness, the sweetness, and the constancy of the tender mercies of the Lord *will do much to fortify and protect us in the troubled times* in which we do now and will yet live."[3]

As I afterward reflected on that conference session, two scriptures came to mind. The first was counsel given by the Lord through the Prophet Joseph Smith to the Saints in Missouri. This was at a time when they were being mercilessly driven from Jackson County, Missouri, by howling mobs:

> Fear not, let your hearts be comforted; yea, *rejoice evermore,* and *in everything give thanks*; waiting patiently on the Lord. . . . Therefore, he giveth this promise unto you: . . . *all things* wherewith you have been afflicted *shall work together for your good.* (D&C 98:1–3; see also D&C 90:24, 100:15)

All things work to our good? Can that really be? Can the infidelity and betrayal of a spouse actually work to one's good? Can we truly rejoice and give thanks even when a deadly disease invades our bodies? Those two sisters did not cite that scripture, but they both testified of what it teaches.

The other scripture that came to my mind was Matthew 7:24–25—about building our house upon a rock. These sisters knew personally about the storms of life. The wind and the rain and the floods had descended and beat upon them, yet the rock of their testimony was such that their faith stood fast through it all. As I sat and listened to them, I wondered where that strength had come from. Then the second sister shared something that answered that question, at least for her.

Tender Mercies in Times of Challenge

As I mentioned, the sister who had struggled with leukemia said that Heavenly Father "so wanted to bless us." That struck me as a curious way to express it. He wasn't just *willing* to bless her, He *wanted* to bless her. She then shared a recent personal experience to illustrate her point.

She said that her husband was a student at the local university. He worked part-time, but his job provided no insurance benefits. As a result, she had to take full-time employment outside the home to not only help support the family, but also for the insurance benefits. She felt terrible about having to leave her young children every day in the care of others. She felt a great desire to be home with them. But she also knew that with her current medical problems, maintaining insurance coverage was critical. So she began to pray and ask God if He would help her find a way to stay at home with her children.

After much prayer, she had a strong feeling that she should quit her job. This went counter to all logic. It wasn't just that she felt impressed to quit her job *sometime,* the feeling was that she quit *now.* That surprised and troubled her. In one way, it seemed completely insane. What would they do without insurance? But she could not shake the feeling, and so, after a time, with great hesitancy and the approval of her husband, she gave notice to her employer. Then, fighting back the tears, she said that the very next day, her husband was offered a job at the university that carried full insurance benefits. That was how she knew the Lord *wanted* to bless her.

Elder Bednar noted that the Lord's timing of tender mercies can help us both discern and acknowledge them. That was certainly the case here. After she quit her job, not even one full day passed before her answer came. But it was more than just the remarkable timing. It was not just *when* it came, but *how* it came, and *what* was given. She was able to be home with her children and still have full medical benefits. Here was another example of a divine signature, and it brought tears of joy to her eyes as she recounted it for us.

Not all tender mercies become such defining experiences. Many are general blessings that enrich our lives and make them better. But there are times when blessings are sent at just the right time, and under such unusual circumstances, that they are not only blessing experiences, they become *learning* and *confirming* experiences as well.

A Hispanic Grandmother

We don't have to be in extreme difficulty to receive such confirmation blessings. Here is another experience I had in a stake conference. This one came so quietly and so naturally that I almost missed it when it happened.

I was presiding at a stake conference in Southern California. One of the things I most enjoy about stake conferences is being able to sit on the stand and watch the faces of the members. That morning, I noticed a Hispanic family sitting in the congregation. The family occupied one side bench about six rows from the front. There was an older woman and her husband, a younger woman (clearly her daughter) and her husband, and a handsome young lad of about two. This grandson was full of energy and a bit of a handful. While he paid occasional attention to Grandpa, Mom, and Dad, it was clear that Grandma was the center of this little boy's life. He sat on her lap as she read to him or helped him color something. Twice I watched him convince her to take him out in the hall for one reason or another. As I watched this interaction, I was touched by her obvious love for this little boy and by his adoration for his grandmother.

As was my usual pattern, I had asked the stake presidency to speak following the testimonies from some of the sisters in the stake. Usually that took us to the top of the first hour of the conference. On this morning, though, each speaker had taken less time than allotted to them, and as we approached eleven o'clock, we were running about five minutes ahead of schedule. Just before the stake president was to stand and speak, I leaned over and suggested we have another testimony from the audience. I called his attention to the grandmother and suggested he call on her.

I watched her as he did so. There was a moment of shock, followed by momentary confusion, but she stood and came to the stand. When she came to the pulpit, her first words were: "Well, I suppose it is my fault that I am up here." That startled all of us a little. She then explained, "As my family and I came into the chapel this morning, I said to my husband, 'I wonder if they will call people out of the audience to bear their testimony this morning.' Then with irritation I added, 'Have you noticed that when they do that, they never call on Hispanics? Why is that, do you suppose? Do they think we can't speak English, or that we don't have strong enough testimonies? Or maybe they just don't think about us in that way.'" Then, very sheepishly, she added, "I guess it serves me right, because here I am."

Everyone got a chuckle out of her comment, as did I. But as she spoke, it suddenly hit me. The Lord knew the heart of this good woman; He knew how she felt. Even the fact that we had extra time was a bit unusual. It is far more typical in stake conferences for people to take more time than they are assigned so that other things must be shortened. I felt a sudden rush of gladness that Heavenly Father had called my attention to this woman and put the thought into my mind to call her up.

Maybe others didn't think of her "in that way," but she learned that morning that her Heavenly Father did.

"I Thought I Was Dying"

Let me share one other example of a divine signature that has special significance for me personally. This was a tender mercy in the fullest sense of the word *tender*. My father, typical of many other men from his generation, did not express emotion openly very often. In all my growing-up years, I can never remember him telling me or any of my brothers and sisters that he loved us. We knew that he did, because he was a good father. He read stories to us almost every night. He taught us to work and how to be responsible.

The one exception to his emotional reticence was with my mother. With her, he was openly expressive of his love. He would often take her in his arms in front of us and tell us how she was the best thing that ever happened to him. Then he would kiss her soundly. It always embarrassed Mom but delighted us. One of the quickest ways to trigger Dad's wrath was to be sassy to Mom. That behavior was corrected instantly and in a way that was not quickly forgotten.

Mom's early life was hard. When she was six, her father was killed in a farming accident. When she was sixteen, her mother broke her hip, and Mom had to drop out of school to care for her and her younger siblings. When my father met my mother at a dance when she was eighteen, he was instantly smitten. A few months later they were married.

After more than sixty years of married life, my father died of colon cancer in 1995. As I watched Mom as the months and years moved on, I came to understand in ways I had not understood before what it meant to grieve for a person. She went on with life as a widow for the next nine years, but never quite got over the loss of Dad. She lived close to us and my siblings for a time, then moved in with our family for three years before we were called to go to England.

One day while we were having breakfast together, we were talking about Dad, and I said something about how protective and caring he had always been toward her. Her eyes immediately misted up as she nodded. Then she told us that in the latter part of their life the tenderness had only increased.

"He was always so tender with me in those last years," she said. "For example, every night when we went to bed, we would lay there and talk for awhile. Finally, as we prepared to go to sleep, he would reach across to me and lay his hand on my cheek." By now the tears were flowing. "Then he would say, 'I love you, Evelyn.'"

By that time, both my wife and I were a little teary-eyed too. But she wasn't through. "I have something I want to share with you about your father that I've never shared before. This happened about a year after he died." She then reminded us of how she did not like the dark. I had to smile. That was an understatement. Mom *hated* being alone in the dark.

She continued with her story:

> One night, I had gone to bed. The house was pitch-black and as I lay there all alone, the old feelings of fear and anxiety began to rise. I started thinking about your dad and how much I missed him. I missed him comforting me when I became frightened of the dark. As I was thinking about that, suddenly my heart began to pound. It was racing so fast and so hard that I was gasping for breath. I was terribly frightened. I was sure I was having a heart attack. What was even worse was the thought that I would die there alone in the dark and it might be days before anyone even knew.

She had to stop then, she was crying so hard. For all of her gentle spirit, my mother was not one to show her emotions either. Finally, regaining enough composure to go on, she said:

I was so terrified that I involuntarily cried out in my mind, "Heavenly Father, please don't let me die here alone."

For a moment, nothing happened. Then suddenly, I felt a hand rest against my cheek. And I heard your father say, "I love you, Evelyn." That was all. But instantly, I was at peace. My heart slowed; my fear disappeared. A few minutes later, I fell into a deep sleep and slept through the rest of the night.

Mom passed away in August 2004. Even now, years after she told us that story, I cannot think of it without getting emotional all over again. Talk about tender mercies! And not just for her. My wife and I were also greatly blessed that morning. I silently thanked my Heavenly Father for allowing Dad that brief penetration of the veil. It enriched Mom's remaining life, and it certainly enriched ours.

To Summarize

In the richness of His love for us, God sends down blessings upon His children, especially on those who are striving to be faithful and to serve Him. The scriptures call these blessings "tender mercies" because they reflect the merciful nature of our Father and His Beloved Son and their desire to add joy and happiness to our lives.

Sometimes these blessings come in such an unusual manner and with such precise timing that they accomplish something in addition to blessing us. They so clearly confirm the reality of God's existence that they buoy us up in times of trials.

Joseph Smith said if we are to have strong faith we must have a correct idea of God's attributes, character, and perfections. These divine signatures do exactly that. They teach us about His love, His power, His perfect knowledge of us, and His long-suffering and forgiveness. They directly strengthen our faith and deepen our testimony. They are a sweet answer to that aching question: "Heavenly Father, are you really there?"

Joseph Smith also said that to have faith we must have an actual knowledge that our lives are pleasing to God. These special tender mercies confirm that as well. Maybe we aren't perfect. Maybe we're still struggling to overcome some problems. But to receive one of His blessings in such a special way lets us know that, at least to some degree, He is pleased with us. And that also strengthens our faith.

In the introduction I said that my purpose in this book is to answer this question:

How do we strengthen our faith and deepen our testimony to the point that we can endure whatever life holds in store for us and come out stronger than before?

There are many ways to answer that question, but I hope you are beginning to see that one answer is through the tender mercies and divine signatures of the Lord. In the following chapter, we shall see why they are so necessary as we make our way through mortality.

A Suggestion

Elder Richard G. Scott has often taught the value of recording impressions and promptings when they come so that they are not forgotten. He also taught that doing so can show the Holy Ghost that we are willing to be taught of Him as well and thus actually bring more revelation. For example, Elder Scott gave this counsel to students at a BYU devotional:

> Write down in a secure place the important things you learn from the Spirit. You will find that as you write down precious impressions, often more will come. Also, the knowledge you gain will be available throughout your life. Always, day or night, wherever you are, whatever you

are doing, seek to recognize and respond to the direction of the Spirit.[4]

President Henry B. Eyring taught a similar principle in general conference:

When our children were very small, I started to write down a few things about what happened every day. . . .

I wrote down a few lines every day for years. I never missed a day no matter how tired I was or how early I would have to start the next day. Before I would write, I would ponder this question: "Have I seen the hand of God reaching out to touch us or our children or our family today?" As I kept at it, something began to happen. As I would cast my mind over the day, *I would see evidence of what God had done for one of us that I had not recognized in the busy moments of the day.*[5]

I would suggest that you keep a paper and pencil by your side as you read this book, particularly the stories and examples shared here. I am confident that as you read the stories of others, you will be reminded of times in your life when the Lord has given you special blessings. Or perhaps thoughts will come that will teach you what to do to have your own tender mercies. Write them down, and, if appropriate, share them with your families.

Notes

1. David A. Bednar, "The Tender Mercies of the Lord," *Ensign,* May 2005, 99–102.

2. Emma Bull, as cited by Jerry Earl Johnston, "Ideally Speaking," *Deseret News,* January 2, 2010, E8.

3. Bednar, "The Tender Mercies of the Lord," 100.

4. Richard G. Scott, "To Acquire Knowledge and the Strength to Use It Wisely," *Ensign,* June 2002, 32.

5. Henry B. Eyring, "O Remember, Remember," *Ensign,* November 2007, 66, 67.

Turning Points—
A Nudge from Heaven

While in Liberty Jail, the Prophet Joseph wrote letters to the Saints in Illinois. In one of those letters, he made this observation: "There are many yet on the earth among all sects, parties, and denominations, who are blinded by the subtle craftiness of men, whereby they lie in wait to deceive, and *who are only kept from the truth because they know not where to find it*" (D&C 123:12).

That is why we send missionaries out into the world. That is why the Church in recent years has used the media and the Internet to let people know about the Church and our message. But in talking with converts to the Church over the years, I have learned something else. In some cases, there are people whose circumstances are such that it is highly unlikely that the missionaries would ever *find them*. They are too isolated or inaccessible. Sometimes they have been so blinded by negative things they've heard about the Mormons, that they would never consider even speaking to the missionaries.

In those cases, a special nudge is required to bring them into the kingdom. These are other manifestations of how the Lord works with His children.

New Convert Meetings

President Gordon B. Hinckley asked that, as part of our stake conference assignments, the presiding authority hold what we called "new convert meetings." Recent converts, investigators, and those who had recently returned to Church activity were invited to attend. These meetings proved to be one of the choice meetings of the conference.

The mission president, the stake president, and I would speak briefly, and then we would invite those present to bear their testimony if they were inclined to do so. But I specifically asked the people if, as part of their testimony, they would tell us what had been the "turning point" for them in finding the Church, deciding to talk to the missionaries, or coming back to full activity in the Church. What I was looking for were those pivotal moments that made a difference.

The results of that simple request were astonishing. The stories that were shared were touching, confirming, and very often downright amazing. Here are just a few stories that illustrate how the Lord can reach out and find His lost children. Three come from new convert meetings, while one happened to me when I was a young missionary.

"So This Is What It Was Like for Jesus?"

In one new convert meeting, I noticed an older man who came into the room accompanied by two missionaries. He caught my attention because he didn't look like someone you would normally expect to see in a Church meeting. He was a short man in his mid-sixties with a leathery face and tattoos up and down both arms. He wore casual clothes, gym shoes without stockings, and his hair was tied in a long ponytail that reached halfway down his back.

When I extended the invitation to share their own personal turning points with the group, I noticed a look of momentary alarm cross his face. As others stood and talked, he watched and listened closely. Each time there was a pause, I noticed him start to fidget. I guessed that he wanted to speak but was too nervous to do so. To my surprise, he finally stood up about halfway through the meeting and began speaking in a quiet voice.

Here, as best I can remember it, is his story.

He apologized in advance for not being good with words. He explained that he had been baptized just a couple of weeks before. He told us that he had been a sailor in the merchant marines for his country for his entire working life. He said that he had been in most of the world's great ports and had partaken of most of the temptations those ports had to offer. As he approached retirement age, however, he began to feel that his life had been a wasteland. He began to hunger for something more satisfying, something of worth. However, he wasn't sure what he was even looking for or where to turn to find it. But the yearning to find something of lasting value grew deeper and stronger, and he began to read and study. Occasionally he visited different churches. But he found nothing to satisfy the hunger he was feeling.

One day he was out in his yard, pruning back the dead leaves on a large palm tree. This particular palm tree had long, swordlike leaves with a needle point on the end. He had neglected the tree for a long time, and there was a lot of dead foliage that needed to be trimmed, especially around the base of the tree. This required him to crawl in among the dead leaves beneath the tree to clear them out.

As he worked in that tangle, the needle points of the leaves kept scratching his bare arms, face, and head. After several minutes, he realized that he was bleeding slightly from numerous places. He especially noticed a light trickle of blood coming down his forehead from the scratches on his head. As he went to wipe it off, suddenly a thought came into his mind with great power: "So this is what it was like for Jesus when they put the crown of thorns on his head?" In that moment, he knew with absolute clarity that Jesus Christ was the answer to his quest, that in the Savior, he would find that for which he was seeking.

Excited with this discovery, he crawled out from beneath the tree and stood up, wondering what to do next. And who should come riding by on their bicycles at that very moment? That's right. Two young men wearing white shirts and black name tags.

Doing what missionaries are supposed to do, they stopped and introduced themselves, then said, "We are out here on a mission because we have a message about Jesus Christ that we would like to share with you. Would that be all right with you?"

Then, with his eyes shining brightly, and in a choked voice, this man looked directly at me and said, "And you wonder why I decided to listen to the missionaries?" And he sat down.

A Strange Day in the Park

Here is another story shared in one of the new convert meetings. This is unquestionably one of the stranger stories I heard, and it is not without its humorous moments.

After I asked the people to bear their testimonies about turning points in their lives, a well-dressed and well-groomed gentleman in his mid-fifties stood. He motioned to a young woman in her mid-twenties to join him and introduced her as his only daughter. She too was dressed nicely. Both looked to be very cultured and intelligent people.

He introduced himself and her, saying that they had joined the Church about four months before. "We are Jewish," he announced, which surprised us all a bit. Here is his story:

I grew up in a Jewish household, though we were not what you would call observant Jews. However, I married a woman who was also Jewish, and we honored the Jewish holidays and some of the other Jewish customs in our home.

Several years ago, my wife passed away unexpectedly. This hit both my daughter and me very hard. She was the light of our lives. In the grieving process, my daughter and I began to feel that we were missing something in our lives—a spiritual dimension that might give more meaning to our loss. Together we decided that we needed religion in our lives again, and we determined to work together to find it.

We returned to our mother faith and began attending synagogues in the various branches of Judaism, but they did not satisfy us. We finally determined that Jesus Christ had what it was we were looking for, so we began attending different Christian churches. We enjoyed some of these experiences more than others, but again we felt that they did not have what we were searching for.

One evening, while we were watching television, we saw an advertisement by the Mormon Church. It talked about the importance of families and said something about families being together forever. It then invited us to learn more. As the advertisement finished, I turned to my daughter and said, "Maybe we ought to investigate that church too, though I have no idea how to begin." [He hadn't thought to write down the contact information shared on the TV.]

My daughter agreed and then told me that Mormon missionaries came to the large park in the center of the city every Sunday afternoon to talk to people about their church. "Let's go meet them this Sunday," I said.

The next Sunday afternoon we went to the park and began looking for the missionaries. Sure enough, a few minutes later my daughter spied them and pointed them out to me.

"Let's go talk to them," I said. The two missionaries were easily recognizable, being the only people in the entire park wearing white shirts and ties on a warm summer's afternoon. The two elders were not standing right together, but were about thirty or forty feet apart. We approached the nearest one, obviously intent on speaking to him.

When he saw us coming, he smiled warmly. When we were about ten feet away, he said, "Hello. My name is Elder Smith. I am a missionary for The Church of Jesus Christ of Latter-day Saints. My companion and I have a message about Jesus Christ for you."

That pleased me. "I know," I said. "That is why we have come to the park. We would like to talk with—"

To my surprise, the elder held up a hand, cutting me off. "Excuse me a moment," he said. Then he half turned and looked toward his companion. He cupped a hand to his mouth. "Did you get it, Elder Jones?" he called.

The other missionary waved in disgust. "No. Sorry."

Elder Smith then turned back to us. "Hello," he started again, in exactly the same tone. "My name is Elder Smith. I am a missionary for The Church of Jesus Christ of Latter-day Saints. My companion and I have a message about Jesus Christ for you."

Completely taken aback, I tried again. "I know," I said. "That is why my daughter and I have come—"

Again his hand shot up, stopping me in mid-sentence.

He turned away. "Did you get it that time, Elder Jones?"

"No. It didn't work. Try again."

For the third time, the elder turned to us. "Hello, my name is Elder Smith. I am a missionary for The Church of Jesus Christ of Latter-day Saints. My companion and I . . ."

The man stopped his story there and, smiling, looked down at the two missionaries who were sitting beside him and his daughter. Both of their faces were quite red by now.

He continued, "As you can imagine, my daughter and I were completely taken aback. This was really strange. What was going on? Had he not heard us? Didn't he want to talk to us? Did he think I had poor hearing? But I started again, and finally he acknowledged me. We began to talk. We liked what we heard, and after several minutes of conversation, we agreed to have them come to our home and teach us."

He looked at the elders again. "Care to tell these people what you were doing, Elder Smith?"

Very sheepishly the missionary said, "My companion and I were making a video of us contacting people in the park to send home to our families."

Well, that brought a lot of appreciative laughs from everyone present. It was a delightful story. But as soon as the meeting concluded, I went right over to that man and his daughter. I thanked him for sharing their experience with us, and then I said, "I'm sorry, but I just have to know. After that kind of strange reception, why in the world didn't you just turn and walk away?"

He looked me straight in the eye and said, "Good question. Because, even as I wondered what in the world was going on and if this young man was somehow a little deranged, I had the strongest feeling come into my heart. It was almost like an inner voice speaking to me. And it said, 'Don't turn away. These young men have what you're looking for.'"

The Church of Evans

One of the choice conversion experiences I personally experienced happened while I was serving as a full-time missionary in the West

Central States Mission. At that time I was assigned to a town in central Wyoming. One day in sacrament meeting, one of the sisters in the ward approached my companion and me and said that she had a referral for us. It was her mother.

This member had been raised on a cattle ranch about forty-five or fifty miles outside of town. Since her marriage, she had lived in town. There she and her husband had met the missionaries and were converted to the Church. In recent years, her father had passed away and now her widowed mother lived out on the ranch, all alone except for a few ranch hands who worked for her.

This sister asked if we would go out and meet her mother and see if she might let us teach her the gospel. However, and she was quite emphatic about this point, we couldn't tell her mother that it was her own daughter who had sent us out there. The daughter had tried to talk with her about the Church but had been abruptly cut off. Her mother had told her that she had her own church and wasn't interested in anything else.

We were thrilled, of course, and agreed to meet her mother during the upcoming week. The daughter gave us detailed directions because the ranch was a long way out in the country and accessible only by gravel roads. We set out and, following her directions, eventually found the ranch. I can still remember pulling up in front of the house and startling three antelope that were grazing on the lawn. That's how isolated the ranch was.

When we introduced ourselves, the mother, probably in her mid-sixties at that time, was quite surprised that we had found her. We told her we were missionaries and that we had a message for her. She frowned. She said that she already had a church and wasn't interested in changing. When I pressed a little, she became quite firm and turned cool. However, since we had come so far, she graciously invited us in for some cold lemonade.

As we visited, we asked her about the ranch and her life there. It was obvious that she was lonely and glad for the company. Then, at an appropriate moment, as senior companion, I took the lead and again mentioned that we were missionaries for The Church of Jesus Christ of Latter-day Saints, often called the Mormons. Again she cut me off. She knew about the Mormons because her daughter had become one. She repeated what she had said before with even greater emphasis. She already had a church and was very happy with it.

Disappointed, but not quite ready to give up, I asked her which church she belonged to.

"To the Church of Evans," she said.

My companion and I looked at each other blankly. "The Church of Evans?" Then, trying to recover, I added, "I guess I'm not familiar with that church. Tell me a little about it."

That seemed to please her. "Well," she said, "it's not a church in the normal sense of the word. I mean it's not a church that I attend on Sundays. I'm too far from town to do that. But this is a church that comes over the radio. I listen to it every Sunday morning. The Tabernacle Choir sings this beautiful music, and a minister by the name of Evans then preaches a short but wonderful sermon. I never miss it. So that's my church. The Church of Evans."

I gaped at her. "Do you mean Richard L. Evans?" At that time, Richard L. Evans, a member of the Quorum of the Twelve, was the voice for *Music and the Spoken Word,* the radio broadcast by the Mormon Tabernacle Choir.

Surprised, she nodded. "Yes, that's his name."

"But Richard L. Evans is one of the apostles in our church," I exclaimed. "That broadcast comes from our church."

She was instantly skeptical and actually bristled a little, thinking this was some kind of manipulative trick on my part. She invited us to leave. Fortunately, I carried in my scriptures a folded sheet of paper with the pictures of the First Presidency and the Twelve. Eagerly I whipped it out and showed it to her. "There," I said, pointing. "That is Richard L. Evans. He is a leader in our church."

For a long moment she just stared at us, and then abruptly she stood up. "Stay right there," she said and disappeared down the hallway. A moment later she came out carrying a large, gallon-sized Miracle Whip jar. It was stuffed to the top with bills and coins. "Here," she said, handing it to me. "Mr. Evans talked about the law of tithing a year or so ago, and I was so impressed with what he said that I started paying my tithing immediately. But I didn't know where to send it, so I've been putting it in this jar. I want you to have it since it is your church."

In a bit of a daze, we explained that we couldn't accept it personally, but that we would take it to the bishop and he would pay it to the Church. We then taught her the first discussion. We returned several more times, now with her daughter and her daughter's husband, and taught her the rest of the lessons. About a month later, she was baptized into The Church of Jesus Christ of Latter-day Saints, sometimes known as "The Church of Evans."

It is no surprise that the Lord would love a daughter like that. To pay tithing in a Miracle Whip jar when you didn't even know what to do with it? That's remarkable faith. But there was a problem. We never went tracting out in the countryside. Houses were widely scattered and it took too much gas. There was no way that we would have found her on our own. So the Lord made sure I had a picture of Richard L. Evans with us—something that I don't remember doing either before or since—and prompted me to ask what church she belonged to. It took a little nudge from heaven to bring it all together, but it worked. She remained faithful to the Church until her death a few years later.

An Albanian Monastery

My wife and I were in France for a stake conference. During a new convert meeting, I noticed two young men in their mid-twenties sitting together. One of them stood and introduced himself. He said that he was a refugee from Russia. He had come to France to escape oppression and there had found the Mormon missionaries and joined the Church. When he sat down, the other young man got to his feet. Speaking in halting French, he told his story. The mission president, who was sitting beside me, translated for us. Here, as best as I can remember it, is what he said:

I, too, am a refugee, come to France to escape persecution. But I am from Albania. I should like to tell you how I came to meet the Mormon missionaries. I was born a Roman Catholic, and my family and I were devout members of the Catholic faith. When I reached my teen years, with the encouragement of my family, I decided I wanted to be a priest. I was accepted for training and was sent to a monastery there in Albania.

At first I was happy in my training for the priesthood. But as the months went by, I began to feel a vague sense that there was something lacking. It was hard for me to describe, but my experience just wasn't satisfying me as I thought it should. This troubled me, and I tried harder. But my sense of dissatisfaction kept growing. I began to spend a lot of time in the monastery library, trying to find answers, or, at least, something that would satisfy this sense of unrest growing within me. Nothing seemed to help.

One day as I was in the library, I moved through the stacks absently looking at the titles to see if anything might catch my eye that could help me. Between two thicker books, I saw a thin book with a black cover. There was no title on the spine. Curious, I pulled it out. On the cover, I read in Albanian: *Excerpts from the Book of Mormon.**

The Book of Mormon? I had no idea what that meant. I had never heard the word Mormon before. Curious, I began to read. What I read deeply impressed me. I checked the book out of the library and took it to my room and continued to read. The more I read, the more deeply impressed I was. Here was something to satisfy my hunger. Here was something that I could believe in.

When I finished the book a short time later, I had made up my mind. I did three things. I returned the book to the library. I went to the head priest and explained that I could not continue in the program. Then I left the monastery.

Some time after that, due to political unrest and other events, I chose to leave my native country and come to France to live. When I got off at the train station here in town, I had no idea what to do. I knew no one. I had no place to stay. I spoke a little French, but my funds were limited.

Then I noticed a large board on the wall of the train station where people were allowed to post notices. There I saw a card written in both Russian and French. I could read Russian, so this caught my eye immediately. The card was advertising for a roommate in an apartment here in the city. This was my answer. I called the number to see if the vacancy was still available.

At that point, the young man laid his hand on his friend's shoulder

---

* In languages where there are not many members of the Church, it was a common practice to print excerpts from the Book of Mormon. These included the more significant passages in the Book of Mormon, and normally was about a third to a fourth of the total book.

and told us that this was the person who answered the phone that day. He was the one who had advertised for a roommate. They agreed to meet so the Albanian could see the flat. When he got there, he was pleased. It was a small apartment but sufficient for the two of them. The rent was reasonable, and he would have a roommate with whom he could communicate. He told the other man that he wanted it.

He continued:

> When I said I wanted to take the flat, there was a moment's hesitation. Then my new Russian acquaintance said, "There's one thing I have to tell you. You need to know this before you make your final decision."
>
> Puzzled, I asked him what was wrong.
>
> "I am meeting with two young men who are teaching me about their religion. We meet here in this apartment. You don't have to listen to them, but I wanted you to know."
>
> I asked him which church they were from. He told me they were Mormon missionaries.
>
> "Mormons," I cried. That was the word on the book which had so moved me back in Albania. Ever since I had left the monastery I had tried to find out what the word Mormon meant and where the book came from. No one knew. Now here I was about to move into an apartment where Mormons were coming to teach my roommate about their Church. I assured my friend that it would not be a problem for me to have Mormons in the flat so long as he would let me sit in with them and be taught as well.
>
> We were both baptized several weeks later.

Someday I hope to learn how a copy of excerpts from the Book of Mormon, written in Albanian, ended up in the library of a Catholic monastery. That should be quite a story.

Fear thou not; for I am with thee: be not dismayed; for I am thy God: I will strengthen thee; yea, I will help thee; yea, I will uphold thee with the right hand of my righteousness. . . . For I the Lord thy God will hold thy right hand, saying unto thee, Fear not; I will help thee.

Isaiah 41:10, 13

CHAPTER THREE

Defining Experiences

Sometimes the tender mercies of God can come in such an unusual way that they have a tremendous impact on our minds and hearts. In this way, they become defining experiences. I'm not saying that the blessings are always life-changing in and of themselves, only that they do change how we think and feel about things.

A Lost Check

When I was twelve or thirteen years old, I had a daily newspaper route. Like many other boys my age, I was responsible for delivering the *Deseret Evening News* to about eighty homes, seven days a week. Unless the weather was bad, I did my route on my bicycle. Back in those days, there was no central billing service for newspaper subscribers as there is today. Instead, the delivery boys were given a monthly bill from the *Deseret News* for the papers we received, then it was up to us to collect the monthly subscription rate from each of our customers. This was usually about twenty dollars more than what we owed the *News,* so that became our "salary" for the month.

One summer afternoon, I was collecting subscription fees as I delivered the papers. Back then, most people paid in cash, and so

I needed to have change as I went along. I carried a small pouch in which I kept the change and the money I collected. While I was collecting one day, a woman apologetically told me that she didn't have any cash. Then she explained that she had a personal check from a neighbor for twenty-seven dollars.

"If you have enough change," she said, "I can sign the check over to you and pay you today." Though that was unusual, I found that I did have just enough to make change for her.

Near the end of my route another woman had only a twenty-dollar bill. I assured her that I could make change and opened the pouch. As I drew what I had from the sack, I suddenly realized that there was no check. It was gone! I was instantly aghast. That couldn't be. I searched in the pouch again, but the check was gone. I must have gone gray because the woman asked me with great concern if I was all right.

I felt like I had been kicked in the stomach. I could hardly breathe. Twenty-seven dollars not only took *my* total salary for the month, but that meant my family was going to have to come up with what I owed the *Deseret News* for the month. Finances were tight in our home, and I knew this would be bad news.

Sick in heart and mind—and stomach!—I finished delivering the papers to the last few houses and then began to retrace my steps. I didn't ride my bike. I walked, pushing it along as I searched for the check. I'm sure I picked up every scrap of paper along that mile-long route. But I found nothing. I turned around and covered the route again. Nothing! I did it a third time with the same results. There was no check to be found.

As I look back on it now, I'm not sure why it took me so long (more than an hour) to come to the realization that I wasn't going to find the check. It simply was not there. But then it hit me. "You may not know where it is," I thought, "but the Lord does. Why don't you ask Him for help?" That thought came with such clarity and power that I stopped right there on the side of the road. Holding the handlebars of my bike with both hands, I bowed my head. It wasn't a very elegant prayer, unless desperation creates elegance. It was something like, "Heavenly Father. I need that check. Help me find it. *Please!*" I don't think my eyes were closed for even thirty seconds.

When I opened my eyes, I was looking at the ground just a few feet in front of my bicycle. There, to my utter astonishment, lodged in the top of a tumbleweed, was my check. I stared at it for a moment or two. It couldn't be. This paper was in plain sight. There was no way I could have missed seeing it before. I took no more than two or three steps, reached down, and picked it up. I stared at it for several seconds. I couldn't believe it. It was the check. I had found it! The relief almost made me dizzy. My prayer had been answered.

"Just Go Home"

A few years later, when I was a junior in high school, I worked at the Murray Theater, which was located in downtown Murray, Utah, on the corner of State and Vine streets. (The theater is still there today.) Since there were usually two showings of the movie each night, I typically worked until after midnight. After my brother left for his mission, my parents allowed me to take his car to work so they wouldn't have to pick me up from work each night.

I loved having access to a car. The sense of freedom was exhilarating. I soon developed a pattern when I got off work. Instead of going directly home, I would turn onto Vine Street and drive slowly along up to Ninth East. It added only about ten minutes to my drive, but I enjoyed the chance to be alone and unwind a little after my shift.

One evening, I left work as usual and got into the car. I started it up and turned right onto Vine Street from the parking lot. Then there came the thought, "Oh, just go home." Nothing unusual or dramatic. No sense of premonition or warning. It was just a simple, fleeting thought. At first I shrugged it off. Why would I want to do that? However, I looked at the clock on the dashboard and noted the time: 12:40 a.m. I was tired, and I had school the next morning. So I made a U-turn on the deserted road and took the direct way home, giving it no further thought as I did so.

The next afternoon, when I returned home from school, Mom was at the kitchen sink. As I got something from the refrigerator, she pointed to the newspaper on the kitchen table. "You may want to look at that," she said. "Second section." Mother never asked me to look at the newspaper. Curious, I picked up the second section. What I saw shocked me. There was a large black-and-white photo of a crumpled mass of steel. It took me a moment to realize that what I was looking at had once been an automobile. Beneath it was the headline: "Four Teens Killed in Early Morning Crash." I quickly read to see if they were from Murray High School and if that was why Mom had shown it to me. They were not. But as I continued to read, I was suddenly stunned. The report stated that the accident had taken place on Vine Street, just below Ninth East. I gaped at the words. That was where I drove every night on my way home.

I read on. Based on the skid marks on the road, the police estimated that the car was traveling at more than ninety miles an hour when the driver tried to negotiate one of the sharper curves. Murray was a mostly rural area then, and there had been no witnesses, but the police were able to determine the exact time of the crash because the dashboard clock in the car had been smashed, stopping the clock at 12:47 a.m. I stared at those words with a sickening feeling in the pit of my stomach. I had started up Vine Street at 12:40. The crash had occurred at 12:47. Could it be that . . . ?

After dinner, I left for work early and reversed the route of my evening drive. It wasn't hard to find the crash site. The wreckage was gone, but there was a lot of shattered glass and small pieces of metal. A deep, ugly scar marked the bark of the tree. To say that I was deeply sobered would be an understatement. Four people, just my age, had died here the previous night. Were they laughing and having a good time when they lost control of the car? Where were they now? What were they doing?

I don't remember how long I stood there, but I finally got back into the car. I carefully checked the clock on my dashboard and then continued on Vine Street. I was careful to drive at about the same speed as I did when I made my nightly loop.

When I turned into the parking lot of the theater, I checked the clock again. It had taken me exactly seven minutes from the crash site to the theater.

Selling a Home

The next example happened much later in my life. Lynn and I were married and our family contained six of our eventual seven children. Our house was bulging at the seams, and we decided it was time to move into a larger home. We had a friend who was both a general contractor and a real estate agent. When he learned that we were thinking of moving, he made us an attractive deal. If we would list our current home with him as our agent and also let him be the general contractor for the new house, he could offer us some significant savings. It was a good deal, and so we decided to do it.

This was in the mid-seventies when things were much different in the home financing business. When we spoke with the bank about our plans, they offered to finance both the construction loan and the new mortgage. In addition, they said that they would lock in the current interest rate for a period of six months. However, they warned us that if we didn't close within six months of signing, we would have to accept whatever the current rate was at that time.

Our friend assured us that he could have the new home done in six months and that half a year was more than enough time to sell our old home in the current housing market. That made sense, and so we moved ahead.

I do remember feeling slightly uneasy. It was not that it felt wrong. It was knowing that if we didn't sell our current home—or if the new one wasn't finished on time—we would be in a financial crisis. I would then have three mortgages to pay—the old home, the new one, and the construction loan. My salary and benefits were good as a Church employee, but my resources were hardly sufficient to handle three different house payments. Nonetheless, we signed the papers in early March.

At first, things went well. Construction moved along smoothly. We had numerous prospective buyers coming through our home. The one downside was that interest rates began to shoot up. By early summer the rates had climbed by more than two points. We had to close by the deadline or our house payment would be a couple hundred dollars more per month.

Then other things began to go wrong. By June, the number of people coming through our home had dwindled to a trickle. By early July, no one was looking at our home. My uneasiness turned to open anxiety. We renewed our efforts to make the house an attractive purchase—I mowed the lawn every three days, put new floor tile in the kitchen, repainted several rooms. Lynn and I prayed earnestly every day for help in selling the house. We lowered the cost, not once, but twice. It made no difference. By the end of July, we had not had a single person look at our house in more than five weeks. By mid-August, we were not sleeping well. What were we going to do?

It is interesting to me to think back on what we were feeling then. My wife and I didn't question that God *could* help us sell our home. The question in our minds was, *would* He? It seemed like He had abandoned us, and we began to wonder why. Had this all been a terrible mistake, and this was our punishment? Were we being too worldly for wanting a bigger home for our family? What was wrong? It wasn't just that He wasn't answering us. Things were actually going downhill, and fast.

Then I remembered a story from the New Testament about a man who brought his son to Jesus to be healed. From the descriptions given, it appears the boy had what we would call epilepsy. He was having seizures, which caused him to foam at the mouth and sometimes threw him into the fire. The father said he had asked the disciples to heal his son, but they could not. Jesus took the boy and immediately healed him (see Matthew 17:14–21; Mark 9:14–29; Luke 9:37–42).

Afterwards, the disciples came to Jesus and asked why they had been unable to heal the child. Jesus bluntly told them that it was because of their lack of faith. But then he added, "Howbeit this kind goeth not out but by prayer and fasting" (Matthew 17:21). That was it. The Master was saying that some problems are of such magnitude that it takes both fasting and prayer to solve them.

That was on a Sunday afternoon. That night I told my wife that beginning the next day I was going to start fasting. I decided that I would fast for one day and then go off my fast for a day. Then I would fast for another full day, and so on. I told her I had determined in my mind that I would keep up that pattern for as long as it took to get an answer.

I can remember saying something like this to her: "Perhaps the Lord's answer will be, 'No, I am not going to intervene on this one. You're on your own.' But if that is the answer, I want to know so we can prepare how we're going to cope with it."

I began my fast that night and went without food all of Monday. I ate normally on Tuesday, then fasted again on Wednesday. I ate Thursday, fasted Friday. When I started the process, I fully expected that I might have to follow that pattern for as long as two weeks to get an answer. But on Saturday morning—after fasting only three times—we got a call from our agent/builder. A real estate agent had just called. We had an offer on our home, and they wanted to close as soon as possible!

Lynn and I were ecstatic. It had worked! We had our answer, and it was more wonderful than we had dared hope. We set an appointment for five o'clock that afternoon to meet with their realtor and review the offer.

So imagine our stunned surprise when a couple of hours later our agent called again. As soon as I heard his voice, my heart plummeted. The buyers had changed their mind, I thought. Not so.

"You're not going to believe this," our agent said, "but I just received a second written offer from another realtor."

That afternoon, Lynn and I, still half-dazed with wonder, sat across the table from two different realtors. Both buyers they represented were so determined to purchase the home that they actually bid each other up, and we ended up getting fifteen hundred dollars more than the asking price![1]

The Hand of the Lord—The Love of the Lord

President Joseph F. Smith made a statement many years ago that has come to have great importance for me:

It has not been by the wisdom of man that this people have been directed in their course until the present; it has been by the wisdom of Him who is above man and whose knowledge is greater than that of man, and whose power is above the power of man. . . . The hand of the Lord may not be visible to all. There may be many who can not discern the workings of God's will in the progress and development of this great latter-day work, but there are those who see in every hour and in every moment of the existence of the Church, from its beginning until now, the overruling, almighty hand of [God].[2]

President Smith spoke of the hand of the Lord in the affairs of the kingdom of God. By this time in my life, thanks in part to a lost check, a trip up Vine Street, and two buyers bidding for the right to buy my home, I had come to know that the hand of the Lord also operates on a more personal level. Elder James E. Talmage put it this way: "The Lord's hand is in our lives; if we will but feel for it, in the darkness, we can grasp it and be lifted thereby."[3]

Those who do not believe in a God who watches over His children and cares for them will openly scoff at such a notion. That is all right. As a popular saying notes, "Those who danced were thought to be quite insane by those who could not hear the music." Those who believe that God lives and is a loving Heavenly Father hear a music that others do not.

I was so grateful to the Lord the day that I found my lost check and the day that I stood before that scarred cottonwood tree. I knew that I had seen the hand of the Lord in my life. It was only later that something else gradually began to crystallize in my mind. As I pondered both of those events, I began to wonder about something. What I had prayed for on the day that I lost the check was that I would find the check. I didn't ask that it happen immediately or that it would be laying just two feet away. Had I spent another hour retracing my steps and then found it, I still would have been ecstatic. But it wasn't another hour. It wasn't even another minute. I opened my eyes and there it was.

The same was true of the Vine Street experience. Where had that thought to go home come from? It wasn't some dramatic warning that started the hair on the back of my neck prickling. It was just a thought. But it registered enough to matter. And what prompted my mother to show me the paper? And wasn't it interesting that the news article had the exact time of the crash? Would I have been there when that car came hurtling around the corner? I'm not sure. But it certainly looked like it.

Then it occurred to me that if the Lord had protected me, He didn't have to show me that He had. I am sure there are many times in our lives when we are protected, but we go blithely on our way, never knowing how close we came to tragedy. But it was like the Lord made a special effort to make sure that I knew. Why was that? I could only think of one reason—one that had a profound influence on me: He *wanted* me to know that He was involved in my life.

By the time Lynn and I sold our house, I was more familiar with these unique blessings of the Lord. And again I marveled. We didn't need two buyers. One offer would have been absolutely wonderful. But after not having a single person come through the home in more than a month, we suddenly had two buyers. And then to have them bid each other up so we received the fifteen-hundred-dollar bonus? I can remember telling Lynn that the extra money was "icing on the cake."

Now I have a better word for it. I call it a divine signature. And sometimes divine signatures can become defining experiences.

Notes

1. I recounted this story in *Hearing the Voice of the Lord: Principles and Patterns of Personal Revelation* (Salt Lake City: Deseret Book, 2007), 312–14. I did not indicate there that this story came from my own life. I do so here because it became another defining experience for me.

2. Joseph F. Smith, in Conference Report, April 1904, 2.

3. James E. Talmage, in Conference Report, October 1914, 101.

Answers to Prayers—
Miracles Big and Small

Not all blessings that come from the Lord have to be dramatic, defining experiences. Often we pray and get answers that come quietly, so gently that we may not even notice.

On the other hand, there are occasions when the righteous and the faithful are thrust into extreme circumstances. Now the prayers become earnest, yearning, even desperate. And if the Lord chooses to, the answer may come, not as a whisper, but like a clap of thunder. Though such experiences qualify as examples of divine signatures, even that title seems inadequate. The word we more often use is "miraculous."

The following are three examples of how prayers are answered. The first is the gentle brush of the Lord's hand. The others are miracles in the fullest sense of the word.

A Lost Shoe

Quite a few years ago, my wife and I were visiting in another ward on fast Sunday. A young mother came to the pulpit to bear her testimony. She indicated that she was the wife of one of the counselors in the bishopric. They had a young family of five children, which meant that each Sunday morning it was up to her to get them ready for Church because her husband attended bishopric meeting at 6:30 A.M. She then said she wanted to share a special experience that she had had that week.

She explained that she was a teacher in Relief Society. The previous Sunday she was to teach a lesson about how we can have the Spirit in our lives. As she prepared, she realized that it would be very important for her to have the Spirit in class if she was to teach the concept effectively. Her ward had the nine o'clock block, and sacrament meeting was last. That meant that she had to be ready, and have the Relief Society room ready, well before nine. This would be a challenge because her husband was already at the church performing his bishopric duties and she wouldn't have any help with getting the children ready.

She determined that, with proper planning, she could manage. Early Saturday evening, she and her husband started getting the children ready. The children all took baths. The parents laid out the Sunday clothes. She gathered all of her teaching materials and put them in the car. Here, in her approximate words, is what happened next.

> The next morning, I saw my husband off to his meetings, did some final preparations on my lesson, and then woke up the children. We had a quick breakfast, and then we all trooped off to get dressed for church. Everything went like clockwork, and I was thrilled. Then it happened. Just ten minutes before departure time, my four-year-old came into my bedroom holding up one of her shoes. "Mommy, I can't find my other shoe."
>
> I couldn't believe it. I had checked her shoes along with everything else the night before. But it didn't make any

difference. She had only one pair of Sunday shoes, and now we had only one of those. This was a mini-crisis. I immediately called the other children in. "We have a lost shoe. We have to find it. Go to work." As they scattered, I hurriedly finished my own preparations and joined the hunt.

We looked everywhere, upstairs and down, and even outside. Nothing. As I saw the minutes ticking by, I started to panic. It was really important for me to be to church early to get the Relief Society room set up. I so much wanted to have everything perfect for this lesson.

By the time we should have been leaving, I was frustrated, I was fuming, and I was shouting at the children to find that shoe. Then suddenly I realized that even if I did make it to church on time, I was hardly in a mood conducive to having the Spirit.

Suddenly, I wanted to cry. In desperation I bowed my head. For a moment, I hesitated. Could I really approach God on a matter as trivial as this? Surely in the great cosmic scheme of things, a child's shoe was not high on His priority list. I was in the kitchen at that moment, so I leaned back against the counter and closed my eyes. My prayer was short but fervent. "Heavenly Father, I know that a lost shoe is a small thing in Thy sight, and perhaps I am wrong to ask, but I so want to have Thy Spirit with me today for my lesson. Wilt Thou help me find that shoe?"

It was that simple, she said. For a moment she didn't move, her eyes still closed, wondering if she had just crossed a line. Then she opened her eyes. Directly in front of her was the refrigerator. And there, in the small gap between the refrigerator and the wall, was a little girl's Sunday shoe.

She stopped talking. Tears were flowing freely now, as they were down several cheeks in the congregation. Finally she was able to close with this:

> Do you know how that made me feel? First of all, God knew where the shoe was. Second, He had prompted me to say the prayer in the kitchen where the shoe would be the first thing I would see when I opened my eyes. And most of all, He knew how important this was to me. He wanted me to know that, in this case, even a child's shoe was not beneath His notice.

Saints in War

One of the "inevitable tragedies" of life is war. Whether localized or global, war brings with it the most severe kinds of tribulation. President James E. Faust said: "None of us knows the wisdom of the Lord. We do not know in advance exactly how He would get us from where we are to where we need to be. . . . We encounter many bumps, bends, and forks in the road of life that leads to the eternities."[1]

For some of the Lord's people, even when they are living righteously, the "road of life" takes them through the carnage and horror of war. It is another example where the Lord may choose not to deliver them from their circumstances. Faithful Latter-day Saints are killed or wounded in combat, driven from their homes, lose their lives in bombing raids, and so on. Yet out of these extreme difficulties come examples of divine signatures, where the Lord reaches out and blesses His children. Here is one example from World War II.

> On the night of Jan. 30, 1945, Latter-day Saints Margarete Hellwig and her daughter Gudrun fought their way through the crowds that thronged the piers of the Baltic

Sea port and secured passage on the *Wilhelm Gustloff.* Along with thousands of other German women and children, they had fled their home in East Prussia, leaving husbands and sons to hold off the Soviet army as it advanced relentlessly toward the heart of Germany. Originally designed as a hospital ship, the *Wilhelm Gustloff* had been converted into a rescue transport vessel to carry the Germans on the Eastern front across the Baltic Sea to Germany and safety. The ship was meant to carry fewer than 2,000 passengers. On the night Margarete and Gudrun boarded, the vessel groaned under the weight of more than 10,000.

The Hellwigs were lucky to have made it aboard the ship, and their good fortune continued—they found a place to sit next to the warm engine room, deep within the ship. Just as they settled in, a loudspeaker announced that the ship was overloaded and that the crew was looking for volunteers to disembark before they set sail. At that moment, Margarete received a clear impression from the Holy Ghost. She recalled:

"It seemed as if somebody wanted to push me out. I told my daughter, 'I'm not staying in here, I've got to get out!'

"She answered, 'Mommy, it's so warm, let's stay here!'

"'No, I'm not staying here, I have to get out!' I was so very frightened."

Margarete followed her impression, and the two found themselves once again on shore. They located a smaller ship that was departing at the same time and were soon at sea.

At about 9 P.M. the *Wilhelm Gustloff* was struck by Soviet torpedoes, and from the deck of her ship, Margarete watched it sink into the Baltic. In what is still the most deadly maritime disaster in history, approximately 9,000 people lost their lives. Had she ignored the prompting to get off the ship,

Margarete and her daughter would have been among them. Mother and daughter arrived safely in Berlin, where they were taken in by Church members. Both survived the war.[2]

Here is another powerful example of how the Lord's hand is extended to help His children in times of extremity. I cannot help but note again that here, as in other cases of divine signatures, events unfolded in such a way that within hours, this mother learned for herself that her prompting was indeed from the Lord. Even in such terrible circumstances, the Lord confirmed to her that He was with them.

Amanda Barnes Smith—Exiled to Missouri

Warren Smith and his wife, Amanda Barnes Smith, were among the first to hear and accept the gospel after The Church of Jesus Christ of Latter-day Saints was organized. They were baptized in 1831 and moved to Kirtland, Ohio, the following year. There they were privileged to participate in many of the early events of Church history, including the building of the Kirtland Temple and the marvelous events surrounding its dedication.

In 1838, the Smiths, along with many other Saints, were forced to leave Kirtland by the enemies of the Church, including many who were former members turned apostate. The exiles became part of the "Kirtland Camp," a group of just over a hundred families and more than five hundred individuals. The Smiths and their five children left Kirtland in July 1838 and headed west for Adam-ondi-Ahman, Missouri, a distance of more than eight hundred miles.

Unfortunately, although they were hoping to find peace and safety, the Kirtland Camp moved from the proverbial frying pan directly into the fire. By the time the Smiths approached Far West, all of Missouri was in an uproar. As they neared their destination, the

Smiths and a few other families were delayed, and the main camp moved on without them.

On October 27, 1838, the situation in Missouri exploded. Governor Lilburn W. Boggs issued his famous order to drive the Mormons from the state or exterminate them. On receiving word of the governor's order, the Prophet Joseph sent messages to the outlying Mormon settlements and told them to come into Far West for protection.

October 30, 1838

The day after the extermination order was issued, a band of Missourians stopped the small party that included the Smiths and confiscated all their firearms. The following day, October 29, the group stopped at a small settlement just twelve miles east of Far West to rest and repair their equipment. Stopping there proved to be a fateful decision. The town had been founded by a man named Jacob Haun and was called Haun's Mill. One of those in the Smiths' group later recorded what happened the next day:

> More than three-fourths of the day had passed in tranquility. . . . The banks of Shoal creek on either side teemed with children sporting and playing, while their mothers were engaged in domestic employments, and their fathers employed in guarding the mills and other property, while others were engaged in gathering in their crops for their winter consumption. The weather was very pleasant, the sun shone clear, all was tranquil, and no one expressed any apprehension of the awful crisis that was near us—even at our doors.[3]

At about 4:00 P.M., the settlers heard what sounded like distant thunder. Suddenly they saw a band of about 250 men riding hard toward them. As mothers screamed for their children and husbands and fathers came running from the fields, a fusillade of rifle shots erupted.

In an instant, all was pandemonium. The women and children ran for the woods, while the men raced for the protection of the black-smith shop with its thick log walls and heavy door.

Screaming for his three boys to join him, Warren Smith also darted into the blacksmith shop. Alma and Sardius followed. But Willard, the oldest, was thrown back by some invisible force when he tried to pass through the door. He tried again and again, but with the same result, before he raced to a woodpile and dove behind it with bullets flying around him.

The blacksmith shop proved to be a death trap. Although the logs were heavy and thick, there were great cracks between them. The mob dismounted and surrounded the building, then put the muzzles of their guns to the openings and unleashed a withering fire.

Warren went down immediately, gravely wounded. Alma and Sardius crawled beneath the blacksmith's bellows to escape the gun-fire. When the mob broke in, they found Warren Smith crawling toward his boys. They stripped him of his boots, then killed him.

One mob member shoved his rifle under the bellows and fired. The bullet hit Sardius in the head, killing him instantly. Another mobber heard Alma whimpering in terror. He jammed the muzzle of his rifle against the boy's body and blew the entire hip joint away.

Nor were the women and children spared. As Amanda grabbed her two girls and sprinted for the trees along with the other women, volley after volley was sent in their direction.

When the mob finally retreated, a pall hung over the village. Slowly people began appearing—weeping, dazed, deep in shock. Willard Smith was the first to enter the blacksmith shop. What a terrible thing for a young boy to see. In addition to several other bodies, he found both his father and his brother Sardius dead. Alma, his youngest brother, was nearly unconscious and in terrible agony. He picked him up and took him outside.

"Heavenly Father, What Shall I Do?"

Here is Amanda Smith's account of what happened that terrible day:

> When the firing had ceased I went back to the scene of the massacre, for there were my husband and three sons, of whose fate I as yet knew nothing. . . . Passing on I came to a scene more terrible still to the mother and wife. Emerging from the blacksmith shop was my eldest son, bearing on his shoulders his little brother Alma. "Oh! my Alma is dead!" I cried, in anguish.
>
> "No, mother; I think Alma is not dead. But father and brother Sardius are killed!"
>
> What an answer was this to appal me! My husband and son murdered; another little son seemingly mortally wounded; and perhaps before the dreadful night should pass the murderers would return and complete their work! But I could not weep then. The fountain of tears was dry; the heart overburdened with its calamity, and all the mother's sense absorbed in its anxiety for the precious boy which God alone could save by his miraculous aid.
>
> The entire hip joint of my wounded boy had been shot away. Flesh, hip bone, joint and all had been ploughed out from the muzzle of the gun, which the ruffian placed to the child's hip through the logs of the shop and deliberately fired. We laid little Alma on a bed in our tent and I examined the wound. It was a ghastly sight. I knew not what to do. It was night now. . . . Yet was I there, all that long, dreadful night, with my dead and my wounded, and none but God as our physician and help.
>
> "Oh my Heavenly Father," I cried, "what shall I do?

Thou seest my poor wounded boy and knowest my inexperi-
ence. Oh, Heavenly Father, direct me what to do!" And then
I was directed as by a voice speaking to me. The ashes of our
fire was still smouldering. We had been burning the bark of
the shag-bark hickory. I was directed to take those ashes and
make a lye and put a cloth saturated with it right into the
wound. It hurt, but little Alma was too near dead to heed it
much. Again and again I saturated the cloth and put it into
the hole from which the hip joint had been ploughed, and
each time mashed flesh and splinters of bone came away with
the cloth; and the wound became as white as chicken's flesh.

Having done as directed I again prayed to the Lord and
was again instructed as distinctly as though a physician had
been standing by speaking to me. Near by was a slippery-elm
tree. From this I was told to make a slippery-elm poultice
and fill the wound with it. My eldest boy was sent to get the
slippery-elm from the roots, the poultice was made, and the
wound, which took fully a quarter of a yard of linen to cover,
so large was it, was properly dressed. It was then I found vent
to my feelings in tears, and resigned myself to the anguish of
the hour.

Still greatly fearing a return of the mob, the next morning the
Saints quickly took stock. The exact number is not known, but there
were at least seventeen dead. There was no time to dig graves, so the
survivors carried the bodies to a dry hole that was being dug for a
well. They hastily threw dirt over the bodies and prepared to leave
Haun's Mill.

"I'll Never Forsake"

But Alma Smith was not going anywhere. Amanda continues her account:

> I removed the wounded boy to a house, some distance off, the next day, and dressed his hip; the Lord directing me as before. I was reminded that in my husband's trunk there was a bottle of balsam. This I poured into the wound, greatly soothing Alma's pain. "Alma, my child," I said, "you believe that the Lord made your hip?"
> "Yes, mother."
> "Well, the Lord can make something there in the place of your hip, don't you believe he can, Alma?"
> "Do you think that the Lord can, mother?" inquired the child, in his simplicity.
> "Yes, my son," I replied, "he has showed it all to me in a vision."

That interchange between mother and son is quite astonishing. Her husband and two sons are dead, yet Amanda has not turned bitter. In fact, she teaches her son about the attribute of God's power. This is a powerful example of how a *correct* idea of God's character and attributes strengthens faith.

> Then I laid him comfortably on his face and said: "Now you lay like that, and don't move, and the Lord will make you another hip."
> So Alma laid on his face for five weeks, until he was entirely recovered—a flexible gristle having grown in place of the missing joint and socket, which remains to this day a marvel to physicians. On the day that he walked again I was

out of the house fetching a bucket of water, when I heard screams from the children. Running back, in affright, I entered, and there was Alma on the floor, dancing around, and the children screaming in astonishment and joy.

It is now nearly forty years ago, but Alma has never been the least crippled during his life, and he has traveled quite a long period of the time as a missionary of the gospel and a living miracle of the power of God.

During the five weeks in which Alma was recovering, the persecution continued. Far West fell and was ravaged. Joseph and other leaders were dragged off to jail. The Saints were forced to leave. The surviving women of the Haun's Mill massacre were threatened by the militia who said they would come back and kill them if they didn't stop praying to God for help.

Amanda describes her reaction to this further difficulty:

This godless silence was more intolerable than had been that night of the massacre. I could bear it no longer. I pined to hear once more my own voice in petition to my Heaven[ly] Father. I stole down to a corn field, and crawled into a stalk of corn. It was as the temple of the Lord to me at that moment. I prayed aloud and most fervently. When I emerged from the corn a voice spoke to me. It was a voice as plain as I ever hear[d] one. It was no silent, strong impression of the spirit, but a voice, repeating a verse of the Saint's hymn:

That soul who on Jesus hath leaned for repose,
I cannot, I will not, desert to its foes;
That soul, though all hell should endeavor to shake,
I'll never, no never, no never forsake!

From that moment I had no more fear. I felt that nothing could hurt me.[4]

"If God is a loving God as you say," some might ask, "why did he allow Amanda's husband and two of her boys to be killed in the first place? Why didn't he warn them not to stop at Haun's Mill?"

Those are difficult questions, and we don't have easy answers for them except to say that the Lord does not always reveal His purposes to us. As He has said, "For my thoughts are not your thoughts, neither are your ways my ways" (Isaiah 55:8).

The better question is this: Where did Amanda Smith find such astonishing faith and courage? It came directly from her unshakable faith in God's power to heal, and her belief that He had not forgotten her, even in such a terrible hour.

Amanda Smith's story is a powerful example of the truthfulness of what Joseph Smith taught in the School of the Prophets about faith and having a knowledge of God. This is what sustained Amanda Smith through a terrible tragedy. This is what allowed her to say, "From that moment on I had no more fear."

Notes

1. James E. Faust, "Where Do I Make My Stand?" *Ensign*, November 2004, 21.

2. Nathan N. Waite, "Steadfast German Saints," *BYU Magazine* (Winter 2010): 53–54.

3. Joseph Young, in Joseph Smith, *History of The Church of Jesus Christ of Latter-day Saints,* 7 vols., edited by B. H. Roberts (Salt Lake City: The Church of Jesus Christ of Latter-day Saints, 1932–51), 3:184.

4. "Amanda Smith," in Andrew Jenson, *LDS Biographical Encyclopedia,* 4 vols. (Salt Lake City: Andrew Jenson History Company, 1914), 2:796; paragraphing modernized. Some information also comes from the entry on Willard Smith, 1:473.

Mortality is a school of suffering and trials. We are here that we may be educated in a school of suffering and of fiery trials, which school was necessary for Jesus, our Elder Brother, who, the scriptures tell us, "was made perfect through suffering." It is necessary that we suffer in all things, that we may be qualified and worthy to rule, and govern all things, even as our Father in Heaven and His eldest son, Jesus.

L ORENZO S NOW

CHAPTER FOUR

The Paradox of Life

Joy and Happiness, Sorrow and Tribulation

There is a puzzling paradox in life as we know it.

A paradox is a statement or a set of facts that seems contradictory, but which is nevertheless true. And life is a paradox. Mortality, or this probationary state as the scriptures call it, contains what appears to be an enormous contradiction. Note the following scriptural passages:

Lehi taught that "Adam fell that men might be; and *men are, that they might have joy*" (2 Nephi 2:25).

Yet God said to Adam and Eve, "I will greatly multiply thy *sorrow* and thy conception. In *sorrow* thou shalt bring forth children. . . . Cursed shall be the ground for thy sake; in *sorrow* shalt thou eat of it all the days of thy life" (Moses 4:22–23; Genesis 3:16–17). (*Note:* The Hebrew word used in Genesis that is translated as "sorrow" conveys more than just grief. It includes the idea of labor, toil, pain, and travail.[1])

In his vision, Lehi saw that the fruit of the tree of life "was desirable to *make one happy*" (1 Nephi 8:10); and that it filled the "soul with *exceedingly great joy*" (1 Nephi 8:12). It was "the most desirable above all things. . . . Yea, and *the most joyous* to the soul" (1 Nephi 11:22–23).

The prophet Jacob said of his life: "Our lives passed away like as it were unto us a dream, we being a *lonesome and a solemn people*, wanderers, cast out from Jerusalem, *born in tribulation*, in a wilderness, and hated of our brethren, which caused wars and contentions; wherefore, *we did mourn out our days*" (Jacob 7:26).

Alma taught that the plan of salvation is also known as "the *great plan of happiness*" (Alma 42:8, 16).

Yet both Nephi and Alma described this life as a "vale" or "*valley of sorrow*" (2 Nephi 4:26; Alma 37:45). Isaiah said, "I have chosen thee in *the furnace of affliction*" (Isaiah 48:10; see also 54:16); and the Psalmist noted, "Many are the *afflictions of the righteous*" (Psalm 34:19). In Proverbs we read, "*Even in laughter the heart is sorrowful*" (Proverbs 14:13).

To the twelve disciples in America, the resurrected Christ said, "Ye shall have *fulness of joy*; and ye shall sit down in the kingdom of my Father; yea, *your joy shall be full*" (3 Nephi 28:10).

To the twelve apostles in Jerusalem, the mortal Jesus said: "These things I have spoken unto you, *that in me ye might have peace*. In the world *ye shall have tribulation*: but *be of good cheer*; I have overcome the world" (John 16:33).

A Bishop's Experience

When I was called as a new bishop some years ago, I received some wonderful advice from a good friend and experienced priesthood leader.

"When I was a new bishop," he said, "I used to sit on the stand in sacrament meeting and look out over the congregation. I would notice a new family sitting in the audience and think to myself, 'Oh, that must be the Jones family who just moved in by the Browns. I wonder what we could call them to do.' But after I had been a bishop for a year or so, I would sit on the stand and look out and see a new family, and say to myself, 'Oh, a new family. I wonder what problems they have?'"

At first I thought his statement was a bit of an exaggeration. When he said that everyone had "problems," I thought he was talking about "spiritual problems"—sins or transgressions. But as my service as a bishop continued, I quickly learned something that I believe is true of virtually every bishop and branch president in the Church. I could pass through my ward and point to almost any house and name a problem that family was facing. The list included aging parents living in the home; wayward children who were breaking their parents' hearts; a personal or family health crisis; deep depression or clinical anxiety in a loved one; a crumbling marriage; addictions to pornography, drugs, or alcohol; loss of employment and the resulting financial crisis that follows; a crippling accident; or the tragic, unexpected death of a family member.

And those were just the problems I knew about!

The Challenges of Good Times

Not all the problems I saw were caused by some kind of tragic twist of fate or personal disaster. We lived in a peaceful, beautiful setting with a low crime rate and much harmony in the community. Our ward was not a wealthy ward, but we had strong, stable families, experiencing, for the most part, a comfortable level of affluence by the world's standards.

I learned as a bishop, and it has been validated many times since, that not all trials come from tragic circumstances, no more than all sin and transgression comes from open rebellion. Life is complex, and human beings are complex. Good times bring their own kind of challenges. Mormon gave this warning as he abridged the history of the Nephites: "We may see at the very time when he doth prosper his people, . . . yea, then is the time that they do harden their hearts, and do forget the Lord their God, . . . yea, and this because of their ease, and their exceedingly great prosperity" (Helaman 12:2).

Some years ago, Elder Melvin J. Ballard issued a similar warning:

> The sorest trials that have ever come to the Church in any age of the world are the trials of peace and prosperity. But we are to do a new thing, a thing that never has before been done—We are to take the Church of Christ not only through the age of persecution and mob violence, but through the age of peace and prosperity. *For we must learn to endure faithfully even in peace and prosperity. . . .*
>
> For it was not the design and the intention of the Lord to have this people always in suffering in bondage and distress. They shall come to peace and prosperity, but it is the sorest trial that will come to them.[2]

Priesthood leaders frequently see problems arising from this happier side of life as well as from the darker and more challenging side. It is not uncommon to hear of families with three or four times the average income of others being the ones who end up deepest in debt. Some individuals, in their desire to be successful and provide a comfortable lifestyle for their family, set the "good things of life" as their highest priority. Surely these good things of life are not evil in and of themselves, yet the quest for them may bring unexpected and unintended consequences.

During my service in an area presidency, and then for two years with the Missionary Department, I dealt with several missionaries who insisted on going home early because their missions just weren't "fun." In many of those cases, I learned that their family's affluence had allowed them to live a lifestyle filled with ATVs, jet skis, skiing, surfing, playing video games, taking vacations to exotic places, and so on. Is there anything wrong with those things? Of course not. But this "ease" and "prosperity," as Mormon called it, were now having their effect. And parents and families were devastated.

When I asked one young man what he planned to do if he did go home, he said that his primary goal right now was to achieve level seven of some video game he had played before coming into the field. I felt like weeping for him, for his family, and for his future wife and children.

I have learned something else as a priesthood leader. Lehi spoke of those who fall away into "forbidden paths" and are lost (1 Nephi 8:28). In my early years I tended to stereotype such individuals as rebellious and steeped in sin. And there is no question that sometimes some people just want to be bad. But I've learned that it is far more common for us to fall into sin and transgression for more human reasons—boredom, loneliness, low self-esteem, a desire to love and be loved, laziness, a longing to be accepted by peers, simple curiosity, or just plain lack of good sense.

Several years ago, a priesthood leader told me of another tragic case. He was working with a girl of seventeen or eighteen who was having an affair with a married man twice her age. She had been active in the church and still was. Her parents were active members, but there were a lot of problems in the home. Her father left the family for another woman when this girl was in her early teens. The mother had so many emotional problems of her own that this young woman had been basically pushed aside.

When this priesthood leader realized that nothing he was saying was getting through to her, he said, "But don't you understand? What you are doing has eternal consequences. If you continue in this relationship, it could stop you from entering the celestial kingdom."

She looked at him for a long moment, then, in a low voice, said, "Don't *you* understand? I would rather be loved for one hour right now, than have an eternity in the celestial kingdom."

A Side Note

It has been my experience that there are some individuals in life whose problems and challenges greatly complicate the process of gaining faith and testimony for them. I speak of sexual abuse, same-gender attraction, and clinical depression or mental illness.

These circumstances are often so emotionally and spiritually crippling that they leave an individual feeling deeply alienated from God. This may be reflected as deep anger because God allowed this to happen to them or that "He made me this way." In other cases, they don't directly blame God, but they feel so totally unworthy that they believe they are unloved and unlovable. And therefore they are without hope. They may turn to alcohol, drugs, or promiscuous sex in their desperation to cope with the pain.

Usually these problems require much more than well-intentioned admonitions to "try harder," or "be more faithful." Such individuals may need the help of trained professionals and might require prolonged use of medications, or even hospitalization, in the case of mental illness. This book does not attempt to address those specific problems and was not meant to suggest that what is discussed here may be the solution to such deeply rooted challenges.

Unfortunately, these difficult challenges not only affect those who are struggling with the problems, they directly impact friends, family members, and other caregivers. This can create heavy burdens for them as well. For those looking for answers within the Church, the following can provide help:

- Bishops and stake presidents can provide information and access to resources produced by the Church to help people struggling with these challenges. That includes referring them to LDS Social Services or other professional individuals or organizations.
- LDS Social Services provides not only counseling but an extensive library on how to deal with social, emotional, and spiritual problems. These can be accessed in person (usually through a referral from a priesthood leader) or online at www.ldsfamily services.org.

Here are some recently printed resources that may help:

- M. Russell Ballard, *Suicide: Some Things We Know, and Some Things We Do Not* (Salt Lake City: Deseret Book, 1993).
- "Bipolar Disorder: My Lessons in Love, Hope, and Peace," *Ensign,* January 2009, 62–67.
- Jeffrey R. Holland, "Helping Those Who Struggle with Same-Gender Attraction," *Ensign,* October 2007, 42–45.
- Alexander B. Morrison, "Myths about Mental Illness," *Ensign,* October 2005, 31–35.
- Alexander B. Morrison, *Valley of Sorrow: A Layman's Guide to Understanding Mental Illness* (Salt Lake City: Deseret Book, 2003).
- Dallin H. Oaks, "Same-Gender Attraction," *Ensign,* October 1995, 7–14.

- Ann F. Pritt, "Healing the Spiritual Wounds of Sexual Abuse," *Ensign,* April 2001, 58–63.
- Richard G. Scott, "To Heal the Shattering Consequences of Abuse," *Ensign,* May 2008, 40–43.
- *Understanding Same-Sex Attraction: Where to Turn, and How to Help* (Lehi, Utah: Foundation for Attraction Research, 2009).

Life Is Good; Life Is Hard

So there is the paradox. Life is good in so many ways. We are blessed in so many ways. There is joy and peace and happiness to be had. But just around the next corner, even lurking close by, we may find, as Brigham Young said, "sorrow, grief, mourning, woe, misery, pain, anguish and disappointment."[3]

This is because we were sent to earth to gain experience and to prove ourselves. Unfortunately, the strongest and most resilient plants grow outside of the hothouse. That means that the Garden of Eden just wouldn't do as a proving ground. Or, to use another metaphor, the most precious metals are refined in the fire. As the Lord said, "Behold, I have created the smith that bloweth the *coals in the fire,* and *that bringeth forth an instrument for his work*" (Isaiah 54:16).

For those who desire to become an instrument in the hands of God, those are sobering words.

Elder Bruce R. McConkie tied adversity, in its many forms, to this testing, purifying process:

I say that this life never was intended to be easy. It is a probationary estate in which *we are tested physically, mentally, morally, and spiritually.* We are subject to disease and decay. We are attacked by cancer, leprosy, and contagious diseases. We suffer pain and sorrow and afflictions. Disasters strike; floods sweep away our homes; famines destroy our food; plagues and wars fill our graves with dead bodies and our broken homes with sorrow. . . .

Temptations, the lusts of the flesh, evils of every sort—all these are part of the plan, and must be faced by every person privileged to undergo the experiences of mortality.[4]

George Q. Cannon, of the First Presidency, explained it this way:

The Saints should always remember that God sees not as man sees; that he does not willingly afflict his children, and that if he requires them to endure present privation and trial, it is that they may escape greater tribulations which would otherwise inevitably overtake them. If He deprives them of any present blessing, it is that he may bestow upon them greater and more glorious ones by-and-by.[5]

The Threshing Sled

Threshing is the process whereby the edible kernels of various cereal grains, such as wheat or oats, are separated from the inedible chaff that surrounds them. In ancient times, this was a laborious and tedious process. The Romans, with their usual engineering ingenuity, developed what came to be known as a "threshing sledge," or sled, as we would say, to make the process more efficient and less labor-intensive.

Similar to a modern toboggan, only wider and shorter, a threshing sled had pieces of metal or sharp stones driven into the underside of the wood in order to provide a rough cutting edge. The harvested stalks of grain were spread out on a flat, hard surface called the threshing floor, and animals would drag the sled around and around over the grain stalks.

In Latin, the threshing sled was called the *tribulum*. Yes, that's right. This is the source of our word "tribulation." Sometimes life has a way of feeling like one giant threshing sled, doesn't it? Perhaps if all adversity came in quick, short bursts, or if all toil could be done in the cool of the morning, we could endure it better. But so often the demands of life are unyielding and the pressure is never ending. It feels like *we* are the stalks of grain spread out on the threshing floor, and life keeps going around and around over the top of us, pressing down, grinding away, stripping away any joy and happiness we might have known.

Someone once quipped: "The thing about life is, it's so *daily*!" Words like relentless, implacable, unsparing, persistent, inexorable, and merciless describe some aspects of our mortal experience. Sometimes grief piles upon grief, adversity turns into tribulation, sorrow pushes aside happiness, joy is swallowed up in suffering. Poverty, war, anarchy, and tyranny all bring their own form of tribulation. But as we have seen, peace and prosperity are no guarantee that life will be merry and filled with perpetual gaiety either. One might say that tribulation and adversity are "equal opportunity" employers. There is no discrimination on their part. They are generous with the rich and the poor, the famous and the obscure, the happy and the sad, the righteous and the wicked, the healthy and the sick, the whole and the maimed.

Tribulation is part of mortal life. But it will not always be so. When we leave this life, if we have sought to be faithful, we shall enter into "a state of happiness, . . . a state of rest, a state of peace, where they shall rest from all their troubles and from all care, and sorrow" (Alma 40:12). Until then, the *tribulum* awaits.

To Summarize

We are told in several places in the scriptures that we must "endure to the end" (e.g., 1 Nephi 22:31; 2 Nephi 31:20; D&C 14:7).
That's an interesting choice of words, isn't it? It doesn't say that we
shall "coast along until it's over," or "skip happily on our way, singing,
and strewing rose petals along the path." It doesn't even say that we
must "persevere to the end," though, obviously, perseverance will be
required. It says that we must endure. "Endure" comes from the Latin
root, *durare,* which means to last, to be strong, or to become hard.[6]

My daughter shared this experience with me that had been told
to her by a close friend:

> My friend Roberta was complaining to her mother that
> her life was not going like she had hoped and planned that
> it would. "Mom, I'm keeping the commandments," she said,
> "honoring my covenants, serving in the Church. I'm doing
> everything, but my life is not working out."
>
> Her mom looked her in the eye and said, "Roberta, you
> have it backward. This life isn't the reward. This life is the
> test."

My mother taught me a similar lesson when, at a family gathering, one of our children asked her: "Grandma, you've lived more
than eighty years now. What changes have you noticed?" I'm not sure
what I expected her to say, but it sure wasn't what she said. She fired
right back with this:

> People never said "Have a nice day" until the 1970s. We
> didn't expect to have a nice day. We knew it would be hard.
> Our life was hard. Our friends' lives were hard. It had always
> been hard for us, and we figured it would always be hard. But

we were all in it together, and so it was all right. Then in the '70s everyone started saying, "Have a nice day." And then people felt gypped if they weren't having a "nice day" kind of life.

While Paul and Barnabas were preaching the gospel in a city called Lystra, some of Paul's enemies came and stirred up the town against the missionaries. Paul was stoned and left for dead. Fortunately, he survived, and the next day he and Barnabas left the city and travelled to Derbe. There Paul exhorted the Saints to "continue in the faith," and told them that "we must *through much tribulation* enter into the kingdom of God" (Acts 14:22).

The purpose of this book is not to dwell on the more difficult side of life, nor to fully explore the question of tribulation and adversity. Our question is: *How do we strengthen our faith and deepen our testimony to the point that we can endure whatever life holds in store for us and come out stronger than before?* What we have learned in this chapter is that this will not be easy. The challenges will not come only intermittently to us, and they may come in good times or bad.

Notes

Epigraph. Lorenzo Snow, in Clyde J. Williams, *The Teachings of Lorenzo Snow* (Salt Lake City: Bookcraft, 1984), 119.

1. See William Wilson, *Wilson's Old Testament Word Studies* (Peabody, Mass.: Hendrickson Publishers, 1990), 406.

2. Melvin J. Ballard, in Conference Report, April 1929, 66. Note the date of his address; the Great Depression began just six months later.

3. Brigham Young, as cited in Daniel H. Ludlow, ed., *Latter-day Prophets Speak* (Salt Lake City: Bookcraft, 1948), 28.

4. Bruce R. McConkie, "The Dead Who Die in the Lord," *Ensign,* November 1976, 106.

5. George Q. Cannon, in *Millennial Star* (3 October 1863): 25:634.

6. *Random House Webster's Unabridged Dictionary* (New York: Random House Reference, 2010), s.v. "endure."

A Strengthening Hand in
Times of Extremity

A Calendar of Exile

O ne day while reading in the history of the Church, something occurred to me. I had noticed, of course, that from the earliest beginnings of the Restoration, there had been persecution. (Who could miss that?) But over and over the persecution would become so intense that either the leaders or the Church as a whole were forced to move to escape danger. As I was thinking about that pattern, I noticed something else. Let me illustrate what I eventually called "A Calendar of Exile."

December 1827. Persecution in Palmyra forces Joseph to take Emma to Harmony, Pennsylvania.

January 1831. The Lord commanded the Saints to move to Ohio. Joseph and Emma left early that month and arrived in Kirtland the first week of February. The Saints followed soon after.

October/November 1833. The Saints are driven from Jackson County, Missouri.

January 1838. Joseph flees Kirtland because his life is threatened.

The same month, a large body of members called Kirtland Camp followed.

October/November 1838. The extermination order is issued in Missouri. The Haun's Mill massacre and the fall of Far West quickly follow. Joseph, Hyrum, and other leaders are imprisoned.

January/February 1839. Under the direction of Brigham Young and Heber C. Kimball, the Saints in Missouri are forced to flee east to Illinois for refuge.

February 1846. Under threat of mob violence once again, the Saints leave Nauvoo, and the first wagons head west across Iowa Territory.

Notice anything unusual about that pattern? Sometimes there's such a thing as bad timing, but seven out of seven times the Saints' exiles happened in the winter. That's more than a run of bad luck.

We know that the testing and proving process is part of this mortal life. And it is particularly true for the Lord's people. Paul said it well: "All that will live godly in Christ Jesus shall suffer persecution" (2 Timothy 3:12). But must the way be so hard? Must there always be the refining fire or the constant grinding of the *tribulum?* A June or July might have been nice in the calendar of exile. Even a May or April would have been acceptable. Such was not the case. As if being driven from their homes was not a challenge enough, they had to do it at the worst time of the year.

Quoting Elder Orson F. Whitney, President Kimball had this to say about adversity:

> No pain that we suffer, no trial that we experience is
> wasted. It ministers to our education, to the development
> of such qualities as patience, faith, fortitude and humility.
> All that we suffer and all that we endure, especially when

we endure it patiently, builds up our characters, purifies our hearts, expands our souls, and makes us more tender and charitable, more worthy to be called the children of God . . . and it is through sorrow and suffering, toil and tribulation, that we gain the education that we come here to acquire and which will make us more like our Father and Mother in heaven.[1]

It may help to know that a trial is for our good, but it doesn't make the suffering any less intense. However, one of the lessons that becomes abundantly clear in the study of Church history is that while the Lord may place His people into extreme circumstances, that doesn't mean that He abandons them. He doesn't remove the challenges, but He is there to support, sustain, and strengthen. As Elder Neal A. Maxwell once observed, "[God's] grace will cover us like a cloak—enough to provide for survival but too thin to keep out all the cold."[2]

Such was the case in 1856.

Blessings in the Midst of Suffering

The story of the Martin and Willie Handcart companies of 1856 is well-known in the Church. While other companies had come earlier in the season without serious incident, these two companies, with well over a thousand emigrants, were late leaving England. When they arrived in Iowa City, supplies were already severely depleted. Worse, in Salt Lake City, Brigham Young didn't know any more travelers were coming west, so he called in the resupply wagons that had been meeting the other companies in eastern Wyoming with food and other critical supplies.

Due to one delay after another, the Willie Company didn't get underway until July 15, and the Martin Company was two weeks behind them. This was well over a month past the deadline for the last companies to head west. The high plains of Wyoming and the mountain passes of Utah Territory are six and seven thousand feet in elevation, and winter storms can strike early and hard. Some areas along that trail can see frost in any month of the year. This combination of circumstances set the stage for a crisis of enormous proportions.

What followed as the two companies made their way westward would turn into one of the most difficult challenges any pioneers ever faced. Men who had traveled the trail many times later reported that the storms that struck in mid-October were the worst they had seen. Food ran out, and there was no more to be had. They had to ford ice-choked rivers. The weather at one point dropped to minus ten below zero. Frostbite was endemic. Before the companies made it to Salt Lake, about one-fifth of their number had died. They suffered almost beyond comprehension.

For whatever purpose, God chose not to soften their circumstances. But through the darkness of their terrible sufferings shines the light of God's tender mercies and the mark of His divine signatures. I cite only three examples out of many.

From Liverpool to Salt Lake City in Seventy Days

A member of the Quorum of the Twelve, Elder Franklin D. Richards was serving as the president of the British Mission, and it was his responsibility to help emigrants get to America and on to the Valley.

The *Horizon,* the last emigrant ship for the season, left Liverpool on May 25, 1856. After getting the last two shiploads of Saints on their way from Liverpool, President Richards then began to make preparations for his own departure for Salt Lake. He had sent letters to Brigham Young advising him that two more companies were on their way, but communication between Europe and the Utah Territory was slow. A letter could take two months or more to go one way.

A close examination of what few records we have of the journey gives us a fairly detailed account of how long the journey from Liverpool to Salt Lake took. Five handcart companies came in 1856. They crossed the Atlantic in four different sailing ships: the *Enoch Train,* the *Samuel Curling,* the *Thornton,* and the *Horizon.* Three of the four sailed to Boston, while the *Thornton* disembarked at New York City. The entire journey from Liverpool to the Great Salt Lake Valley varied somewhat according to how long each company stopped along the way. The accompanying chart shows the various ships and their companies and how long their journeys took.[3]

Name of Ship	Atlantic Crossing	Time from Arrival to Leaving Florence	Total for Entire Journey to Salt Lake City
Enoch Train	39 days	79 days	185 days
Samuel Curling	35 days	67 days	167 days
Thornton	42 days	94 days	221 days
Horizon	37 days	62 days	195 days
Average	38 days	76 days	192 days

Now compare that with the journey of Elder Richards' party. They left Liverpool on July 26, more than two months later than the previous departure. They took a steamship instead of a sailing ship, which helped. They went to New Orleans and then took a riverboat all the way up the Mississippi and Missouri rivers to Florence, arriving there on August 21. They departed Florence two weeks later, on September 3.

There's the first miracle. Where it took the other companies an average of 114 days from Liverpool to their departure from Florence, it took the Richards' party only 38 days! Even though the route through New Orleans was several hundred miles longer, they made the journey in almost one-third the time it took the others.

Elder Richards and his group traveled in light carriages drawn by horses and mules. They literally raced westward. They arrived in Salt Lake City in the afternoon of October 4, just thirty-two days later.[4]

Let's put that in the proper perspective. The Richards' party came from Liverpool, England, to the Salt Lake Valley—a distance of 4,700 miles as the crow flies—in an astonishing seventy days! To put it another way, they made the trip in less than half the time of the fastest group, and a third of the time of the slowest company. If we take out the two weeks the company spent in Florence, and assume the actual distance was more like 5,500 miles, it means they averaged nearly one hundred miles per day. That is an incredible feat for that day and age.

It is not just the speed of their journey that is significant. As noted, they arrived in the Valley in the afternoon of October 4. They immediately reported to the First Presidency that two more handcart companies with about a thousand people were still on the plains with winter closing in.

The next morning, Sunday, October 5, was the first general meeting of the Church's 26th Semiannual General Conference. At the beginning of the meeting, President Young stood and told the congregation what he had just learned. He put aside his prepared text and told the other speakers to do the same. Their message that day would be, "Go out and rescue the handcart people." He called for teams, wagons, teamsters, flour, clothing, bedding, and medical supplies.

The response was amazing. The people immediately sprang into action. Less than forty-eight hours later, early Tuesday morning, the first wagons were rolling eastward. Had the Richards' party been even a week later, they would have missed the conference. That was a critical component in what followed. The Church leaders didn't have to send riders out to all the settlements to spread the word; everybody was already in Salt Lake for conference! That saved them at least a week and probably more. As it turned out, when the rescue party did find the Willie Company, the handcart pioneers were out of food and had stopped, unable to go any farther.

Here is another case where the timing of the Lord's blessing proved to be critical, as Elder Bednar said.[5] Thanks to the timely (we may even say, *miraculous*) arrival of the brethren from England, one of the greatest, if not the greatest, rescue efforts in early U.S. history was launched, and hundreds of lives were saved.

"This Act [Was] the Means of Their Salvation"

Here is another example of when the precise timing of another of the Lord's signatures averted disaster.

As the rescue wagons, filled with desperately needed supplies, moved east from the Valley, they kept expecting to receive word of the whereabouts of the two handcart companies. By the time they reached the Green River crossing, a week into their journey, they still had no idea how much farther they had to go to find them. George D. Grant, captain of the rescue party, decided to send an express party of four scouts forward to try to locate the companies.

On October 17, a raging blizzard swept out of the north, lasting for three days. This was a terrible blow to the handcart companies who were already near total exhaustion. When the Willie Company reached the Sixth Crossing of the Sweetwater River, they stopped. They were exhausted, out of food, and unable to go any farther. It was here that the four scouts of the express party found them. They were welcomed like angels from heaven. The scouts distributed what little food they had, then moved on to find the Martin Company, telling those in Captain Willie's group that more wagons were coming.

What the express party didn't know was that the blizzard had stopped the rescue wagons too. The storm was so fierce that Captain Grant finally ordered the wagons off the trail a few miles east of South Pass. He pulled them down into sheltering willows along a creek and settled in to let the storm blow itself out. They had no way of knowing that the Willie Company had been found and was expecting them to arrive at any time.

Back at the Sixth Crossing, the Willie Company was in a deep crisis. It was bitter cold, and they were completely out of food. Finally, in utter desperation, Captain Willie and Joseph Elder decided to set out in the storm to try to find Captain Grant's party.

Ranchers in Wyoming can tell stories of people getting lost and freezing to death within two or three hundred yards of their cabins. Wyoming blizzards are so fierce that even today sections of Interstate 80, which crosses southern Wyoming, are frequently closed to traffic because the wind whips the snow into deep drifts and causes complete whiteout conditions. For those two men to set off in such blizzard conditions shows just how critical their situation was. And they had no way of knowing that the rescue wagons were not on the trail, but were camped out of sight in some nearby willows.

What happened next was a little thing, hardly noticed by anyone at the time. A man by the name of Harvey Cluff, one of Captain Grant's rescue party, explains what happened in his own words:

> For protection of ourselves and the animals, the company moved down the river to where the willows were dense enough to make a good protection against the raging storm from the north. . . . Quietly resting in the seclusion of the willow copse, three miles from the road, I volunteered to take

a sign board and place it at a conspicuous place at the main road. This was designed to direct the express party who were expected to return about this time. So they would not miss us. In facing the northern blast up hill [and in deepening snow] I found it quite difficult to keep from freezing.[6]

If I may interject some speculation here. When Brother Cluff first decided to take the signboard back up to the trail, I'm sure he could have thought of a hundred reasons for not going. Surely no one would be out on the trail in this storm. If the express party was on their way back, they were likely holed up somewhere too. It was so much more comfortable sitting by the fire and out of the wind.

And not only was it going to be difficult bucking his way back up through the snow to the trail, but dangerous, too. In that kind of storm a man could easily get lost and perish before anyone found him. Yet the feeling that he should place the board was strong enough and clear enough that he felt he had to respond. By the time he returned to camp, he probably wondered if it had not been an exercise in futility. But confirmation that those feelings were from the Lord was not long in coming.

Cluff continues: "I had only been back to camp *a short time* when two men [Willie and Elder] rode up from Willie's handcart company. The signboard had done the work of salvation."[7]

Note his words. He had only been back in camp "a short time." A storm that bad would have covered the sign and made it virtually invisible very quickly, so Captain Willie and James Elder must have reached the spot where Cluff placed the signboard within minutes of him putting it up. Had Cluff hesitated even for a few minutes, or rationalized that it was a futile effort, James Willie and Joseph Elder would have passed on by and been lost. In addition to the almost certain deaths of those two faithful brethren, how many more of the

Willie Handcart Company would have died as a result of further delays?

Brother Cluff ended his account with these words: "I have always regarded this act of mine as the means of their salvation. And why not? An act of that importance is worthy of record and hence I give a place here."[8]

"Every One of Us Came through with the Absolute Knowledge That God Lives"

Francis Webster was twenty-five years old when he joined the Martin Handcart Company and started west. His wife, Ann Elizabeth Parsons, was pregnant at the time. She gave birth to a baby daughter somewhere in western Nebraska by the Platte River. The baby was barely a month old when the October storms hit, yet she survived and was carried by her mother all the way to Utah.

The Websters eventually settled in Cedar City in Southern Utah. One day, many years after the ordeal of 1856 was over, a Sunday School teacher began criticizing the decision of the Church leaders to bring those last two companies across the plains when it was so late in the season. Brother Webster was present. Incensed at what he was hearing, he spoke up:

> I ask you to stop this criticism. You are discussing a matter you know nothing about. Cold historic facts mean nothing here, for they give no proper interpretation of the questions involved. . . . I was in that company and my wife was in it. . . . We suffered beyond anything that you can imagine and many died of exposure and starvation, but . . . every one of us came through with *the absolute knowledge that God lives* for we became acquainted with him in our extremities.
>
> I have pulled my handcart when I was so weak and weary

from illness and lack of food that I could hardly put one foot ahead of the other. I have looked ahead and seen a patch of sand or a hill slope and I have said, I can go only that far and there I must give up, for I cannot pull the load through it. . . .

I have gone on to that sand and when I reached it, the cart began pushing me. I have looked back many times to see who was pushing my cart, but my eyes saw no one. And I knew then that the angels of God were there.

Was I sorry that I chose to come by handcart? No. Neither then nor any minute of my life since. *The price we paid to become acquainted with God was a privilege to pay,* and I am thankful that I was privileged to come in the Martin Handcart Company.[9]

That is a wonderful summary of the importance of divine signatures. To have help from the other side of the veil in pushing your handcart is incredible, a marvelous blessing in and of itself. But Brother Webster didn't emphasize that. What had the deepest impact on him was that coming through that experience had given him "the absolute knowledge that God lives."

It is unlikely that many of us will face anything as arduous and dangerous as what those early pioneers experienced. But we have challenges of a different nature, and spiritually they may be even more dangerous than a Wyoming blizzard. Elder Neal A. Maxwell once said:

These really are our days, and we can prevail and overcome, even in the midst of trends that are very disturbing. If we are faithful the day will come when those deserving pioneers and ancestors, whom we rightly praise for having overcome the adversities in their wilderness trek, will praise today's faithful for having made their way successfully through a desert of despair and for having passed through a cultural wilderness, while still keeping the faith.[10]

What experiences does the future hold for us that will help us become acquainted with God? We do not know. Perhaps nothing that would compare to the experiences of these handcart pioneers. But note this counsel from President James E. Faust:

> In the heroic effort of the handcart pioneers, we learn a great truth. All must pass through a refiner's fire, and the insignificant and unimportant in our lives can melt away like dross and make our faith bright, intact, and strong. There seems to be a full measure of anguish, sorrow, and often heartbreak for everyone, including those who earnestly seek to do right and be faithful. Yet this is part of the purging to become acquainted with God.[11]

If we are called to experience "a full measure of anguish, sorrow, and often heartbreak," may we be buoyed up and strengthened by the divine signatures that came through Franklin D. Richards, Harvey Cluff, and Francis Webster. Their experiences teach us a great deal about what kind of God it is that we worship.

Notes

1. Orson F. Whitney, in Spencer W. Kimball, *Faith Precedes the Miracle* (Salt Lake City: Deseret Book, 1972), 98.

2. Neal A. Maxwell, *Even As I Am* (Salt Lake City: Deseret Book, 1982), 109.

3. These calculations come from figures provided in LeRoy R. Hafen and Ann W. Hafen, *Handcarts to Zion* (Glendale, Calif.: The Arthur H. Clark Co., 1960), 46, 193.

4. See Hafen and Hafen, *Handcarts to Zion,* 97, 218.

5. See David A. Bednar, "The Tender Mercies of the Lord," *Ensign,* May 2005, 99.

6. Harvey Cluff, in Stewart E. Glazier and Robert S. Clark, *Journal of the Trail,* 2d ed. (N.P.: Crescent Handcarts, 1997), 85.

7. Ibid.

8. Ibid.

9. Francis Webster, in David O. McKay, "Pioneer Women," *Relief Society Magazine* (January 1948): 8.

10. Neal A. Maxwell, *If Thou Endure It Well* (Salt Lake City: Deseret Book, 1996), 28.

11. James E. Faust, in "Faith in Every Footstep: The Epic Pioneer Journey," *Ensign,* May 1997, 63.

Fear not even unto death; for in this world your joy is not full, but in me your joy is full.

DOCTRINE AND COVENANTS 101:36

CHAPTER FIVE

Hardened Hearts or Softened Hearts?

When No Tender Mercies Come

I f adversity and misfortune followed simple rules or came in pre-
dictable patterns, it might help us better cope with them. But it
just isn't so. At times it seems as though there is some cosmic game
of spin-the-bottle underway, and all we can do is hunker down and
hope and pray that the bottle doesn't end up pointing at us. This is,
by its very nature, deeply unsettling and disturbing.

We have shared several stories now about God's rather dramatic
intervention into people's lives—a lost shoe and a lost check found,
a voice telling a bereaved mother how to treat her critically wounded
son, a Brazilian missionary who miraculously found his sister, a comforting touch on the cheek in the night. All are marvelous examples
of God's tender mercies to His children.

Yet not all stories end so happily. I am certain that there will be
readers who say to themselves, "But my mother, or my little brother,
had leukemia and wasn't healed. Why?"

Thousands of faithful women who were betrayed by their husband's infidelity have not seen their husband's priesthood and temple
blessings restored nor their marriage saved. In fact, in many cases,

just the opposite is true. Some endings are as tragic as the circumstances that brought them on.

One woman told me, "In addition to cheating on me with a woman he worked with, my husband siphoned off all the funds from our family business before he left me. Since I was co-owner of the business, I was left with a mountain of his unpaid bills. I had to go to work, something I had not done since we were married, but it was not enough. Eventually I lost the business and the house, the one thing I thought I had salvaged out of all this. Even now, many years later, we still have not fully recovered."

Thorny Questions

We have been exploring questions about faith and testimony. We're trying to discover what it is in the faith and testimony of some people that give them this astonishing amount of courage, but which is lacking in others.

All of us who live very long on this earth will sooner or later face challenges and misfortunes that will test us to the core of our being. These "inevitable tragedies of life"[1] become a crisis of faith. They raise questions about God and our relationship to Him and, since faith rests on having a correct knowledge of God and His nature and upon our own standing with Him, this can create a spiritual crisis within us.

When we are experiencing such intense sorrow or suffering, it is only natural that we seek understanding. We want to know why this is happening to us. If we know there is purpose in such experiences, perhaps that can help us better deal with the challenges that accompany them.

But so often the setbacks and problems of life seem so random, so undeserved. They seem to come into our lives independent of any action—good or bad—on our part. They strike without warning, and we have little or no control over them. And they smack directly in the face of our sense of justice, our sense of right and wrong.

A lifetime of observance of the Word of Wisdom doesn't guarantee freedom from disease. A drunk driver can wipe out an entire family who never touched any form of liquor in their lives.

Years of diligent and loyal employment can be lost in a single day because of the greed or dishonesty of corporate executives.

An innocent child is sexually or physically abused, sometimes by the very ones who should be the most trustworthy, and a lifetime of sorrow and pain follows.

We can carefully pray about our choice of a mate, choosing someone active and worthy so we can marry in the temple, then a few years later see him run off with an associate at work, or see her decide that the burden of children isn't "her thing" and abandon them and her husband.

When faced with such difficult circumstances, we want answers. We seek some kind of resolution so that we can cope with the challenges better. Here are but a few of the questions that naturally rise in the hearts of even the most faithful and committed:

- If God is the Creator of all things and has all power and perfect love for us, then why do bad things happen to good people?
- I have tried my whole life to do as He asks, to keep His commandments, to be faithful. And now this. Why, God? Why are you doing this to me?
- If God is good and loves His children, why does He tolerate evil in the world, especially when it impacts the good and the innocent in terrible ways?
- When women all over the world are able to bear children whom they will neglect or abuse, and millions of others are

terminating their unwanted pregnancies through abortion, why doesn't the Lord hear our prayers and grant us our righteous desires for a child?

- If my mother (or father, or brother, or child) is going to die anyway, why won't God just take them now and spare them weeks or even months of intense suffering?

- My wife and I decided we wanted her to be a mother in the home for our children, and so we have lived modestly so that could happen. But I have been out of a job for almost a year now, and my wife is working to help us survive. Why won't God help us find work?

- Why was a faithful young man in the prime of his life taken by a freak industrial accident just days before he was to begin his mission?

- If there is a God, why would He allow the tsunami in Indonesia, or the earthquake in Haiti, to take the lives of nearly a quarter of a million people in each case. Is this some kind of punishment for their wickedness? If so, why were some members of the Church killed? And what about all the innocent children? Why weren't they spared?

- My best friend is a much better person than I am. So why has she suffered so much more pain and tragedy in her life than I have?

- I have fasted and prayed and wept and pleaded over this affliction for so long now. Why doesn't God answer me?

- Why am I, your chosen prophet, languishing in a filthy cell in Liberty Jail while my wife and children and my people are being mobbed and driven from their homes?

- "O God, where art thou? And where is the pavilion that covereth thy hiding place? How long shall thy hand be stayed, and thine eye, yea thy pure eye, behold from the eternal heavens the wrongs of thy people?" (D&C 121:1–2).

Similar Circumstances, Different Responses

Earlier we raised the question about why people of faith (as judged by outward signs of their commitment such as church attendance, service, their expressed values, temple attendance, how they are bringing up their children, etc.) are caught in this crisis of faith. The downside of life—the setbacks, the pain, the problems, the suffering—is pretty much universal (though not always in equal amounts in the lives of individuals), but the reactions to these circumstances vary widely.

While abridging the history of the Nephites, Mormon took note of something unusual that happened in the midst of the Nephite's prolonged warfare with the Lamanites.

> Because of the exceedingly great length of the war between the Nephites and the Lamanites many had become *hardened,* . . . and many were *softened* because of their afflictions, insomuch that they did humble themselves before God, even in the depth of humility. (Alma 62:41)

Earlier, we noted Mormon's warning about peace and prosperity turning people away from the Lord. Yet note these passages, also written by Mormon in that same record:

> And the people of Nephi began to prosper again in the land, and began to multiply and to wax exceedingly strong again in the land. And they began to grow exceedingly rich. But notwithstanding their riches, or their strength, or their

prosperity, they were *not* lifted up in the pride of their eyes; neither were they slow to remember the Lord their God; but they did humble themselves exceedingly before him. Yea, they did remember how great things the Lord had done for them. (Alma 62:48–50)

It is not surprising that people are hardened by the effects of war, but softened? That is not what we would normally expect. And there are so many examples in the Book of Mormon of people falling away in times of prosperity that it is a little surprising to find a case that runs counter to that.

Had we personally known the Nephites of whom Mormon spoke, could we have identified specific traits that would help us predict whether they would be hardened or softened by war, or remain faithful in peace and prosperity? Can we do the same with people like Amanda Barnes Smith, or the mother with the lost shoe? Why did these women feel like they could turn to the Lord for help? Was it the way they were brought up? Was it some inner quality that they brought with them from the premortal world?

Think how valuable it would be if we could identify and articulate factors that make the difference. For those of us who live in these perilous times, that seems to be an issue of some consequence. Let us first look at things that do not explain this difference, even though they are often cited as the primary reason.

Human Frailty and Weakness

Some would say these differences are simple to explain. It is because people are different. Some people are stronger by nature, some weaker. Some have great confidence, others struggle with low self-esteem. Some seem to be blessed with a remarkable courage, while others are timid and easily frightened.

Of course people are different. That is a reality of life. But can we use those differences to justify our failure to stand strong? I don't think so. The Lord has made it clear that even though there are individual weaknesses or differing levels of ability, He will compensate for those shortfalls through His grace and mercy. I'll note just one passage here since this idea will be discussed in more detail in chapter 11.

If men come unto me I will show unto them their weakness.
I give unto men weakness that they may be humble; and *my grace is sufficient* for all men that humble themselves before me; for if they humble themselves before me, and have faith in me, *then will I make weak things become strong* unto them. (Ether 12:27)

While I served as a member of the Seventy, my wife and I conducted numerous mission tours and often spoke at the local Missionary Training Centers. It was our privilege to meet literally thousands of missionaries. Some of these individuals—elders, sisters, and senior missionaries—struggled with a deep sense of inadequacy. They were so painfully shy, so awkward, so lacking in confidence that they found the demands of missionary work to be pure agony. One sister told me that speaking to people was so utterly frightening to her that even the thought of it made her physically sick. In saying this, they were trying to explain why they were not being more effective missionaries.

I tried to let them know that I understood their pain, but I also felt compelled to teach them that the Lord has made his expectations quite clear. Consider, for example, what he said to early missionaries in the Church: "You shall open your mouth to declare my gospel; therefore, *fear not*" (D&C 30:5). And to a later group:

With some I am not well pleased, for they will not open their mouths, but they hide the talent which I have given unto them, *because of the fear of man.* Wo unto such, for mine anger is kindled against them. And it shall come to pass, if they are not more faithful unto me, it shall be taken away, even that which they have. (D&C 60:2–3)

When Moses was called to return to Egypt and confront Pharaoh, his reaction was open dismay. "O my Lord," he said, "I am not eloquent, . . . but I am slow of speech, and of a slow tongue." The Lord rebuked him, saying, "Who hath made man's mouth? . . . have not I the Lord?" (Exodus 4:10–11).

Enoch had pretty low self-esteem at the time of his call as well. His response to the Lord was "Why is it that I have found favor in thy sight, and am but a lad, and all the people hate me; for I am slow of speech; wherefore am I thy servant? And the Lord said unto Enoch: Go forth and do as I have commanded thee, and no man shall pierce thee. Open thy mouth, and it shall be filled, and *I will give thee utterance*" (Moses 6:31–32).

Moses went on to not only deliver Israel from Egypt but also led them in the wilderness for forty years and wrote the first five books of the Old Testament. Those books are to this day still classed among the great literature of the world. Not a bad accomplishment for a man who believed he had no eloquence.

As for Enoch, we read: "And so great was the faith of Enoch that he led the people of God, and their enemies came to battle against them; and he *spake the word of the Lord,* and the earth trembled, and the mountains fled, . . . *so great was the power of the language* which God had given him" (Moses 7:13).

Trying to excuse our failure to remain strong when adversity comes simply won't do. There are too many promises of help from the Lord. There are too many examples of individuals who, through faith, overcome such weakness.

The Intensity and Duration of Our Suffering

Here is another explanation frequently put forward to explain the differences in how individuals react to tragedy and tribulation: "But my burdens are so much heavier than yours. My trials are so much more intense than those that others are asked to face. That is why I gave up. I couldn't bear it any longer."

Sorry, but that doesn't stand up to examination either. Some years ago, a popular author made this observation about life:

> Life is difficult.
>
> This is a great truth, one of the greatest truths. . . .
>
> Most do not fully see this truth that life is difficult. Instead they moan more or less incessantly, noisily or subtly, about the enormity of their problems, their burdens, and their difficulties as if life were generally easy, as if life *should* be easy. They voice their belief, noisily or subtly, that their difficulties represent a unique kind of affliction that should not be and that has somehow been especially visited upon them . . . and not upon others. I know about this moaning because I have done my share.[2]

Others refuse to view themselves as victims, either of fate or of God's wrath, no matter how intense the challenge may be. They simply lower their heads and plow through whatever comes. In the history of the Church we find numerous examples of both types of people.

The Pioneers

When we speak of the Mormon pioneers, we tend to focus on the stories and accounts of those people who made their way to Utah and the Great Basin. We tell and retell the stories of their courage, their fortitude, and their indomitable faith. And rightly so. They earned their place in history, sometimes at a terrible cost. Indeed, the vast majority of Saints who started out for Zion persevered through every hardship and made their way to Zion.

But not all.

A careful study of the journals and accounts of those who came across the plains reveals numerous examples of people who found the way too hard, the trail too long, the price too high. Some crossed the oceans on Mormon emigrant ships, but once they disembarked in America, they never traveled again. There are towns in present-day Nebraska that were founded by Mormon pioneers who decided they had gone far enough. A few individuals came all the way to the Valley, only to turn around and leave again as soon as possible.

Poor health and physical exhaustion were factors, of course. On the other hand, there were others who were also in poor health or physically weak, and they refused to quit. In addition to physical exhaustion, some seemed to develop what might be termed "spiritual fatigue," or "soul fatigue." This is more a problem of the mind and heart than of the body. There is no question that these difficult circumstances were enough to try even the hardiest of souls. But on the other hand, the distance from Iowa City to the Salt Lake Valley was the same for all the pioneers. But for some it was too much.

There are examples in Church history of people who left the Church for what we might call trivial reasons. Symonds Ryder, who left the Church shortly after his conversion because his name was misspelled on his mission call, is one of the best examples of that.[3] One family left the Church because they had actually seen the Prophet come down out of the translating room and play with his children. And when Joseph read the dedicatory prayer for the Kirtland Temple, "this was a great trial of faith to many. 'How can it be that the prophet should read a prayer?'"[4]

Thomas B. Marsh, who was president of the Quorum of the Twelve at the time, turned so completely against Joseph Smith and the Church, that he made statements to the Missouri militia that did enormous damage to the Church and directly contributed to the tragedy at Far West and Haun's Mill. What happened in his life that was so terrible and made him so bitter? The First Presidency had earlier sided against him and his wife in a dispute over a few ounces of butter cream.[5]

Today we find similar examples. I personally know of a returned missionary who was so hurt when he wasn't invited to play on the Church softball team that he refused to come to church any longer. A long-time friend of our family decided to come back to the Church after years of no activity. A few weeks later, as she entered the chapel, the bishop—who was always there to welcome her—was talking to others and didn't see her. Deeply hurt, she left the meeting and never went back again as far as I know. A woman who had been one of the stalwarts in her ward was unexpectedly released as Primary president in sacrament meeting. She had not been told this was going to happen. She became convinced that the bishop was "getting even" with her for disagreeing with him in an earlier meeting. Fortunately, after a couple of months of nonattendance, she realized how foolish she was being, and returned. As it turned out, a counselor in the bishopric had been asked to speak with her before her release, but he simply forgot.

Stillman Pond

Compare the previous examples with the story of Stillman Pond and his family, as told by President James E. Faust:

> Stillman Pond was a member of the Second Quorum of Seventy in Nauvoo. He was an early convert to the Church. . . . Like others, he and his wife, Maria, and their children were harassed and driven out of Nauvoo. In September 1846, they became part of the great western migration. The early winter that year brought extreme hardships, including malaria, cholera, and consumption. The family was visited by all three of these diseases.
>
> Maria contracted consumption, and all of the children were stricken with malaria. Three of the children died while moving through the early snows. Stillman buried them on the plains. Maria's condition worsened because of the grief, pain, and the fever of malaria. She could no longer walk. Weakened and sickly, she gave birth to twins. They were named Joseph and Hyrum, and both died within a few days.[6]

Another account adds this detail:

> Stillman Pond, unable to walk, lay upon his stomach in his wagon. Bracing himself with one arm and peering through a knot hole in the dash board he drove his team with his other hand hanging over the dash board. In this manner he drove the last one hundred and fifty miles of Iowa territory.[7]

I can't help but wonder what feelings Stillman Pond had by this point. Did he question whether this new religion of his was really worth it? Did he feel that God had abandoned him? It is hard to believe that sometime during his ordeals he was not at least tempted to say, "O God, why? Where art thou? Why aren't you hearing my cries?"

President Faust continues:

> The Stillman Pond family arrived at Winter Quarters and, like many other families, they suffered bitterly while living in a tent. The death of the five children coming across the plains to Winter Quarters was but a beginning.
>
> The journal of Horace K. and Helen Mar Whitney verifies the following regarding four more of the children of Stillman Pond who perished:
>
> - "On Wednesday, the 2nd of December 1846, Laura Jane Pond, age 14 years, . . . died of chills and fever."
> - Two days later on "Friday, the 4th of December 1846, Harriet M. Pond, age 11 years, . . . died with chills."
> - Three days later, "Monday, the 7th of December, 1846, Abigail A. Pond, age 18 years, . . . died with chills."
> - Just five weeks later, "Friday, the 15th of January, 1847, Lyman Pond, age 6 years, . . . died with chills and fever."
> - Four months later, on the 17th of May, 1847, Stillman's wife, Maria Davis Pond, also died.[8]

Driven from Nauvoo at the point of a bayonet; driving one hundred and fifty miles looking through a knothole; losing his wife and nine of his eleven children—would it surprise any of us if the record showed that at this point Stillman raised his fists and shook them at the heavens, crying, "Enough! I will endure no more"?

But no. He went on to Utah and, as President Faust notes, "'became an outstanding colonizer in Utah.' . . . Stillman Pond did not lose his faith. He did not quit. He went forward. He paid a price, as have many others before and since, to become acquainted with God."[9]

An Apostle's Witness

Over the years I have collected a group of what I call my "humility" scriptures. When I begin feeling sorry for myself, I take them out and read them again. They quickly put things back into their proper perspective. The life of Paul of Tarsus is one of those examples.

Paul was a missionary for more than thirty years. He traveled through much of the Roman Empire at a time when travel was slow and ponderous and dangerous. He suffered ridicule, rejection, persecution, and eventually martyrdom. When some of the Saints in Corinth questioned Paul's credentials and claimed to be more qualified leaders than he was, he answered them with a summary of his ministry.

> Are they Hebrews? so am I. Are they Israelites? so am I. Are they the seed of Abraham? so am I. Are they ministers of Christ? . . . I am more; in labours more abundant, in stripes [i.e., the lacerations that come from scourgings] above measure, in prisons more frequent, in deaths oft. Of the Jews five times received I forty stripes save one.*
>
> Thrice was I beaten with rods, once was I stoned, thrice I suffered shipwreck, a night and a day I have been in the deep;

---

* Under Jewish law, a man accused of heresy, as Paul often was, could retain his membership in the synagogue if he accepted the punishment imposed, which was to be lashed with thirty-nine blows: thirteen on the right shoulder, thirteen on the left, and thirteen across the chest. This punishment was so brutal that there are records of men dying from it. But Paul was a Roman citizen. He could not be scourged without being tried under Roman law. Yet he submitted to it five different times. He does not say why, but it is likely that by accepting the punishment, he could not be banished from the synagogues, which were often his bases of missionary work as he opened new towns and cities to the work.

In journeyings often, in perils of waters, in perils of robbers, in perils by mine own countrymen, in perils by the heathen, in perils in the city, in perils in the wilderness, in perils in the sea, in perils among false brethren; In weariness and painfulness, in watchings often, in hunger and thirst, in fastings often, in cold and nakedness. (2 Corinthians 11:22–27)

That one man experienced—and endured!—so much is almost beyond comprehension.

One night my wife and I were flying back from southern Italy after a mission tour. All was well when we took off from Sicily, but as we landed in Milan, heavy fog rolled in and we missed our connecting flight back to Birmingham, England. And so began one of those "travel experiences" that frequent flyers run into from time to time. We were supposed to arrive back in Birmingham at three o'clock that afternoon. After sitting in an open-air airport transport bus for more than an hour and a half in twenty-eight-degree weather, we were diverted to London, which was a hundred miles from where we lived. We arrived in London at an hour when the trains and buses had stopped running and the rental car counters were closed for the night. We finally paid a taxi driver a hundred and fifty pounds to drive us to Birmingham (even at three hundred dollars it was cheaper than the airport hotels). On the way, we had a flat tire, and the cabby discovered he didn't have a spare. After waiting for another cab to be sent from London, we finally arrived home about two o'clock the next morning. We were exhausted, irritated, frustrated, and downright angry. What a day! Then came this thought as I walked into the house: *It's still better than being shipwrecked.* That stopped my "poor me" mumblings on the spot.

Though the scriptures do not say what happened to Paul, very strong traditions indicate that he was arrested, probably in Rome during the Christian persecutions under the Emperor Nero, and was beheaded about A.D. 65. That's not much of a happy ending, and yet Paul consistently bore witness of the Lord's love and sustaining power through all of his adversities. Despite the difficulties he endured during his ministry, Paul said, "I take pleasure in infirmities, in reproaches, in necessities, in persecutions, in distresses for Christ's sake: for when I am weak, then am I strong" (2 Corinthians 12:10). And one of the last things he wrote before his death was this declaration:

> I am now ready to be offered, and the time of my departure is at hand. I have fought a good fight, I have finished my course, *I have kept the faith*: Henceforth there is laid up for me a crown of righteousness, which the Lord, the righteous judge, shall give me at that day. (2 Timothy 4:6–8)

Compare that attitude, or that of Joseph Smith, or Stillman Pond, or Amanda Barnes Smith to leaving the Church because your name was misspelled on your mission call, or because the First Presidency decided you were in the wrong about the buttermilk dispute.

To Summarize

There it is, then. That is the issue before us. *What makes the difference between those who falter and those who endure?* If it's not individual differences, or the intensity of the challenge, or some natural gifts that some have and some do not, then what is it?

In chapter one we reviewed Joseph Smith's teaching that the basis for strong faith lies in knowing God, in believing that He exists, in understanding the perfections of His character and attributes, and in knowing that our lives are in harmony with His will.

So with that, let us now begin to examine how people perceive God, and what they believe and feel about Him. Note that. It's not just what we *believe,* it's what we *feel* about God and toward God. That is the basis for a strong faith. And a strong faith is the precursor to a deep testimony.

Notes

1. Harold B. Lee, *The Teachings of Harold B. Lee,* edited by Clyde J. Williams (Salt Lake City: Bookcraft, 1996), 190.

2. M. Scott Peck, *The Road Less Traveled* (Kansas City, Mo.: Andrews McMeel Publishing, 2001), 15; emphasis in original.

3. See Joseph Smith, *History of The Church of Jesus Christ of Latter-day Saints,* 7 vols., edited by B. H. Roberts (Salt Lake City: The Church of Jesus Christ of Latter-day Saints, 1932–51), 1:261, in footnote no. 4.

4. As cited in Karl Ricks Anderson, *Joseph Smith's Kirtland* (Salt Lake City: Deseret Book, 1989), 227.

5. See Gordon B. Hinckley, "Don't Drop the Ball," *Ensign,* November 1994, 49.

6. James E. Faust, "The Refiner's Fire," *Ensign,* May 1979, 54.

7. Kate B. Carter, *Heartthrobs of the West,* 12 vols. (Salt Lake City: Daughters of the Utah Pioneers, 1939–51), 2:108.

8. Faust, "The Refiner's Fire," 54; bullets added.

9. Ibid., 54–55.

A Softened Heart Brings
Strength to Endure

Drusilla Dorris Hendricks

Mormon taught that some of the Nephites reacted in one way to prolonged warfare, and others reacted quite differently. He credited this to the hardness or softness of the people's hearts. It is hard to determine which comes first. Did the conditions of war soften their hearts, or were they able to endure the conditions of war because their hearts were softened? Probably both are true.

We shall now examine an example of the heart of a woman that could have been hardened immeasurably by the afflictions that came upon her. But it wasn't. When the tragedy came, terrible as it was, she accepted it with resolute strength and carried on. Later, her heart was further tested when the Lord asked yet another sacrifice of her. But she softened her heart and accepted. And that brought tremendous strength and comfort into her life.

The life of Drusilla Dorris Hendricks is another wonderful example of how the Lord gives us blessings so that we know of His love and desires for us.

"Don't Get Shot in the Back"

As war and mobocracy erupted in western Missouri late in 1838, the Saints were once again in grave danger. One night, the Missouri militia, which was often little more than an organized and authorized mob, began raiding some of the outlying Mormon settlements. On October 24, they raided one homestead, burning haystacks and shooting livestock. Then they took three men prisoner and vowed they were taking them out to be executed. On hearing the news, Joseph Smith called out the militia in Far West. Led by David W. Patten, senior member of the Quorum of the Twelve, seventy-five men set out in pursuit.

One of the men who answered Joseph's call was James Hendricks, a native of Kentucky. In 1827 James had married a young girl named Drusilla Dorris, who lived just across the border in Tennessee. They joined the church in 1835, in spite of strenuous objections from their families. In the spring of 1836, they moved with their family to Missouri, settling first in Clay County, and then eventually moving north to Caldwell County, where they lived in a dugout. For a time they and their fellow Latter-day Saints lived in peace.[1]

But as October drew to a close that all changed. James was a member of the Mormon militia and so was called out in the night to help rescue the three men. Drusilla later wrote of that night:

> We had prayer and went to bed and fell asleep. I dreamed that something had befallen him and I was gathering him in my arms when Bro. C[harles] C. Rich [one of the captains of the militia] called at the door for him and told him what he wanted. They had word that the mob was on Crooked River ten miles south of us and was a strong band. He said they had two [it was actually three] of our brethren as prisoners and were doing all the damage that lay in their power. . . . He bid

me goodnight and got on his horse, and I took his gun from the rack and handed it to him and said, "Don't get shot in the back."[2]

The Battle of Crooked River

Two companies of the brethren, under the command of Charles C. Rich and David W. Patten, rode all night. As dawn came, they approached a ford on the Crooked River. But they were traveling eastward, so the light was in their eyes, and they didn't see that the Missourians were camped in the brush on the other side. As the Mormons started across the ford, one of the guards saw them coming and opened fire, shouting at his comrades that they were under attack. An intense firefight followed. Silhouetted by the dawn light, the Mormons were easy targets.

One man was shot in the face and killed instantly. David Patten took a ball in the stomach and would die later that day, becoming the first apostle to be martyred in this dispensation. James Hendricks turned when the firing erupted and started back across the river to find cover. Tragically, Drusilla's premonition proved correct. A bullet hit him in the back of the neck and he fell into the water, paralyzed.

Drusilla's account continues:

> I had got used to his going, so went to bed and went to sleep.
>
> Just about the time he was shot I was aroused from my sleep suddenly, and I thought the yard was full of men and they were shooting. I was on my feet before I knew what I was doing. I went to the window at the back of the house but all was still. I was afraid to open the door. I could hear nothing, so I ventured to open the door. It was getting light enough, so I could see very little. I went out and around the

house and found there was no one there. Then I was worse scared than ever, for I thought it was a token to me that they had had a battle.[3]

A short time later, Drusilla learned that James had been wounded and was in a house about four miles away.

> My husband lay within three feet of Brother Patten, and I spoke to him. He could speak but could not move any more than if he were dead. I tried to get him to move his feet but he could not. This was Thursday, October 25, 1838. . . . My husband was shot in the neck where it cut off all feeling to the body. It is of no use for me to try and tell how I felt, for that is impossible, but I could not have shed a tear if all had been dead before me. I went to work to try and get my husband warm but could not. I rubbed and steamed him but could get no circulation. He was dead from his neck down.[4]

"I Strained Every Nerve"

As if the tragedy that had befallen her husband was not enough, now the full fury of the Missourians fell upon the Saints. Haun's Mill, the fall of Far West, and the arrest of Joseph and other leaders all occurred a few days later. The Saints were told to leave the state as quickly as possible or face death. Drusilla's oldest boy was eight at that time, and she had four other children, including a nursing infant. All of that, and with her husband paralyzed from the neck down.

Through the dark days ahead, numerous prayers were offered and two blessings given to James. Joseph Smith Sr. blessed James to the point where he could eventually stand on his feet and walk a few steps if he was helped by others. That was a miracle, and Drusilla expressed gratitude for it, but it didn't change her situation a great deal. At one point during those terrible months, James became very ill. Drusilla said, "I had to lift him at least fifty times a day, and in doing so I had to strain every nerve."[5]

Talk about the *tribulum!*

War with Mexico

Along with the rest of the Saints, Drusilla and her family eventually came to Nauvoo, and they entered into a time of peace. Life improved somewhat, but James was still unable to provide for his family. Life for Drusilla was very difficult. Yet in spite of these grinding challenges, she never lost her faith. Looking back many years later, she talked of the myriad of things she did to try to support her family—she chinked and plastered her own chimney, planted a garden, sold things to the crowds on public holidays, took in washing for others. Then she added this: "I paid a good deal of tithing by making gloves and mittens."[6]

The time of peace was short-lived. In 1844, the Prophet Joseph and his brother Hyrum were martyred in Carthage Jail. Within another year, the enemies were on the prowl again, threatening the Saints if they didn't leave the state the following spring. The first wagons crossed the Mississippi River on February 4, 1846, and headed west across Iowa. The main body reached Council Bluffs, Iowa Territory, in mid-June.

By now, Drusilla's oldest son, William, was sixteen years old. He was a great blessing to his mother. Though she had a daughter two years older than William, now she had a man to help take the place of her crippled husband. They secured an outfit, put James in a bed in the back of their wagon, and started west. When they arrived in Council Bluffs, Iowa, in mid to late June of 1846, Drusilla had no way of knowing that another severe test of her faith was about to descend upon her.

In 1845, President James K. Polk decided to accept the petitions of a large group of Texans and formally annexed the area known as Texas into the United States. Most of Texas lay in Mexican territory, and Mexico was understandably angered by Polk's decision. Relationships between the two nations deteriorated to the point that on May 12, 1846, Congress declared war on Mexico.

During this same time, the Church had been petitioning Congress for assistance in their move west, hoping to build forts along the Oregon Trail. The war with Mexico created a different kind of opportunity. On July 1, 1856, Captain James Allen of the U.S. Army came to Council Bluffs with the request that the Mormons furnish five hundred volunteers to march to California and claim that territory for the United States as well.

In spite of the lack of support the Church had received in previous years from the federal government, Brigham Young saw several distinct advantages to this request, and on July 3, he signed an agreement and issued a call for volunteers to join what would become the Mormon Battalion.

"Are You Afraid to Trust the God of Israel?"

When young William Hendricks heard the news, he immediately determined to go. What an exciting adventure for a young man who would not turn seventeen until November of that year. But when he went to his mother, she adamantly refused to consider it even for a moment. She later wrote of her agony at that time.

> One would say to me, Is William going? I answered, No.
> . . . Why, they said, they would not have their son or husband

stay for anything. Then I would say, a burned child dreads the fire.[7]

In other words, she had already seen her husband go off to battle in the Lord's cause, and he had returned paralyzed from the neck down. She wasn't about to send her son to war and risk the same thing.

But it was more than that. She still had to take her family, including her handicapped husband, across a thousand miles of wilderness and make a new home in the Rocky Mountains. We can only imagine her thoughts at that time. Surely the Lord did not expect her to do such a thing without the only man she had to help her? Hadn't she already done enough, sacrificed enough? While her logic may have been good, it didn't work. She noted that even in her adamancy she felt doubts about her decision.

> The whispering of the Spirit would say to me: "Are you afraid to trust the God of Israel? Has He not been with you in all your trials? Has He not provided for your wants?" Then I would have to acknowledge the hand of God in all His goodness to me.[8]

This is astonishing in so many ways. Surely the Spirit wasn't chastising *her* for a lack of faith? She, who had already stood steadfast through eight years of trial and challenge? Why didn't she blurt out, "But, Lord, have you forgotten about my husband? Have you forgotten what I have already been through? Would you really have me cross the plains on my own?" Instead, she acknowledges the goodness of God and His hand in her life. What an amazing woman!

The volunteers were mustered in on 16 July. Before they marched away to California, the Saints treated them to a farewell ball. . . . Drusilla . . . attended the dance with her son William. . . . But William wanted to go with the battalion, and Drusilla struggled to decide what to do. The next morning she watched him go about his work.

"I got ready to get breakfast," she wrote, "and when I stepped up on the wagon tongue to get my flour I was asked by the same spirit that had spoken to me before, If I did not want the greatest glory and I answered with my natural voice, Yes, I did. Then how can you get it without making the greatest sacrifice, said the voice. *I answered Lord, what lack I yet?* Let your son go in the Battalion, said the voice.

I said it is too late, they are to be marched off this morning. That spirit then left me with the heart ache. I got breakfast and called the girls and their Father to come to the tent for prayers. William came wet with dew from the grass and we sat down around the board and my husband commenced asking the blessing on our food, when Thomas Williams came shouting at the top of his voice, saying "Turn out men, Turn out, for we do not wish to press you but we lack some men yet in the Battalion." William raised his eyes and looked me in the face. I knew then that he would go as well as I know now that he has been.[9]

With heavy heart, Drusilla told her son that he had her permission to go. What an amazing example of a softened heart. And what happened immediately afterward was a direct result of that submission to the Lord's will:

I went to milk the cows. . . . I thought the cows would be shelter for me and I knelt down and told the Lord if He wanted my child to take him, only spare his life and let him be restored to me and to the bosom of the church. I felt it was all I could do. Then the voice that talked with me in the morning answered me saying, It shall be done unto you as it was unto Abraham when he offered Isaac on the altar. I don't know whether I milked or not for I felt the Lord had spoken to me.[10]

So how did the story end for Drusilla? Her earnest prayer that her son's life be spared was answered. William survived the long march to California and rejoined his family after they had reached the Salt Lake Valley. Together they went on to help settle Cache Valley in northern Utah.

James survived the trek to Salt Lake and became the first bishop in the Nineteenth Ward in Salt Lake, where Drusilla also became the Relief Society president. He died eleven years before Drusilla, who passed away at the age of seventy-one. In her final years she wrote:

The gospel is true. I have rejoiced in it through all my trials for the Spirit of the Lord has buoyed me up or I should have failed.[11]

Brigham Young spoke highly of such women as Drusilla. "'If the women did not accomplish as much as the men did,' he said, it was because the women 'had no wives to help them.'"[12]

Notes

1. See Leonard J. Arrington and Susan Arrington Madsen, *Sunbonnet Sisters: True Stories of Mormon Women and Frontier Life* (Salt Lake City: Bookcraft, 1984), 26–29.

2. In Kenneth W. Godfrey, Audrey M. Godfrey, and Jill Mulvay Derr, eds., *Women's Voices: An Untold History of the Latter-day Saints, 1830–1900* (Salt Lake City: Deseret Book, 1982), 90.

3. In ibid., 90–91.

4. In ibid., 91.

5. In ibid., 95.

6. Richard Neitzel Holzapfel and Jeni Broberg Holzapfel, *Women of Nauvoo* (Salt Lake City: Bookcraft, 1992), 36.

7. Arrington and Madsen, *Sunbonnet Sisters,* 30.

8. Ibid.

9. Carol Cornwall Madsen, *Journey to Zion: Voices from the Mormon Trail* (Salt Lake City: Deseret Book, 1997), 35–36.

10. Ibid., 36.

11. Arrington and Madsen, *Sunbonnet Sisters,* 31.

12. Ibid., 32.

A little reflection, I believe, will suggest a number of differences [between our Church and other faiths], but the one I wish to emphasize . . . is our beliefs and faith in Jesus Christ—not our belief that there is a God, but rather our peculiar concept about his nature and identity, and our relationship to him.

MARION G. ROMNEY

CHAPTER SIX

Faith, Testimony, and Our Perception of God

A Quick Review

H ere is the premise I have tried to establish so far in the book: A person's concept of God and his or her understanding of God's attributes and dealings with His children will directly influence the strength of that person's faith and the depth of his or her testimony.

This is just another way of stating Joseph Smith's three requirements for faith:

> First, the idea that he actually exists.
>
> Secondly, a *correct* idea of his character, perfections, and attributes.
>
> Thirdly, an actual knowledge that the course of life which he is pursuing is according to his will. For without an acquaintance with these three important facts, the faith of every rational being must be imperfect and unproductive.[1]

If that initial premise is true, which we affirm it is, then two more follow:

The stronger one's faith is, the deeper one's testimony will be.

The deeper one's testimony becomes, the greater the likelihood is that one will successfully cope with the challenges of life and endure to the end.

Since our perception of God and faith are so closely linked together, coming to a correct understanding and acceptance of the nature and character of God has great relevance for those who live in these perilous times. This is what makes the difference between a Stillman Pond and a Symonds Ryder, a Drusilla Hendricks and a Thomas B. Marsh.

With this in mind, let us explore various conceptions and perceptions of God that are prevalent in the world today and are held among Latter-day Saints to one degree or another. These are general summaries rather than a detailed exploration, and I recognize, at the outset, that people's beliefs, suppositions, or conclusions are held with varying degrees of intensity and may change over time or due to specific circumstances. Also, human nature being what it is, often a person holds (to at least some degree) more than one of these concepts of God at the same time, even if the ideas may seem contradictory with each other.

As we examine various perceptions, I shall make a few comments on how this belief might influence an individual's response to the challenges that come in life.

A Nonexistent Deity

While my wife and I were doing mission tours in Europe, we heard many missionaries talk about people they had met who were members of one church or another but declared themselves to be atheists. When asked by the missionaries if they belonged to a church, they would nod and say, "Well, I'm a Catholic (or Anglican, or Lutheran, or Presbyterian, etc.), but I don't believe in God." (I know one or two avowed atheists or agnostics who still hold affiliation in or identify themselves with the LDS Church, strange as that may seem.)

Many educated and highly intelligent people consider themselves in this category. They openly reject or scoff at the idea of a supreme being. Like Korihor in the Book of Mormon, they believe that men fare in this life "according to the management of the creature; therefore every man prospered according to *his* genius, and . . . every man conquered according to *his* strength," and that "when a man was dead, that was the end thereof" (Alma 30:17–18).

To them, a tsunami that kills hundreds of thousands of people is a force of nature. It is not some cosmic punishment, as some would have us think, or part of a grand design for mankind. In fact, this group often points to such events as proof that there is no God. Adversity happens, they say. Tribulation is part of life. Trying to credit every misfortune to some supernatural entity is pure foolishness, and whining about them is an exercise in futility.

An Irrelevant Deity

Many other people in the world do not reject the idea of a God, but they don't see that He has any personal relevance in their lives or any place in the modern world. While serving in the area presidency for Western Europe I saw many examples of this belief. Church attendance among most Europeans is sparse. Often they come to the church for help only in the three great events of life: birth, marriage, and death.

One night on television we saw a news special on religious attitudes and practices in the United Kingdom. When asked to name the individual who had the greatest influence on determining how they lived, the person named first by more people than anyone else was David Beckham, the famous British soccer superstar. Mother Teresa of India was second. Jesus came in fourth.

On another similar news broadcast, a reporter interviewed various people on the street and asked them how they felt about God. I remember clearly the answer of one pleasant-looking young man in his mid-twenties. When asked if he believed in God, he furrowed his brow momentarily and then shrugged and said, "Yeah, mate, I suppose I do. But to be honest, I don't really much care one way or another."

A Distant and Holy God

Most devout and dedicated believers in God believe there is a tremendous gap between man's own inherently evil and imperfect nature and God's majesty and perfect holiness. We feel this difference keenly and this creates a deep sense of reverential awe, perhaps even fear. But this sense of distance can also create a feeling that God is not approachable by people like us. We do not pray to Him because we feel our problems are so far below His exalted station, that it is highly presumptuous to ask for His help.

Some Christians look to Mary or canonized saints to serve as intermediaries between them and God. Since the saints lived exemplary lives of sanctity and righteousness, it is believed they have more ready access to God and thus can enhance the likelihood that one's prayers will be heard by God.

Though we may not carry it out in such a formalized way, this desire to enhance the likelihood that our petitions will be heard by God is quite natural and may be manifested in other ways. For example, members of Protestant churches may ask their pastor to pray for them in difficult times because they feel he or she may be "more in tune" than they are. Some in the Jewish faith write their petitions on small pieces of paper and insert them into the cracks of the Wailing Wall in Jerusalem, the only remaining remnant of God's holy house in Israel. Sometimes in our own church, a father will seek out the bishop, stake president, or even a General Authority to give a priesthood blessing to a family member because the father doesn't feel that he is as faithful as one of his leaders. Another common practice is to ask family members or friends to join us in fasting and praying for help from the Lord. This desire for greater power with God is a human reaction to our very keen awareness of the difference between God's holiness and our humanity.

Another common, yet more concerning manifestation of this sense of distance, comes when an individual engages in a lifestyle contrary to Church standards. This creates a sense of guilt and unworthiness and adds to one's feeling that he or she cannot approach God directly anymore. It is not that they believe that God isn't there, or that He doesn't care. It is that they cannot believe that He could still care for them after all they have done.

This point of view is well illustrated by the words of a young woman who had grown up in the Church and had a strong testimony of God's reality. At age ten she was sexually abused. She hid the abuse and the growing sense of utter worthlessness and guilt that rose in her. Eventually she entered a same-gender relationship. Though this met her longing for love and acceptance, it added to her guilt, and she began abusing alcohol and drugs. She struggled constantly to overcome the addictions. She met with priesthood leaders, studied the scriptures, fasted, and prayed. Sometimes she made progress; other times she fell back. She described her struggle in these words:

> I continued to abuse alcohol in an attempt to fix the pain and build a bridge across the great abyss. The pain was debilitating. The darkness was all-consuming. It was as if my very identity was being ripped apart. . . .
>
> When I needed strength from the Lord, I often could not grasp it. I believe He was holding out His hand, but I felt

terribly unworthy to respond. I mistakenly believed His love had to be earned.[2]

Here's how another victim of sexual abuse expressed it:

> Because of things which had been done to me in my childhood, it was very difficult for me to want to establish a close relationship with God. . . . It was much easier for me to worship him from a distance. I had no desire for him to know me, and I thought I could hide myself from him. In my opinion, he didn't really want to know someone like me anyway. I had been through such awful experiences, and I was sure that God, in all of his perfection, would be abhorred to know who I really was.[3]

These individuals do not question God's reality, and the one even mentions His perfection, but they still view Him as unapproachable. That is an excellent example of how a person can hold two conflicting perceptions of God at the same time.

A Living but Uninvolved Deity

Another perception of God is that He is real, that He exists, but that His relationship to us is not personal. Such people refer to God in more general terms such as Providence, or the First Cause, or the Grand Designer. They do not in any way doubt the existence of God, but neither do they perceive Him to be a deity who is intimately, or even distantly, involved in our lives. They typically do not believe in supernatural (i.e., miraculous) events. They do not think of God as hovering in the heavens above us, watching our actions and intervening in our behalf.

To them, when tragedy or misfortune strikes, they do not look to God for help. They feel that it is something that is a natural result of the divine creation, and they feel they have to learn to accept it and deal with it as best they can.

A Harsh and Vengeful Deity

In the scriptures, especially in the Old Testament, there are many references to God's anger, and numerous warnings that He will take vengeance upon the wicked. In one instance, He sent down fire from heaven to destroy them (see 2 Kings 1:10). In another case, the earth opened and swallowed up those who had been disobedient (see Numbers 26:10). The New Testament also speaks of a "lake of fire burning with brimstone" to which the wicked will be consigned for eternity (Revelation 19:20). During the Dark Ages and Medieval times, this view was taken quite literally, and there are numerous lurid and gruesome depictions of such a punishment in both art and literature.*

Even those who reject the idea of a literal burning in hell may still view God as a stern, harsh, judgmental deity. They see God as hovering over us, but with a critical eye, scrutinizing our every action, looking for the tiniest infraction of the rules.

Here is one novelist's depiction of how one of her characters viewed God. Though fictional, the description accurately portrays the feelings of some people.

He would shroud God in [dark] clouds and terrible lightnings and make of Him, not a loving Father, merciful and full of lovingkindness, but a Judge armed with terror and vengeance, seeking out the smallest sin or error in order to punish it most cruelly, and delighting not in His children

---

* The Book of Mormon makes it clear that the fire is a metaphorical or symbolic description of the eternal torment experienced by those who reject God in mortality (e.g., see 2 Nephi 9:16, 19, 26; 28:23; Jacob 6:10; Mosiah 3:27; Alma 12:17).

but regarding them as an oppressive king regards his people, suspecting them of crimes and rebellions, and preparing for them the most hideous flagellations and death.[4]

Such a perception of God could easily lead a person to conclude that adversity, tribulation, or natural catastrophes are the direct result of God's punishment for man's wickedness. Even personal tragedy is viewed as the penalty for some infraction of the law.

A Grandfather in Heaven

On the other hand, some people think of God in quite the opposite manner. They picture Him to be so filled with love, kindness, and mercy that there is nothing to fear at all in our relationship with Him. Nephi, the son of Lehi, prophesied that such attitudes would be prevalent in our day:

> There shall be many which shall say: Eat, drink, and be merry, for tomorrow we die; and it shall be well with us. And there shall also be many which shall say: Eat, drink, and be merry; nevertheless, fear God—he will justify in committing a little sin; yea, lie a little, take the advantage of one because of his words, dig a pit for thy neighbor; there is no harm in this; and do all these things, for tomorrow we die; and if it so be that we are guilty, God will beat us with a few stripes, and at last we shall be saved in the kingdom of God. (2 Nephi 28:7–8)

This view reflects a perception of God as a benign, mellow, generously tolerant, forever long-suffering and forgiving Deity. Much like overindulgent parents who spoil their children and rarely hold them accountable for their actions, they perceive God as too loving, too merciful, and too nice to really punish a person for being bad. Well, yes, He may be annoyed when we misbehave, but after a sharp rap or two on the wrist, He will take us into His arms and assure us that everything is okay.

C. S. Lewis, the great defender of Christianity, saw this as a prevalent attitude among some Christians:

> What would really satisfy us would be a God who said of anything we happened to like doing, "What does it matter so long as they are contented?" We want, in fact, not so much a Father in Heaven as a grandfather in heaven—a senile benevolence who, as they say, "liked to see young people enjoying themselves", and whose plan for the universe was simply that it might be truly said at the end of each day, "a good time was had by all."[5]

The problem with this perception—or rather, this misperception—is that when life is good and all is in peace and harmony, our feelings about God sustain us adequately. But continual peace, comfort, harmony, and joy are not the natural conditions of this life, as we have discussed. Thus when things go wrong, people who view God more like a grandfather in heaven, can be completely knocked from their moorings. Suddenly life contradicts their warm and fuzzy picture of the divine nature. "This isn't fun," they cry. "I thought God loved me. Doesn't He know how very unpleasant all this is for me?"

This view runs completely contrary to their perception that God is like a divine Santa Claus or some "cosmic errand boy"[6] who stands around anxiously awaiting orders from us. They think God's whole purpose is to keep us happy: doing our chores and cleaning up our messes after us. When we no longer need Him, then He should just go away and not bother us again until we call.

If God does not conform to that expectation, they grow petulant and annoyed. "If He isn't careful," they warn, "we'll punish Him by withholding our acceptance of Him. We'll stop praying to Him, and that will show Him."

To Summarize

The great paradox of life—joy and sorrow, happiness and pain—is all part of the testing, proving, refining process that God has designed for us. How we deal with that paradox, how we cope with the opposition that life naturally provides, will be greatly influenced by our perception of God. Indeed, it could be said that the very core of the testing process of mortality is to see whether we accept God or reject Him, whether we follow Him or turn away, to see how we feel about Him when the *tribulum* begins grinding over our heads, driving out any expectations we might have had that we were going to "have a nice day."

We have discussed perceptions of God that may leave us floundering when life comes rolling over us. Let us now discuss the "correct" idea of God that will give us the strength we need to construct our lives on the bedrock.

Notes

Epigraph. Marion G. Romney, in Conference Report, April 1959, 9.

1. Joseph Smith, *Lectures on Faith* (Salt Lake City: Deseret Book, 1985), 38; emphasis in original.

2. Erin Eldridge, *Born That Way? A True Story of Overcoming Same-Sex Attraction with Insights for Friends, Families, and Leaders* (Salt Lake City: Deseret Book, 1994), 14.

3. "The Journey in Healing," *Ensign*, September 1997, 21.

4. Taylor Caldwell, *Great Lion of God* (San Francisco: Ignatius Press, 2008), 91.

5. C. S. Lewis, *The Problem of Pain* (New York: HarperCollins, 2001), 31.

6. It is hard to determine who first coined this title. Examples of its use can be found on the Internet by searching the phrase "cosmic errand boy."

Confirmation Following Obedience

In the section titled "Turning Points," we shared stories of how the Lord, using His tender mercies, helped people open up their hearts to the gospel message and eventually come into the Church.

Here we have what might be thought of as the opposite end of the spectrum. Sometimes the Lord gives a special blessing, another of His divine signatures, but *after* His children have proven themselves obedient. These are more confirmation blessings than introduction blessings, but they still bear witness of the Father and His personal knowledge of our circumstances, our wants, and our needs. Here is an example of such a blessing of which I was privileged to be a part.

Restoration of Blessings

When I was called to the Seventy, as part of my responsibilities, I was assigned from time to time by the First Presidency to perform what is known as a restoration of blessings. When a person transgresses to the point that full Church fellowship, or even membership, is taken away, the blessings and privileges of the priesthood and temple ordinances are withdrawn as well. These can only be restored with permission of the First Presidency. The restoration itself is an ordinance done by the laying on of hands. (For many years, only General Authorities were given these assignments. Now area seventies and some stake presidents receive those assignments as well.)

As part of the packet sent out by the First Presidency, we received a brief summary of the actions taken by various Church disciplinary councils held for these individuals. It was sobering to see how far astray some people could wander. It also verified the reality of Alma's warning to his son that "wickedness never was happiness" (Alma 41:10). On the other hand, over and over I marveled at the extent of the Savior's forgiveness. Here was evidence of a life torn apart by spiritual tragedies, and yet they had come back. The process of repentance and the ensuing forgiveness was bringing them back into full fellowship once again.

These were always sweet experiences for me. The men and women who sat before me wept with sorrow for the past and shed tears of joy for their Savior and Redeemer. The only person allowed to attend the restoration with the recipient was his or her spouse. They, too, would share tears as they described what this blessing meant for them. Usually, just before we performed the ordinance, I asked the candidate to share his or her feelings and testimony. Almost without exception, with choked voices and glistening eyes, they bore witness of the power of the Atonement, of the reality of their Savior, and of the love their Father had for them.

One of these experiences proved to be particularly significant. Though it involved me personally, I was only the instrument used to fulfill the confirming experience this individual was given. I have decided to share it because it is a particularly sweet example of the Lord's divine signature.

"This Was God's Way of Telling Me That I Was Truly Forgiven"

After opening the meeting with prayer, I always take a few minutes to get acquainted by asking the people to tell me a little about themselves—about their family, what they did for a living, where they lived. Fortunately, because the First Presidency's office had reviewed the past history of transgressions, we did not recount all the past. I was to confirm that the person was still worthy to have his or her blessings restored before proceeding. So these preliminary conversations were only to help put them at ease and for me to get to know them better.

On this occasion, the restoration of blessings took place while I was in another state for a stake conference. The person was a man in his late fifties who had been out of the Church for many years. He had his wife with him. As we talked, he told me that he was a long-haul truck driver who averaged about five thousand miles a week with his driving partner. It was a regular route, and so he was home on most Sundays and could attend church. I was impressed. That was an average of about eight hundred miles per day between the two drivers. We talked about his family and where he grew up and so on. It was a warm and comfortable few minutes together.

After confirming that he was worthy to have the ordinance performed, I asked him to share any feelings he might have and to bear his testimony. Instantly tears came to his eyes. Poor choices he had made many years before had taken him out of the Church. He said that he had thought about coming back to the Church numerous times, but never could make up his mind to do so until a couple of years before. He then expressed his deep sorrow for the things he had done and for the people he had hurt along the way. He told me that another major factor in his reluctance to return was that he didn't think it was possible that God could ever forgive him for what he had done.

At that point he stopped, struggling to regain his composure. Finally, his head came up and he looked me in the eye. "Would you like to know what finally turned me around?" When I nodded, he continued. "When you're a long-haul truck driver," he said, "you have a lot of time alone on the road. Many truckers listen to audio books to pass the time. I've done that for years now."

He managed a smile. "About three years ago, my wife gave me a set of audio books as a gift. There were nine volumes. They were historical novels about the history of the Church. Some people might be overwhelmed by nine books, but I was pleased, for that meant I had a lot of hours in the truck with something to do."

Now there was a faint smile. "As I began listening to them, something happened to me. Those books had a tremendous impact on me. They rekindled old feelings that I had long suppressed. They reminded me of long-held cherished beliefs about Joseph Smith, about the Church, and about God. These were feelings and beliefs that I had lost many years before. As I listened to them hour after hour, I found my testimony again." He stopped and peered at me. "Do you know what books I'm talking about?"

I thought I did. "You're talking about *The Work and the Glory* series, aren't you?" I said. I had written that nine-volume series of novels long before I was a General Authority. The series told the story of Joseph Smith and the Restoration.

He confirmed that it was that series. That moment was, of course, a very gratifying experience for me. But what he said next held the greatest significance. "It was those stories of Joseph Smith and the early Saints that brought me back to the fold," he said. "I went to the bishop and started the long process of making things right. I was rebaptized. I attended church every week either at home or along the road." Then, openly weeping again, he added, "But I still couldn't believe that the Lord could or would ever forgive me for all the terrible things I had done. I had gone against everything I knew to be true.

"When I received a call from my stake president telling me that a General Authority would be present at stake conference and would restore my blessings sometime during the weekend, I was ecstatic, of course. But when he told me that Elder Gerald N. Lund would be that General Authority, I couldn't believe it. Of all the dozens of General Authorities who could have come to our stake, to have *you* be the one was astonishing to me since it was your series that had reawakened my testimony."

Then deeply moved, he concluded, "At that moment, I knew that this was the Lord's way of telling me that I was forgiven, that the past was finally and forever behind me. I knew then that I was fully accepted of Him and could move on."

We once knew well our Elder Brother and our Father in Heaven. We rejoiced at the prospects of earth life that could make it possible for us to have a fulness of joy. We could hardly wait to demonstrate to our Father and our Brother, the Lord, how much we loved them and how we would be obedient to them in spite of the earthly opposition of the evil one. Now we are here. Our memories are veiled. We are showing God and ourselves what we can do. Nothing is going to startle us more when we pass through the veil to the other side than to realize how well we know our Father and how familiar His face is to us.

Ezra Taft Benson

CHAPTER SEVEN

"Our Father Who Art in Heaven"

"He Called Me by Name"

In the spring of 1820, the great restoration of all things promised by the prophets of old began. On a clear and beautiful spring morning, a young man, troubled about which church he should join, sought out a secluded place where he could ask God for help. He received his answer in a most glorious vision of the Father and the Son. And from that morning has flowed all that we know today—new scripture; priesthood power and authority; a global church with a membership of more than thirteen million; prophets, seers, and revelators; the largest women's organization in the world; temples and meetinghouses all over the world; books, manuals, handbooks, and curriculum; a force of more than fifty thousand full-time missionaries.

But think for a moment. Of all the knowledge that has come from that opening morning, of all the words that have been written and spoken in the Church since the Restoration began, what was the very first *word* of the Restoration?

I saw a pillar of light exactly over my head, above the brightness of the sun, which descended gradually until it fell upon me. It no sooner appeared than I found myself delivered from the enemy which held me bound. When the light rested upon me I saw two Personages, whose brightness and glory defy all description, standing above me in the air. One of them spake unto me, *calling me by name* and said, pointing to the other—*This is My Beloved Son. Hear Him!* (Joseph Smith–History 1:16–17)

"Calling me by name"—think of the significance of that simple statement. These two beings had come from the far heavens where they reigned as gods. Their power and glory and majesty "defy all description," yet the Father did not have to inquire about who Joseph was or what his name was. *They knew him!* He was an unschooled farm boy, living in an obscure village. His family was poor. They lived in a simple cabin. Yet God knew him. And they had heard *his* prayer and came down from heaven to answer it personally.

Joseph learned several things that day—that Satan was real and powerful, that the Father and the Son had greater power than he did, that the godhead was not some amorphous, mysterious, three-in-one, indefinable being. In one glorious blaze of light, this fourteen-year-old lad learned more about God than all the scholars and ministers of Christendom had in hundreds of years. But along with all of that, there was something totally unexpected: *Heavenly Father knew who Joseph was, and He had heard the prayer of his heart.* It cannot be overstated how profoundly that knowledge has affected all that we believe and how we worship.

It is really quite astonishing when we think about it. In a matter of moments, false doctrines and erroneous conceptions that had been held for centuries were totally overthrown and proven false. That was the beginning of the Restoration. The true knowledge of God was restored.

The Character, Attributes, and Perfections of God

In *Lectures on Faith,* Joseph said that the second thing required if we are to have faith sufficient to bring us to salvation, is "a *correct* idea of his character, perfections, and attributes."[1] Joseph then listed those aspects of His character and His attributes and testified that God held them all in perfection. Here is the list he made of God's character:

- He was God before the world was created, and He was the same God after it was created.
- God is merciful and gracious, slow to anger, abundant in goodness, and He was so and will be from everlasting to everlasting.
- God changes not; there is no variableness in Him. He is the same yesterday, today, and forever.
- He is a God of truth and cannot lie.
- God is no respecter of persons but accepts all who fear Him and work righteousness.
- God is love.[2]

The six attributes of God given in the next lecture are:

- Knowledge
- Faith or power
- Justice
- Judgment
- Mercy
- Truth[3]

In regard to God's perfections, the Prophet taught: "What we mean by perfections is, the perfections which belong to all the attributes of his nature."[4] In other words, God not only has knowledge, He possesses all knowledge. He not only has power, He is omnipotent, or all-powerful. He is perfectly just. He is perfect in His judgment and mercy and love. He has all truth, and nothing other than truth in His nature.

Joseph felt this point was so important that he gave example after example of how this worked:

- "Unless he was merciful and gracious, slow to anger, long-suffering and full of goodness, such is the weakness of human nature, and so great the frailties and imperfections of men, that . . . doubt would take the place of faith, and those who know their weakness and liability to sin would be in constant doubt of salvation. . . . [Knowing] he is slow to anger and long-suffering, and of a forgiving disposition, and does forgive iniquity, transgression, and sin . . . does away doubt, and makes faith exceedingly strong."[5]

- "Without the knowledge of all things God would not be able to save any portion of his creatures. . . . Unless God had power over all things, and was able by his power to control all things, and thereby deliver his creatures who put their trust in him from the power of all beings that might seek their destruction, whether in heaven, or earth, or in hell, men could not be saved."[6]

Compare this idea with that held by the Greeks and the Romans. They had a whole pantheon of gods—Zeus, Poseidon, Mercury, Mars, Athena, and so on. (The Romans even believed that there was a god that presided over dung heaps. His name: Beelzebub. Evidently the Christians thought that an appropriate description of Satan.) Their gods were capricious, lustful, selfish, and petty deities. One can hardly generate much real faith in gods like that.

The True Nature of God

In chapter one, we gave a couple of examples of how our knowledge of God's attributes—or lack of knowledge—can affect faith. One woman questioned God's love because she had not been born beautiful. Another rejected the counsel of her doctor to have an abortion, even though the consequences for her could have been enormous.

It seems oddly contradictory, but there are numerous examples where individuals who believe that God is a loving and perfect Being, still question in their mind the reality of His character and attributes. In the previous chapter we discussed the feelings of people who believe that God is there, but who feel that He finds them so evil and abhorrent that they cannot approach Him.

In chapter five, we listed different questions that people ask when tragedy strikes them or someone they love. Let's review a few of those and others to see how such questions really are questions about the nature of God and whether He is really perfect in all things.

- *I have tried my whole life to do as He asks, to keep His commandments, to be faithful. And now this. Why, God? Why are you doing this to me?* Do you really know me? Do you understand what I am going through here? Is this how you demonstrate your love? If you are all-powerful, as they say, then why don't you change things? Maybe you really don't care what happens down here.
- Recently, a drunk driver lost control of his car and hit a minivan, killing an entire family who had been active in

the Church. Couldn't God have intervened just enough to cause the driver to slam into a tree instead of the family's vehicle? Or at the very least, why didn't God give the family a prompting to get off the road or take another route? I don't understand why He wouldn't use His power and foreknowledge to save them. It is so unfair. *Why does God allow the wicked to cause good people so much pain and suffering?*

- *When women all over the world are able to bear children whom they will neglect or abuse, and millions of others are terminating their unwanted pregnancies through abortion, why doesn't the Lord hear our prayers and grant us our righteous desires for a child?* Where is the justice in a system like that? Where is God's mercy? I'm not talking about mercy just for me. Some of those children are terribly abused. If He sent them to our home, they would be loved and accepted and cared for. It just doesn't seem right.

- *If there is a God, why would He allow the tsunami in Indonesia, or the earthquake in Haiti, to take the lives of nearly a quarter of a million people in each case?* I know there is a God. However, it is very difficult to understand how He can be all-powerful, all-knowing, and perfectly loving, and yet still let this happen. Maybe there are some things beyond His control. Or maybe He is a vengeful and punishing deity.

- *My best friend is a much better person than I am. So why has she suffered so much more pain and tragedy in her life than I have?* I'm questioning both the justice of God and His judgment. Doesn't the Lord promise to bless the righteous? If so, then this doesn't make sense. Life is not fair. Can't God change that? And if He thinks I deserve more blessings than my friend, then I guess I'm questioning how well He knows each of us.

Or, let's look at a couple of more positive examples of how an understanding of God's attributes and perfections blessed people in a time of great need. Amanda Barnes Smith lost her husband and two sons at Haun's Mill in a tragedy far beyond what most people ever face. But her first reaction was to turn to God for help in blessing Alma. And that wasn't blind desperation. She believed that He knew of her anguish and that His love for her would not allow Him to forsake her in her time of need. She also had absolute confidence in His power. Remember what she told young Alma? "The Lord can make something there in the place of your hip, don't you believe he can, Alma?"

Another example: When her son begged her to let him join the Mormon Battalion, Drusilla Dorris Hendricks felt the whisperings of the Spirit ask her, "Are you afraid to trust the God of Israel? Has He not been with you in all your trials? Has He not provided for your wants?"

It is absolutely astonishing that Drusilla didn't rise up in indignation at those questions. She had endured eight very difficult years because her husband had been crippled while trying to save others. Yet she acknowledged that God had sustained her. Such faith came from a deep trust and a strong conviction that God knew her and all of her sufferings and sacrifices. While rationally it made no sense to let her son join the Battalion, she knew God would not ask anything of her that was not right and for her best good.

Earlier we asked what made the difference between those who have the faith and testimony to endure and those who don't. Well, here is at least one answer, if not *the* answer: Strong faith and a deep testimony are founded on a correct knowledge of God's attributes,

His character, and His perfections. People like Stillman Pond, Amanda Smith, Drusilla Hendricks, and Francis Webster and so many others didn't just believe in Heavenly Father and Jesus. They *knew* them. Not just *of* them. Not just *about* them. They knew God.

Here were people who understood what Helaman meant when he said to his sons:

> And now, my sons, remember, remember that it is upon the rock of our Redeemer, who is Christ, the Son of God, that ye must build your foundation; that when the devil shall send forth his mighty winds, yea, his shafts in the whirlwind, yea, when all his hail and his mighty storm shall beat upon you, it shall have no power over you to drag you down to the gulf of misery and endless wo, because of the rock upon which ye are built, which is a sure foundation, a foundation whereon if men build they cannot fall. (Helaman 5:12)

Notes

Epigraph. Ezra Taft Benson, *The Teachings of Ezra Taft Benson* (Salt Lake City: Bookcraft, 1988), 24.

1. Joseph Smith, *Lectures on Faith* (Salt Lake City: Deseret Book, 1985), 38; emphasis in original.

2. See ibid., 41.

3. See ibid., 50–51.

4. Ibid., 59.

5. Ibid., 42.

6. Ibid., 51–52.

Divine Signatures That
Fortify Faith

In the scriptures, we are warned against trying to establish faith by demanding some kind of evidence beforehand. So-called "sign seeking" is condemned by the Lord. On two different occasions, the Savior said that it was "an evil and adulterous generation" that sought after signs (Matthew 12:39; 16:4). In a modern revelation, the Lord was even more specific:

> There are those among you who seek signs, and there have been such even from the beginning; But, behold, faith cometh not by signs, but signs follow those that believe. Yea, signs come by faith, not by the will of men, nor as they please, but by the will of God. . . . Wherefore, I, the Lord, am not pleased with those among you who have sought after signs and wonders for faith. (D&C 63:8–10, 12)

Yet there are examples where the Lord asked something of a person that was so overwhelming, or so beyond their limited abilities, that they felt they could not succeed. In those cases, the Lord chose to give them specific signs to fortify their faith. When Moses was overwhelmed with the thought of delivering Israel from Egypt, the

Lord strengthened his courage with three miracles—his staff was turned into a serpent and then back to a staff; his hand was turned leprous and then restored; and water from the river was turned into blood (see Exodus 4:1–9).

Gideon was asked to deliver Israel from the iron hand of the Midianites. It seemed such an impossible task that Gideon bargained with the Lord, asking for evidence that this request was really from Him. He first asked that a fleece of wool on the floor become wet with dew but nothing else around it. When that happened, Gideon asked that the opposite happen—that the floor be wet but not the fleece. Surprisingly the Lord did not chastise him for this lack of faith, but did as Gideon suggested (see Judges 6:36–40). Once fortified, Gideon went on to destroy the Midianites with only three hundred men.

Such examples seem to run counter to what God has said about sign seeking, but in the case of both Moses and Gideon, the signs given were done to fortify faith as they were asked to undertake a very difficult task for the Lord. I have come to believe that sometimes this is true in our modern world as well. God knows all things. He knows the hearts of each individual. Sometimes what the Lord asks of people may be so difficult that they need a special witness so their courage will be strengthened.

Stake Conference in Edinburgh, Scotland

Just a month after my wife and I arrived in England, I was assigned to travel north to Edinburgh, Scotland, for a stake conference. As part of the conference, I was to release President Stephen C. Kerr as he had served a full term of service as stake president. Then we were to reorganize the stake presidency.

We wanted to start interviewing the stake's priesthood leadership early Saturday morning, so my wife and I drove up to Edinburgh on

Friday afternoon. That night we invited President Kerr and his wife, Yvonne, to dinner so we could get to know them and express our appreciation for their service. That proved to be a very pleasant experience, and we quickly became good friends. (Later it was my privilege, under the direction of the First Presidency, to extend a call to Stephen Kerr to be an Area Seventy, a position that he still holds at the time this book was published.)

During the course of the dinner, as I asked the Kerrs to tell us more about themselves, Yvonne mentioned that she had been converted to the Church in her early twenties. Since the factors that lead people to conversion (the *turning points* we spoke of earlier) have always interested me, I asked if she would share her story with us. It turned out to be quite a remarkable account and I was deeply impressed. When I began work on this book, I remembered her story. It was such a great example of the concept of divine signatures that I asked Yvonne if she would be willing to share her story here. She agreed, and I asked if she would mind writing it in her own words. What follows is her story.*

Raised As a Baptist

I was brought up in the town of Ayr, about thirty miles from Glasgow on the west coast of Scotland. My mother and father were members of the Baptist Church in Ayr, as were my mother's family. I remember my grandfather, whom I called Papa, with a lot of kindness because I knew he loved me. He was a tall man, a very fine man, and had a great knowledge of the Saviour. He owned a local clothing store and served as a lay minister and as an elder for the Baptists in his hometown

---

* There are some slight differences in spelling between American English and British English. I have retained Yvonne's spellings throughout her account.

of Maybole. I grew to love the Saviour through my grandfather, and I loved attending church, even on the boring
days!

Because of going to church regularly, I started to read
the scriptures. I loved the feelings I had when reading in
the Bible about Jesus Christ, and I knew that He was the
Son of God. I began to have a deep desire to know both
Him and His Father more.

In time, both my beloved Papa and my father died. One
of the last times I saw my dad before he passed away was
when I was ten years old. He told me that his being ill was
no excuse for my not going to church and that I could cycle
there. As a result I always attended church.

As my knowledge of the Bible increased, I began to realise that not everything was explained in the book that I
held most dear, so I prayed to God for help to understand
more. Some of my church's teachings did not fully make
sense, but as long as I could worship Him then I felt that
would have to suffice. My greatest desire was to meet an
Apostle. I wanted to have more of God's words that I could
study. I also began to realise that whenever I attended church
I felt good—warm and at peace—but those lovely feelings
left when I returned home. I wanted that feeling with me
all the time, so I again prayed hard that one day I would
feel Him with me all of the time and not just at church or
evangelical meetings.

The Mormons

When I turned eighteen, I left home to attend university
in Edinburgh. I enjoyed my time there and attended the local
Baptist Church. It seemed different from the one in Ayr. The

people acted differently, and the things they taught were not the same as at home. I wondered why the same church would teach different doctrines.

One day I saw a group of Mormon missionaries at a bus stop. I thought I knew all about the Mormons! I had been taught by my church that not only were Mormons misled, but that they were also evil! I stood as far away from them as possible in case they noticed me. When they got on the same bus as I did, I again sat as far away from them as possible. They were telling jokes and laughing! I had to admit their jokes were funny, but I was not going to let them notice that I was listening. More than that, though, was that I could feel something from them, but I didn't know what that feeling was. When they spoke to me, I answered them back very curtly.

The following day they passed me in the street. Again, I could feel something from them. The day after that, I saw them again. Then the following day! In fact, I began to notice them daily, much to my annoyance! Scottish people are friendly to each other and when we see people we recognise, even if we don't know them, it is polite to acknowledge them with a nod of the head or a simple "hello." And these missionaries were growing familiar to me! So, when the missionaries passed me, I would condescend to saying "hello," but I refused to smile. Every time I saw them, I would feel something powerful and I didn't know what it was, but I would never have told them that. I was so confused by the good feelings I could feel from them. If they were as bad as I had been taught, then why did I feel this way?

One day they came up to the campus I was attending. Since they knew my face, they stopped me and asked for directions. They wanted to perform a musical number in the theatre there. I was a drama student and had all the contacts, so out of courtesy I told them I would help them. "Helping my enemy," I thought, and I couldn't believe what I was doing. I made introductions and helped as much as possible. They both had very strange first names— they were both called "Elder"! They told me they were missionaries of The Church of Jesus Christ of Latter-day Saints.

A short time later, I was standing in the local post office when I had the very strong impression that two Mormons were about to come in. As I looked toward the door, I saw the missionaries enter, and the feeling that came into the post office with them was so exceedingly powerful that I felt I could hardly breathe. I left as fast as I could without them seeing me, and I cried all the way to my Halls of Residence. I was shaking and scared. I didn't understand what it was that I was feeling from them but knew it was something that I had to pay attention to.

Because I had been taught the Mormons were evil, I would not let myself think that this could be a good feeling. All that day I cried in my room and missed all my classes. The only place I could think of to find out more about the Mormons was the university library, so I checked out the only book they had on the subject. It contained dreadful and impossible things that the Mormons believed. The feelings I got from that book were awful. I later found out that it was an "anti-Mormon" book that was written by someone who hated the Church. Yet, even with all of that, I still could not stop thinking about the missionaries I had met.

Let me note some things about Yvonne's situation. She was brought up in a Baptist home where she was loved and taught to love God. As part of her religious upbringing, however, she was taught as a young girl that Mormons were evil and should be avoided at all costs. When she began to come in contact with the missionaries, she was torn by unexpected feelings about them. As time went on, the Lord seemed to be nudging her more and more toward the missionaries. She saw them again and again. They asked her for help. They came into the post office immediately following a premonition she had. These feelings bothered her enough that she began an investigation into what others had to say about Mormonism, but that only confirmed all the bad things she had heard about them.

This is not like the other examples we read of, where people were nudged toward the Church and there was a natural readiness to respond. Nor is this a case of someone fighting against God. This young woman was searching. She was believing. But she was thrown into an emotional turmoil by conflicting beliefs and values, and conflicting feelings of what she should do. God knew her heart, and He understood that this was going to require something unique to her.

Attendance at a Concert

A few days later I met the missionaries on campus again. The student union president had told them that if they could find a few people who would sign a petition for them to do a performance then they could give a concert on campus. The missionaries asked me if I would send around a letter asking for people to attend the concert, then convince my friends to sign it. I agreed. However, I refused to sign it myself! Although my friends signed the letter, they told me privately they would not attend. In fact, not one person told me they would go along with this request.

Over the next short while, I would bump into the missionaries often. They tried to get me to listen to their message, but I told them I was not interested. Little did they know about the feelings I was having! On the night of the performance, I prayed and told God that if more than a certain number (which I chose) turned up, then I would go into the theatre and listen to the concert. I felt safe that not even one person would go! The missionaries saw me and asked me in. I said "no" and stayed outside to count the number of people entering. I felt quite smug that the missionaries would have no audience.

To my horror, students began to enter one by one. I was astonished! When my count reached exactly the number I had prayed about, I knew I was in trouble. I had promised God that I would go in, so I knew I had no choice. I sat in the back, hidden behind the others. The missionaries' music made me cry, and I was astonished that the things they sang about were things I already believed in and felt familiar with. They taught that we lived with God before we were born and could live with God again one day. They taught about the purpose of life. More than all of that though, they gave me a beautiful feeling inside, and that was what made me cry! What was this that I was feeling?

"I Began to Test God"

After that night, I met with the missionaries often and was taught about the feelings of the Spirit. I began to test God. I was so determined to prove that the elders must be wrong. One day, for example, I was walking down a long hill in Corstorphine in Edinburgh. It was on a very quiet and sunny Sabbath Day. There was no one in sight. I was so confused by the feelings from the elders that as I walked along I prayed with my head down and eyes open. I recited the Lord's Prayer from the Bible and asked God that if the elders were saying words that were true, then "let me bump into the missionaries right now!"

I looked up and there was no one in front of me. What relief! However, at that precise moment, a bus drew up and stopped right next to me. There was no bus stop there so naturally I wondered why it was stopping. To my amazement, two missionaries got off the bus! I tried to pass off the incident as a coincidence, but I could not.

Every time I prayed to God He would directly answer me. I was so determined that the elders must be proved wrong that I was looking for either the missionaries to slip up, or for Heavenly Father to stop answering me. Neither happened! I asked the elders more and more questions. To begin with, I would only let them give me answers from the Bible. I already believed in God, but they had to prove to me that they knew Him and loved Him the way I did. They answered all my questions with ease. The ones they couldn't answer they found out for me.

After about eight months of refusing baptism and struggling to admit that the wonderful feelings that I felt were from the Holy Ghost, I decided to go on a long summer holiday to Canada and America. I wanted to test the members of the Church at its roots in Salt Lake City. To my surprise, I bumped into missionaries wherever I went in Canada. In fact, one day I was staying at the home of an American Baptist preacher and prayed to ask if the

Mormons were telling me the truth. I asked that if they were, then, "let me see some members right here and now!" I got off my knees satisfied that He could not answer that prayer because I was in my bedroom. I turned on the small TV that was there and saw a choir singing. The music was wonderful, and they sang of things the missionaries had taught me. I cried. The feelings were so beautiful! At the end of the programme I read that this had been a broadcast by the Mormon Tabernacle Choir. I had indeed seen Mormons in my bedroom!

After staying with another friend in Canada, I had a fall while water-skiing one day and had to go to hospital. I could not walk, and my ankle was badly sprained. I was told by the hospital that it would be impossible for me to continue my travels across Canada and the States and that I had no alternative but to cancel the rest of my holiday and catch a flight home. That night I prayed. By this time even I realised that the things I had been taught were true. So this time I prayed and told Heavenly Father that if He would heal my ankle miraculously overnight then I would obey the Word of Wisdom as I had been taught.

Early the next morning I awoke with a start. The mother of the house was calling me for breakfast. I had slept in! I jumped up and ran downstairs. The family looked at me with amazement. My ankle was completely better! I was able to carry on with my journey with barely a limp. From that day I started to keep the Word of Wisdom. Once you make a promise to God, you cannot retract it!

A Trip to Salt Lake City

Eventually I arrived in Salt Lake City. This was my final chance to find out what these Mormons were really like and for me to be able to finally walk away from them. The Greyhound bus station at that time was in the heart of Salt Lake City. As I stepped off the bus, the Spirit hit me so strongly and I felt I had come home. Again I cried. What was this place? Everywhere I went I felt I was surrounded by the Spirit, and I could find fault with not one person there. Every single person portrayed the pure love of Christ, and I felt the Spirit strongly with them all. I had many more beautiful spiritual experiences, some too sacred to me to record here.

When I returned home to Scotland, the missionaries continued teaching me with patience and answered my questions. Finally, I determined I wanted to be baptized. One year after first meeting the missionaries, I finally accepted baptism. It was the hardest thing I have ever done as I felt I was betraying my roots. My family were very opposed to my baptism and felt that by doing so I was denying God and also rejecting both my family and my heritage. My grandmother disowned me. A Baptist friend attended my baptism and stood at the font when I went down into the water. She told me that this was not something God wanted me to do and that at that moment my old church was holding a prayer meeting for me! However, I went ahead with the baptism and later was given the gift of the Holy Ghost. Since then I have always felt the Spirit with me.

Many years later I recollected my early youth when I wanted that lovely feeling I felt at church to be with me all the time and remembered that it always left me when I left church. Now I have the gift to have the Holy Ghost with me all the time and I never want to be without it again. It has been the most wonderful, precious gift and I can never take it for granted. I also remember wanting to meet an Apostle. I pleaded with God to one day let me meet an Apostle. Now I have sat and talked face to face with real Apostles and can testify that they are truly men of God. As a youth I had always believed that there must be more scripture, that the Bible could not contain all of God's words. But I didn't know where those words would be or what they looked like. I have found those missing words in my life and am satisfied that the Book of Mormon is indeed another witness of Jesus Christ.

My mother was eventually baptised herself. It may have taken her fifteen years, but she is now a very active member and says that it was partly because of my example in the way I raised my children that she began to investigate the Church. She now wishes she had found the Church earlier in her life. Over the next few years following my baptism, I managed to convince my grandmother that I still believed in Jesus, and she became more accepting of my newfound faith and even defended me to her friends.

All of these experiences in my life have been for my good. I am grateful to missionaries all over the world for serving in order to find people like myself. More than that, I feel so humble to think of the many missionaries who taught me and brought me the gospel restored in its fullness. Since my baptism, I have learned not to test God, but to trust in Him. I have met great people through my membership in the Church, but none greater than those first missionaries who taught me the restored gospel of the One who means the most to me in my life: my Lord, Saviour, and Friend, Jesus Christ. I bear witness that this is His Church.

I believe that our Heavenly Father wants to save every one of his children. I do not think he intends to shut any of us off because of some slight transgression, some slight failure to observe some rule or regulation. There are the great elementals that we must observe, but he is not going to be captious [quick to find fault] about the lesser things.

I believe that his juridical concept of his dealings with his children could be expressed in this way: I believe that in his justice and mercy he will give us the maximum reward for our acts, give us all that he can give, and in the reverse, I believe that he will impose upon us the minimum penalty which it is possible for him to impose.

J. REUBEN CLARK, JR.

CHAPTER EIGHT

The God We Worship

What the Scriptures Teach about God's Nature

Recently, I spoke at a fireside on the topic of God's tender mercies and His love for us. Afterward, a young man came up to me and said, "But Brother Lund, if that is true, how then do you explain all of the scriptures that talk about God's negative qualities?"

I didn't have to ask him what he meant. The scriptures are filled with words like anger, wrath, vengeance, judgment, damnation, indignation, jealousy, punishment, and hellfire, and in most cases these are tied to God. These, too, are part of His nature. There is no question about it. Unfortunately some would have us believe that such attributes are not just *part* of His nature, they *define* His nature. They define *Him.* In other words, God is harsh, stern, and judgmental by nature. And that simply is not so.

Without dwelling on this for too long, let me suggest a couple of ideas to consider.

First, parents who have more than one child understand that no two children are alike. Even though they come from the same gene pool, each child comes with his or her own unique personality, character, gifts, abilities, and temperament.

This holds true for obedience as well. Some children are naturally more compliant and willing to accept counsel than others. They are teachable and seem to internalize concepts and principles quickly. Gentle correction or mild admonishment suffices to keep them moving forward. Others seem to have this inbred inclination to push back against regulation and direction. They are always testing the limits, pushing the boundaries, crossing the line to see what will happen.

Parents set up limits, boundaries, and lines because they know that an uncontrolled and undisciplined life can destroy a person. They feel compelled to try to mold and influence and direct those types of children so they will do those things that will bring them happiness. If they impose consequences and punishments when children do things to their own detriment or to the harm of others, this is a reflection of the parents' love.

So it is with God. We are His children. He wants the best for us. He wants us to be happy. If we are obedient, He blesses us. If we are not, well then . . . He warns, corrects, chastises, punishes, and disciplines. Why? Because He knows better than we do that "wickedness never was happiness" (Alma 41:10)—and never can be—and that "repentance could not come unto men except there were a punishment" (Alma 42:16). So when we read of His jealousy, wrath, vengeance, judgment, punishment, and eternal damnation, let us remember that these are not a reflection of God's imperfect nature. They are the result of man's failings.

As two examples, let's quickly look at the concept of hell and situations where God ordered that the wicked be destroyed.

Many devout and sincere Christians (and Muslims) believe that the lake of fire and brimstone is a literal place of punishment. Fortunately, the Book of Mormon teaches us that the lake of fire is a metaphor for the personal remorse of conscience we will feel if we chose evil over good in this life. But in a modern revelation, our understanding of what happens to the wicked after they die is expanded even further (see D&C 76, 138). Based on what we learn there, Elder James E. Talmage taught this about hell:

> Hell is no place to which a vindictive judge sends prisoners to suffer and to be punished principally for his glory; but *it is a place prepared for the teaching, the disciplining* of those who failed to learn here upon the earth what they should have learned. True, we read of everlasting punishment, unending suffering, eternal damnation. That is a direful expression; but in his mercy the Lord has made plain what those words mean. "Eternal punishment," he says, is God's punishment, for he is eternal; and that condition or state or possibility will ever exist for the sinner who deserves and really needs such condemnation; but this does not mean that the individual sufferer or sinner is to be eternally and everlastingly made to endure and suffer. *No man will be kept in hell longer than is necessary to bring him to a fitness for something better.* When he reaches that stage the prison doors will open and there will be rejoicing among the hosts who welcome him into a better state.[1]

We believe that men are sent to hell in order to help them learn and progress so eventually they can enjoy a greater degree of happiness than they would otherwise have had. Human nature is such that if we had the power, we would send men to hell to punish them. God sends them there in order to help them.

An Interesting Exercise

A careful examination of those scriptures where God speaks of judgment, punishment, and eternal consequences shows that these were given when the children of Israel (or the Nephites or the Latter-day Saints) were straying from the path. In some cases they had turned to gross wickedness and were headed for the destruction of their entire society.

But there are also times in the scriptures when the Lord's people are being obedient, when they are striving to accept His will and live His commandments. An interesting exercise is to go through the scriptures and look for those times of righteousness. Then compare how the prophets speak to those people with how they speak to the wicked. Is the message significantly different? Do we still find warnings and calls to repentance? What things do they speak of in place of judgments and punishment? Do they teach more doctrine? Do they speak more of happiness and blessings than in those other circumstances?

Here are just a few examples of prophets speaking to a righteous people.

- Nephi's closing counsel to his people (2 Nephi 31–33)
- King Benjamin's last address to his people (Mosiah 2–5)
- Alma the Elder's counsel at the Waters of Mormon (Mosiah 18)
- Alma the Younger's counsel to his sons Helaman and Shiblon (Alma 36–38)
- The Savior's visit to the Nephites (3 Nephi 11–27)
- Paul's epistles to the Philippians and to Timothy
- Enoch's speech on the Plan of Salvation (Moses 6:47–68)

Here is another example. One of the things that bothers people about the Old Testament is how harsh God's punishments are. He destroyed all but eight souls in the Flood. He wiped out Sodom and Gomorrah, sparing only Lot and his family. In some cases He commanded Moses or Joshua to destroy entire populations, including men, women, and children. How could that be an act of love? Here is Elder Neal A. Maxwell's answer to that question.

> Being a loving Father, though deeply devoted to our free agency, there are times in human history when He simply could not continue to send spirits to this earth who would have had virtually no chance. This was the case with Sodom and Gomorrah and the cities of the plains. "Hence it was better to destroy a few individuals, than to entail misery on many (John Taylor, *The Government of God* [Liverpool: S.W. Richards, 1852], 53)." . . . "If we were like the people before the flood, full of violence and oppression; or if we, like the Sodomites or Canaanites, were full of all manner of lawless abominations, holding promiscuous intercourse with the other sex, and stooping to a level with the brute creation, and predisposing our children, by every means in our power, to be fully given to strange and unnatural lusts, appetites, and passions, would it not be a mercy to cut us off, root and branch, and thus put an end to our increase upon the earth? . . . The spirits in heaven would thank God for preventing them from being born into the world under such circumstances (Parley P. Pratt, *Journal of Discourses* 1:259)."[2]

In the book of Moses, the premortal Jehovah taught that "all things bear record of me" (Moses 6:63). This is true of all of His divine attributes, including anger, punishment, and judgment.

Let us now look at some passages that we often overlook precisely because they are not grim and threatening. It may surprise us how often in the scriptures we are taught about God's perfect love, mercy, and long-suffering. Some of these passages are rich in imagery and tender in what they teach us about the Father and the Son. It is critical to our faith that we know, understand, and appreciate this aspect of God as well.

God Desires Happiness for His Children

We saw in the chapter on life's paradox that there are many references to the joy and happiness the Father wishes for His children. We shall add only a few more not mentioned there.

- "The morning stars sang together, and *all the sons of God shouted for joy*" (Job 38:7).
- "Thou wilt shew me the path of life: in thy presence is *fulness of joy*; at thy right hand there are pleasures for evermore" (Psalm 16:11).
- "Be glad in the Lord, and *rejoice,* ye righteous: and *shout for joy,* all ye that are upright in heart" (Psalm 32:11).
- "*Happy is he that hath the God of Jacob for his help,* whose hope is in the Lord his God" (Psalm 146:5).
- "The things of the wise and the prudent shall be hid from them [who are puffed up in pride] forever—yea, *that happiness which is prepared for the saints*" (2 Nephi 9:43).
- "There were many who died with old age; and those who died in the faith of Christ are *happy in him*" (Alma 46:41).
- "And for this cause *ye shall have fulness of joy*; and ye shall sit down in the kingdom of my Father; yea, *your joy shall be full,* even as the Father hath given me fulness of joy" (3 Nephi 28:10).

The God of the Old Testament—Merciful and Gracious

The Old Testament is viewed by many as depicting a harsher deity who shows little love and mercy for His people. This view softened, in their way of thinking, into the kinder, gentler god of the New Testament, namely the Son of God who ministers to the poor, who reaches out in compassion to the needy, who forgives a woman taken in adultery, and, even as He is being nailed to the cross, who asks the Father to forgive them.

One of the great achievements of Satan is that most of the Christian world no longer understands that the Jehovah of the Old Testament was the premortal Jesus Christ. But we don't have to dig very deep into the Old Testament to find descriptions of God that are in full harmony with the New Testament or modern revelation. Here is just a small sample of what is there.

Exodus

When Moses led the children of Israel into the wilderness, he was met with immediate and nearly constant rebellion, despite one incredible miracle after another. As someone once wryly noted, "The real challenge was not to get Israel out of Egypt, but to get Egypt out of Israel." If it was not stubbornness, it was murmuring and complaining. When the children of Israel weren't murmuring, they were running off to worship idols or sin in ways that endangered the entire group. Moses was constantly rebuking them and warning them of the consequences of their sins. Yet when Moses went up to Mount Sinai to commune with the Lord, we read: "And the Lord descended in the cloud, and stood with him there, and proclaimed. . . . The Lord, The Lord God, *merciful and gracious, longsuffering, and abundant in goodness* and truth, *keeping mercy for thousands, forgiving iniquity and transgression and sin*" (Exodus 34:5–7).

Deuteronomy

Much later in his life Moses wrote, "It shall come to pass, if ye hearken to these judgments, and keep, and do them, that the Lord thy God *shall keep unto thee the covenant and the mercy* which he sware unto thy fathers: And *he will love thee, and bless thee. . . . Thou shalt be blessed above all people*" (Deuteronomy 7:12–14).

Psalms

As part of the oratorio *Elijah,* Felix Mendelssohn wrote a beautiful hymn called "He Watching over Israel." The text was taken from Psalm 121:4, which reads, "He that keepeth Israel shall neither slumber nor sleep." There are only nine simple words in that verse, but they carry profound meaning. To appreciate what that means, let us compare this with how things are with us today.

When we approach God, we will never get a recorded message like, "Please listen carefully to the following options before choosing: Press one for customer service, two for technical support, etc." We will never be told that He is on His lunch break, taking a holiday, or that this is His day off. Our Father is always there for us. He has put no restrictions on our access to Him. We can turn to Him at any time of the day or night. We can present Him any question, any problem, any petition. We can do this in any language, with no restrictions on the subject or the gravity of the problem. We do not need a visa or a passport to gain access to Him.

I love that concept: "He that keepeth Israel shall neither slumber nor sleep."

Ezekiel

As noted earlier, one of my responsibilities as a General Authority was to perform restorations of blessings when assigned to do so by the First Presidency. As I said, these were always tender and sweet experiences for me. After we finished the ordinance and I completed the necessary paperwork that had to be returned to the First Presidency, I would conclude with a final scripture. When you think about how many references there are to the Atonement, to repentance and forgiveness, and to God's long-suffering nature, I suppose it is somewhat ironic that the passage I preferred to use came from the Old Testament, a book that supposedly paints a picture of a rigid and unforgiving God.

If the wicked will turn from all his sins that he hath committed, and keep all my statutes, and do that which is lawful and right, *he shall surely live,* he shall not die. *All his transgressions that he hath committed, they shall not be mentioned unto him*: in his righteousness that he hath done he shall live. (Ezekiel 18:21–22)

The New Testament Witness of God's Love

The New Testament is dramatically different from the Old Testament in many ways. The first four books contain a history of the mortal Jesus and His teachings. His very presence in that record fills virtually every page with love and compassion and forgiveness. Passages such as these are found throughout the New Testament:

- "In my Father's house are many mansions: if it were not so, I would have told you. I go to prepare a place for you" (John 14:2; see also D&C 98:18).
- "If a man love me, he will keep my words: and *my Father will love him,* and we will come unto him, and make our abode with him" (John 14:23).
- "God *commendeth his love toward us,* in that, while we were yet sinners, Christ died for us" (Romans 5:8).
- "Who shall separate us from the love of Christ? shall tribulation, or distress, or persecution, or famine, or nakedness,

or peril, or sword? . . . *Nay, in all these things we are more than conquerors through him that loved us*" (Romans 8:35, 37).

- "Eye hath not seen, nor ear heard, neither have entered into the heart of man, *the things which God hath prepared for them that love him*" (1 Corinthians 2:9).
- "Behold, what manner of love the Father hath bestowed upon us, that we should be called the sons of God" (1 John 3:1).

However, in addition to these more direct passages, I have found other examples that have enriched my understanding of the Father and the Son. Here are two examples, both from Luke's gospel:

The Synagogue at Nazareth

Early in His ministry, Jesus returned to his hometown of Nazareth. In Luke 4 we read:

And he came to Nazareth, where he had been brought up: and, as his custom was, he went into the synagogue on the sabbath day, and stood up for to read. And there was delivered unto him the book of the prophet Esaias. And when he had opened the book, he found the place where it was written . . . (Luke 4:16–17)

The normal Sabbath service in the synagogues of that time consisted of prayers, readings from the law and the prophets—what today we call the Old Testament—and a lesson by the leader of the synagogue. Any worthy adult male member of the synagogue could read from the scriptures. Though there was a set reading for each Sabbath day, the reader could also select a passage of his own choosing.

The phrase "he found the place" suggests that Jesus specifically selected the passage from Isaiah 61:1–2, but note that He also inserted text from Isaiah 58:7. It is important to understand that the first of these two passages was viewed by the Jews as Messianic, i.e., that it was a prophecy that directly referred to the coming Messiah. This helps explain what happened next.

> The Spirit of the Lord is upon me, because he hath anointed me to preach the gospel to the poor; he hath sent me to heal the brokenhearted, to preach deliverance to the captives, and recovering of sight to the blind, to set at liberty them that are bruised. To preach the acceptable year of the Lord. And he closed the book, and he gave it again to the minister, and sat down. And the eyes of all them that were in the synagogue were fastened on him. And he began to say unto them, This day is this scripture fulfilled in your ears. (Luke 4:18–21)

Almost instantly, the synagogue was in an uproar. The people understood exactly what He meant when He said, "This day is this scripture fulfilled"—Jesus was declaring Himself to be the Messiah. The reaction of the congregation was first astonishment, and then outrage. Was not this Joseph's son? He was a carpenter. How could *he* possibly be the Messiah? It was unthinkable. When Jesus rebuked them, they were filled with wrath and tried to kill him, but He slipped away, and thereafter made Capernaum His residence.

But consider for a moment the implications of this scripture for us. This event occurred at the very beginning of Christ's mortal ministry. Not only did He declare Himself to be the promised Messiah, but He quoted a passage that *defined His ministry.* This is what Jesus came to earth to do:

- Preach the gospel to the poor
- Heal the brokenhearted
- Preach deliverance to captives
- Help the blind to see
- Set at liberty those that are bruised

In a world where virtually every day we are confronted with the paradox of life, I find those definitions of who He is and why He came deeply gratifying and comforting.

"Pressed Down and Shaken Together"

Some years ago, my wife and I were traveling in the Holy Land with a group of seminary and institute teachers. As we were moving through the crowded streets of Old Jerusalem, I noticed a street vendor up ahead of us. He was seated on the narrow sidewalk with several large burlap sacks of grain arranged around him. As we approached, I noticed an Arab woman coming toward him from the opposite direction. She had a large clay pot balanced on her head. As she reached the vendor, she stopped and took down the jar.

Charmed by the scene, my wife and I stopped to watch, for it was obvious that the woman had come to purchase grain, just as people in the Holy Land had done from before the days of Jesus.

After a few words were exchanged, the man took the jar, held it over the large sack of wheat, and quickly filled it up using a metal scoop. The last scoop left a small heap of grain rising above the top of the jar. Then the vendor did an interesting thing. He reached down and picked up a small, flat stick, somewhat like a ruler. Very carefully, holding the jar over the grain sack, he scraped the stick across the top of the jar, pushing any excess wheat back into the sack.

For a moment I was irritated. Was he trying to cheat this woman? But she was not at all upset as she watched him. Then I realized that he wasn't being dishonest. He was giving her an honest measure. She had asked for a full jar of grain and that was what he was giving her. He just wasn't going to sell her one grain more than what she had paid for.

Now compare this with the Savior's description of how the Father blesses us. "Be ye therefore merciful," He said, "as your Father also is merciful. . . . Give, and it shall be given unto you; *good measure, pressed down, and shaken together, and running over*" (Luke 6:36, 38).

What a difference from how man deals with his fellowman. When God fills our jar, He fills it to the top. Then He tamps it down to compress the grain. That is followed by a vigorous shaking, which aligns the kernels of grain so the level in the jar drops perceptibly. Then once the jar is capable of holding more, the Father fills it to the top again. Only with Him, there is no scraping off any excess. He fills it to overflowing, giving us more than our containers can possibly hold. The Psalmist taught the same principle in these words: "My cup runneth over. Surely goodness and mercy shall follow me all the days of my life: and I will dwell in the house of the Lord for ever" (Psalm 23:5–6).

"Pressed down, shaken together, and running over"—that's the Heavenly Father I have come to know.

Notes

Epigraph. J. Reuben Clark, Jr., in Conference Report, October 1953, 84.
1. James E. Talmage, in Conference Report, April 1930, 97.
2. Neal A. Maxwell, *Sermons Not Spoken* (Salt Lake City: Bookcraft, 1985), 91–92.

Preparing the Way

By now, I hope you see that the Lord's tender mercies not only come in many different ways, but they are given for many different purposes as well. Sometimes, they come simply as a way to move the Lord's work forward. The following is a powerful example of a divine signature that did just that.

In 1996, LeGrand Black and his wife, Marcia, of Blanding, Utah, led a group of Church Educational System administrators and their wives on a trip to the Hole in the Rock. Lynn and I were privileged to be part of that trip.

LeGrand and Marcia were the ones who first introduced me to the story of these incredible pioneers and the divine signatures they experienced on their arduous journey. Their love for those early pioneers was influential in my writing the story of the San Juan Mission.[1]

One day, a few months ago, I was explaining the concept of divine signatures to a group where LeGrand was present. Afterward, he shared an experience from his life that illustrated how the Lord can move the work forward by a simple, but divine, intervention. At my request, LeGrand has agreed to share his story here. I am grateful to him for doing so. I am grateful to him and Marcia for providing me with another defining experience as we crossed the red rock country of Southern Utah.

The Lord's Hand in Lithuania

My vocation throughout my life has been teaching for the Church Educational System (CES) as a seminary and institute teacher. In 1999, this career was interrupted for a few years by a wonderful opportunity to work for the Scripture Translation Department of the Church.

Jim Berlin, a former seminary teacher and personal friend, recommended me for the translation job. I remember Jim saying that one of the main differences I would notice between working in CES and in the Translation Department is that in CES the Lord honors agency, while in Translation no person or thing is allowed to stand in the way.

"When the time comes for a people to receive their first edition of the Book of Mormon you will see the Lord work miracles on a daily basis," Jim said. I thought maybe he was being a little facetious, but I soon learned firsthand what he meant.

After my initial training, I was assigned as the project manager for various languages in Scandinavia and Eastern Europe. One of those projects was to translate the first Lithuanian edition of the Book of Mormon.

Nephi prophesied: "And I would, my brethren, that ye should know that all the kindreds of the earth cannot be blessed unless he shall make bare his arm in the eyes of the nations. Wherefore, the Lord God will proceed to make bare his arm in the eyes of all the nations, in bringing about his covenants and his gospel unto those who are of the house of Israel" (1 Nephi 22:10–11).

The small Baltic nation of Lithuania witnessed the

fulfillment of the Lord's promise to move His work forward with great power. One privilege of working in translation is observing how the Lord raises up a "plowboy" in every land. One soon sees the Lord's arm in the translator's preparation. In Lithuania, the Lord's "plowboy" raised up to translate their scriptures was Genadijus Motiejunas.

Genadijus Motiejunas was born in Kaunas, Lithuania. A modified passage from the Prophet Joseph's life perfectly describes Genadijus: "Some time in the second year of our [liberation from the Soviet Union], there was in the place where we lived an unusual excitement on the subject of religion. . . . During this time of great excitement my mind was called up to serious reflection and great uneasiness" (Joseph Smith–History 1:5, 8).

Genadijus joined with the Baptists and became obsessed with the study of the scriptures. He was a very devout and charitable man and soon became one of the respected leaders of the Baptist Church in Kaunas, Lithuania. Together with other ministers, Genadijus made a promise never to speak with representatives or read the scriptures of a new, suspicious sect in Lithuania called "the Mormons."

At this time, the leaders of the Baptist Church desired to write a declaration of beliefs for their membership, and Genadijus was invited to join the effort. After several weeks spent composing their "articles of faith," Genadijus became uneasy that the drafters were interpreting the scriptures too narrowly. He recommended that the scriptures be allowed to stand on their own stated doctrines without undue human meddling or interpretation.

His recommendations were ignored, so Genadijus made his worries a matter of prayer. He felt inspired to persist with his objections. When he again voiced his disapproval of their work, he was dismissed from the Baptist Church and his job—not because he dared to disagree, but because he claimed to have received inspiration from God on the matter. His peers firmly reminded him that personal revelation had ceased with the original Church of Christ.

Genadijus became depressed. He poured out his heart to the Lord. He felt he had been prompted to devote his life to bringing souls to Christ but was now separated from the vehicle that allowed him to accomplish that work.

A very short time later, two LDS missionaries, Sisters Cristal Hammaker and Heather Baer knocked on his door. Genadijus was initially repulsed as he saw the Book of Mormon the sisters were carrying. The very book so feared by his brethren! He was reluctant to hear the sisters or accept any literature from them and sent the missionaries on their way.

After the sisters left the apartment, Genadijus's wife, Alfreda, voiced her disappointment about not having the Book of Mormon to read as she had recently been over-taken with a curiosity about the ancient inhabitants of the Americas. Alfreda wanted to examine the book for herself.

Then a thought flickered in Genadijus's mind: "My re-cent separation from the Baptist Church has freed me from my promise to never touch this strange book." Morally, he could now at least hold the Book of Mormon. Alfreda quickly sent her husband in pursuit of the departing missionaries.

As he and his wife read the book, their faith and testi-mony of this work grew with every verse. He read the Book of Mormon in a month, and then he started reading the Doctrine and Covenants. What he read answered so many of the questions he had been struggling with. Eventually both

Genadijus and Alfreda were baptized into The Church of Jesus Christ of Latter-day Saints.

When I made my first trip to Lithuania I was very nervous about gaining the trust and confidence of our new native translator. Many in this recently liberated Soviet State were reluctant to open up to outsiders or talk freely, especially about matters of religion. It seemed to me that a "bond of brotherhood" would be critical to accomplishing the work of scripture translation, the most spiritually intense work of the Restoration. On that first flight, I prayed all the way across the ocean that the Lord would prepare a way for me to develop this bond of brotherhood.

When I first met with Genadijus and his dear wife in their home, I asked them to relate their conversion story. With great enthusiasm they brought out a large photo album of their "angels," as they called the two sister missionaries who met their family and taught them the gospel. What a surprise it was for me when I looked at the photographs and recognized both of the sister missionaries!

I practically shouted, "I know these sisters! I taught Sister Heather Baer in seminary in Kennewick, Washington. Later, I taught Sister Cristal Hammaker in institute classes in Price, Utah."

Genadijus gazed at me in wonder. "You are the teacher of my angels?" he whispered. "Then you may be my teacher."

This "coincidence" makes one ponder the intricate planning of "Heaven's Correlation Committee." Two of my former students, one from Washington and the other from Utah, were both called to serve in Lithuania. Both traveled halfway around the world to serve as missionary companions in Kaunas, where very few of the missionaries in Lithuania served. They were led to the Motiejunas apartment, one of literally tens of thousands of apartments in the area. And, of course, the timing of their visit had to be perfect. Still bound to his oath never to open the Book of Mormon, Genadijus, would have curtly dismissed the missionaries only days earlier.

Because I knew and had taught the "angels" who introduced Genadijus to the gospel, an instant bond of trust and friendship was forged. This relationship was a powerful blessing as we worked on the translation project together. The Lithuanian Book of Mormon was published in December 2000, a remarkably short time for a first edition Book of Mormon. Genadijus eventually translated into Lithuanian the very Book of Mormon he once vowed never to touch!

I'm not a mathematician, but if I were, I'd love to try to calculate the mathematical probability of having all the necessary elements come together exactly the way they did and at exactly the right time to make this happen. With more than three hundred missions in the world and about fifty thousand missionaries at that time, what are the chances that two girls from different states, who both had been taught by Brother Black, would end up in the same mission, let alone as companions? Those odds must surely be astronomically huge.

"He that keepeth Israel shall neither slumber nor sleep" (Psalm 121:4).

Notes

1. This is a historical novel I wrote titled *The Undaunted: The Miracle of the Hole-in-the-Rock Pioneers* (Salt Lake City: Deseret Book, 2009).

I am perfectly satisfied that my Father and my God is a cheerful, pleasant, lively, and good-natured Being. Why? Because I am cheerful, pleasant, lively and good-natured when I have His Spirit. . . . That arises from the perfection of His attributes; He is a jovial, lively person, and a beautiful man.

HEBER C. KIMBALL

CHAPTER NINE

"I . . . Delight to Honor"

He Wants to Bless Us

There are many passages throughout all the standard works that powerfully teach about the divine attributes of Heavenly Father and Jesus Christ. But I shall focus on only one more here. I choose this one because it provides an insight into what God is like that I find quite precious, and which has greatly expanded my testimony of Him.

A Suggestion

A valuable part of my scripture study in recent years has been to specifically watch for passages that teach about God's perfect love for His children. Keeping a card or a notebook nearby so I can jot down these references and add them to my growing collection has proven to be a beneficial exercise in strengthening my faith and deepening my testimony.

Some of these references can be found by searching in the Topical Guide, but many do not use the word "love" or "mercy" in the passage and so would not be shown. (Two examples would be the passage in Psalms about God not slumbering and the one in Luke about "filling our jars.") The card or notebook serves as a reminder to be watching for these kinds of references. I can promise that you will be surprised how frequently they occur.

In Section 76 of the Doctrine and Covenants—the section that contains the vision of the three degrees of glory—there is one verse I have always loved. It is verse five.

I, the Lord, am merciful and gracious unto those who fear me, and delight to honor those who serve me in righteousness and in truth unto the end. (D&C 76:5)

Isn't it strange how we can read a passage over and over, even marking it, when suddenly a word or a phrase that we had barely noticed kind of leaps out at us? Well, that happened to me with this passage. It was only a few years ago that as I was reading it again, a single word suddenly caught my attention. It was the word "delight." The Lord said, "I *delight* to honor."

Delight? The word struck me as an odd choice. A delighted God? I have pictured Heavenly Father and Jesus in many ways—loving, patient, merciful, long-suffering, happy, joyful, and so on—but I can't say that I had ever pictured them as being delighted. The dictionary defines delight as "a high degree of pleasure or enjoyment; joy; rapture."[1] Rapturous just didn't seem to fit my conception of God. But then, I thought, why not? If He is a happy and pleasant being as Heber C. Kimball said, wouldn't delight be part of His nature, too?

With that on my mind, I found that God's "delight" is mentioned in other places as well.

- "For I, the Lord God, *delight* in the chastity of women" (Jacob 2:28). I find that interesting. He is not just pleased when His daughters are chaste. He is delighted.

- "Hearken and hear, O ye my people, saith the Lord and your God, *ye whom I delight to bless with the greatest of all blessings,* ye that hear me" (D&C 41:1).
- "*My soul delighteth in the song of the heart;* yea, the song of the righteous is a prayer unto me" (D&C 25:12). I like that idea. I delight in beautiful and uplifting music. Why wouldn't He?

This doesn't quite fit the picture some churches teach about God, does it? And yet a gloomy, morose, and dolorous Deity just doesn't feel right to me, not if He's perfect in every respect of His being. So the more I have thought about it, the more I like the idea of a delighted Heavenly Father and Savior. What father does not delight in his children, and is not delighted to do things to make them happy? I know that from my own personal experience as a father and grandfather.

Carlie

One day during a family gathering when we had our entire family in town, I was sitting in the family room with my youngest son. We were just talking together. The rest of the family was outside playing or talking. This son lived out of state at that time, and we didn't often have the chance to talk with each other. So we had slipped inside to do so. Then the door opened, and a granddaughter, who was about three at the time, came inside. She walked over and stood directly in front of me and looked at me. I stopped the conversation and said, "Hi, Carlie. Do you need something?"

She nodded. "Grampa, can I watch TV with you?"

That surprised me since the television wasn't even on, but I nodded, pulled her up on my lap, and turned on some cartoons. About three minutes later, she was fast asleep. As I looked down on that peaceful little face, I understood. She hadn't wanted to watch television at all. She was just tired and looking for a safe and comfortable place to rest. And I was delighted that she had chosen my lap as that place. More—I was delighted to honor her request.

Andrew

Here's another example. A couple of years ago, one of our daughters shared the following with us concerning our grandson, Andrew, who was six at that time. He is very studied and deliberate in the way that his mind works. He thinks things through very carefully to their conclusion. One day he came home from Primary with a small bag of candy hearts. His teacher had given them to the children and asked them to give them away to someone, *after* they had done something nice for that person. She really stressed the idea that they had to do something nice first.

Andrew gave some of his hearts away to family members and friends, but he saved a pink heart for his sister, Katelyn, who was just younger than he. Pink was Katelyn's favorite color.

The problem was that Andrew couldn't think of anything nice that he could do for her. When he asked his mother for advice, she gave him several ideas, but he quickly rejected each one. Finally his mother told him to just give his sister the heart. Katelyn would be so pleased with the candy and that would be a nice thing in and of itself. Andrew flatly refused. His teacher had said they had to do something nice first, and he couldn't give Katelyn the heart until he did so.

A few minutes later he returned to his mother. He clearly had been thinking about his dilemma. "Mom," he said, "what if I just hit Katelyn? That would make her cry. Then I could put my arms around her and tell her I was sorry. That would be nice, wouldn't it? *Then* I could give her the candy."

Don't you find that delightful? Granted, slugging your little sister hardly qualifies as good Christian behavior, but Andrew's motives were so pure and so sweet, I can't help but believe his Heavenly Father perhaps even laughed aloud that day. I surely did when our daughter shared the story with us.

I suppose one of the reasons I feel so strongly about this idea of delight is because my wife and I have an example from our own lives that seems to fit the description of a blessing with which the Lord would delight to honor us. I share this personal experience in the hope that it will affect your faith and testimony as it did ours.

A Blessing for a Thirteen-Year-Old Girl

My wife, Lynn Stanard Lund, was born and raised in Great Falls, Montana. During the years of her youth, Great Falls was not yet a stake, but a mission district. The nearest temple was the Alberta Temple in Cardston, which was about two hundred miles north of Great Falls. Their branch would typically take a temple trip with adults and youth going up together. While the adults did endowment sessions and sealings, the youth would participate in baptisms for the dead.

When Lynn was thirteen, she went on one such trip to Cardston. The youth finished earlier than the adults, so while they were waiting in the nearby chapel, an older man came in and introduced himself. He told them that since Great Falls was a mission district, they did not have a stake patriarch. He explained that he was the stake patriarch for the Cardston Stake and had been authorized to give patriarchal blessings to any of the youth who didn't already have one and who desired to receive it. He had received permission from the parents to make this offer to the youth.

Lynn didn't have a full understanding of all that a patriarchal blessing entailed, but when the patriarch asked who would like one, she raised her hand. Thus it was that one week before she turned thirteen years of age, a man whom she had never met before, who was an ordained patriarch, laid his hands on her head and gave her a blessing.

Lynn's parents were unable to have children for the first sixteen years of their marriage. Her uncle and his wife were never able to have children either. Because of that family history, Lynn was worried, even at that young age, that she might have inherited whatever the cause of that problem was. So when the patriarch pronounced the blessing, she listened carefully for any reference to future children. It came and she was gratified. When she received the printed copy a few weeks later, she eagerly studied the blessing to see if she had remembered correctly.

It was there, but there was also something related to that blessing that quite concerned her. Without going into the details of the exact wording, here is the gist of what was said. First, it talked about the importance of temple marriage and suggested that this would be a key to her eternal happiness. Second, to ensure she didn't marry outside the temple, it cautioned her strongly about falling in love with someone who was unworthy to take her to the temple. She shouldn't assume that she could marry outside the temple and then be sealed to her husband later. Third, in even stronger words, it warned her about rationalizing that she could marry outside the temple and then be sealed to her husband later.

Those words were very sobering to her. So as she entered high school, she made up her mind that though she had many friends who were not members of the Church, she would date only those who were. This was not a simple vow to keep. Lynn attended a high school of about 2,600 students, and there were only five or six young men who were Latter-day Saints. She had a boyfriend in the Church who had already graduated, but only students could attend the dances, so

Lynn rarely got to go to the school dances, although she was often asked.

The King and I

My wife came from a family that loved music. In Lynn's senior year, Great Falls High School announced that they would be performing *The King and I* by Rodgers and Hammerstein. Both Lynn and her brother, who was two years younger than she was, decided to try out. Both were accepted. Lynn was cast as one of the wives of the king who also made up the chorus for the musical. The play was to be put on in late April or early May.

On the last night of the performance, a cast party was planned. Earlier in the week, one of the boys in the play asked Lynn if she would go to the cast party with him. He was not a member of the Church, and she hesitated at first. But school was almost over. She had been true to her decision to follow the counsel in her blessing, and she would be leaving for BYU that fall. What could one date hurt? So she accepted.

During the intermission, her brother sought her out. "Lynn," he said, "I just learned that your date is out behind the auditorium drinking beer with several others. They are already half drunk. Are you still going to go to the party with him?"

Quite devastated, she shook her head and asked her brother to tell the boy the date was off.

"That night," she says, "when the play was over, I went home. I washed out the black dye from my hair (required of all the king's wives) and then went to bed. I began to cry. I was convinced that my romantic life was in ruins, that I would never find someone to take me to the temple. Then I cried myself to sleep."

A Lesson for a Sixteen-Year-Old Boy

Hold that picture of Lynn in your mind for a few moments, while we enlarge the background a little more. I was raised from the time I was six in Murray, Utah, which is just five or six miles south of Salt Lake City. This was mostly a rural area at that time. Since there was a shortage of young girls in the neighborhood, my brothers and I were often asked to babysit for the neighbors.

One night, I had a bad experience while babysitting. The couple, who were not members, came home. The man was quite drunk and they were having a fight. I had grown up in a home where my father never spoke harshly to my mother, so seeing this guy swearing and shouting and cursing to his wife was pretty awful.

I decided that night that who I married was very important if I was to have a happy marriage. So for the first time in my life, I asked Heavenly Father to help me find the right girl to marry, and I made that a part of my daily prayer thereafter.

A Mission Call

Fast forward four years. Back then, young men were not called into missionary service until the age of twenty. I had spent six months active duty in the army so I was past twenty when I turned in my papers. I was called to the West Central States, headquartered in Billings, Montana. This was a huge disappointment to me. I had two older brothers and I felt that I had spent my entire life living in their shadow. My second-oldest brother, Grant, was currently serving in the West Central States at the time I got my mission call. I was actually angry at the Lord for calling me to the same mission as my brother. But he came home a month before I left, so we didn't ever serve at the same time.

In March of 1960, I caught a Greyhound bus and traveled to

Billings to report for full-time missionary service. After a couple of days at the mission home, I received my assignment. My first field of labor was to be Great Falls, Montana. By this time, Great Falls had grown enough that there was a stake and two wards in the city. My companion and I were assigned to cover the east side of Great Falls and attend the ward that included that area.

At church, I noticed a young girl playing the organ. I was told that she was the daughter of President Stanard, who was in the stake presidency. I never met the young organist or talked to her. About six weeks after my arrival in Great Falls, my companion and I were talking about what to do on our preparation day. Just as now, we weren't allowed to go to movies or attend other activities inappropriate for missionaries. But on this day, my companion had an idea. We had seen posters around town advertising a school musical performance of *The King and I.* We were told there was nothing offensive or inappropriate in the play, so we decided to go. My memory is that we attended the show on the last night of the performance, but memory can play tricks on you, so the only thing I can say for sure was that I attended the play on one of the three nights it was presented.

It was not until some years after we were married that Lynn told me the story of her "tragedy" on the final night of the performance. It was only then that we understood fully what had happened without either of us knowing about it. That night, as she cried herself to sleep, sure that all chances for a happy marriage were lost, she had no way of knowing that her future husband had been in the audience one of those three nights.

Briefly, here's the rest of the story. A short time after that, I was transferred out of Great Falls to Glasgow, Montana, a city about four hundred miles away. In September, my companion and I were on our way back to Glasgow from a mission conference that had been held in Helena. It was Sunday, so we stopped in Great Falls to attend church.

This was in the afternoon so it was not the ward that I had attended before. As we went in, we saw a girl whom we had worked with up in Glasgow on our Youth Missionary Committee. We stopped to say hello, and she introduced us to her best friend, Lynn Stanard. She left, we attended church, then continued on to Glasgow. The next morning, Lynn left for BYU.

Eighteen months later, I was released from my mission service and returned home. To my surprise, I learned that through a strange turn of events, my older brother, Grant, had dated Lynn Stanard from Great Falls, Montana, a couple of times. She had been asked to accompany a musical group that was singing at a mission reunion of West Central States missionaries. Since Grant had been in the same mission, he was at the reunion and asked her out.

I went down to Provo a short time later and looked Lynn up. We dated off and on for the summer and then when I enrolled at BYU that fall, things got serious. We were engaged at Christmas and married the following June.

Two Other Promises

In the patriarchal blessing Lynn received when she was thirteen years old, two additional promises were given. The first promise puzzled her for a long time. The second one she barely noticed, for it was only a brief sentence.

In her blessing she was told that it would be her privilege to go into the world and bear testimony of the Father and the Son to those who didn't have a correct knowledge of God. At first she thought it meant she would be called as a sister missionary to some foreign land. But when I married her two weeks before her twenty-first birthday, that put an end to that. For years we wondered how this promise might be fulfilled.

Then our life took a very different turn. On April 6, 2002, I was sustained as a member of the Second Quorum of the Seventy. After a year of training in Salt Lake City, Lynn and I were assigned to the Europe West Area Presidency headquartered in Solihull, England. The Europe West Area covered twenty-two countries, had twenty-two missions, eighty-two stakes, seven major languages, and about 350,000 members of the Church. We served there for three years.

Lynn often traveled with me on assignment to do mission tours and help train auxiliary presidencies throughout the area. One Saturday night, as she spoke in the evening session of a meeting, it suddenly hit me. She was bearing her testimony about her love of God. It was then that I realized I was seeing the fulfillment of that promise. During our three years in Europe, I sat on the stand behind my wife as she taught and bore testimony to nonmembers and recent converts in Ireland, Northern Ireland, Scotland, Wales, England, Holland, Belgium, France, Switzerland, Italy, Spain, Portugal, and the Cape Verde Islands.

I marveled that night and I have marveled many times since. What a testimony of the reality of revelation. There was a patriarch, giving a blessing to a young thirteen-year-old girl he had never seen before, about whom he knew nothing, and, as far as Lynn knows, never saw again. Yet he made a promise that was being literally and richly fulfilled almost five decades later.

The Linking of Families

The third promise in Lynn's blessing was a single sentence. While speaking of the blessings that would come if she did marry in the temple, the patriarch also said something about how this would be the means of linking her family line and her husband's family line together. We had noticed that sentence in her blessing before, but didn't see it as particularly significant. If you go back far enough, most people's ancestral lines begin to cross. We certainly weren't thinking about it when we were serving in Europe.

The first Christmas we were there, our daughter, Rebecca, and her family came over for a visit. Becky and her mother had done a lot of family history research together, and we decided we would visit some of our ancestral villages while she was there. While Lynn was cooking dinner one day, Becky got on the computer and began grouping our family lines by locations. After a while, she called from our office to her mother.

"Mom, you'd better come and see this." When Lynn walked in, Becky explained that she had been searching one of my lines. She tapped on the screen. There was a whole page of names, but listed by town. And there, to Lynn's astonishment, she saw line after line ending in "Solihull, England. Solihull, England. Solihull, England."

Edward Griswolde (or Griswold), born 1607, was one of my great-great-ever-so-great-grandfathers. He had been a member of the landed gentry, and his family lived in Solihull for several generations. Becky had been able to trace one of my family lines to one of Edward Griswolde's daughter, named Ann or Hannah, born in 1642. That afternoon when I got off work, we went to the city library and asked for any old books on Solihull and its prominent families. When we told the librarian we were looking for something on the Griswolde family, she lit up.

"Oh, my yes," she said. "Very prominent family here. In fact, the Griswolde family coat of arms, which was two greyhounds with a red band between them, is incorporated into the official coat of arms for Solihull. And have you noticed the little tea shoppe there on High Street [the main market street of Solihull]? That was built by the Griswolde family around 1495 as their Manor House. And Malvern Hall, which is that private girls' school just east of town? Well, that was their mansion on another part of their estate."

We were amazed. When we were called to serve in Europe, there were nineteen different international areas. We could have been assigned to any one of them. But here we were, just a stone's throw from one of my ancestral homes. In fact, from my office on the third floor of our headquarters office building, I could look out on St. Alphage church, no more than a hundred yards away, where there was a pew dated 1560 and dedicated to the Griswolde family because they had donated money to repair the roof after a fire.

But we still weren't thinking of the promise in Lynn's blessing.

Some months after Becky had returned home, she called Lynn again. "Mom," she said, "I've been doing some research on your family line. Get on your computer. I want to show you something." When Lynn did so, Becky directed her to log onto the Griswolde family group record. Once Lynn had it up, Becky said, "Now, look at Edward Griswolde's other daughter, named Deborah, also born about 1642." There was a long pause, and then she finished. "Your line comes through her."

I suppose it isn't wise to impute motives to Deity, but I can't help but wonder. I think of all that He did—calling me to Great Falls; having my companion and me attend *The King and I*; calling Lynn and me to Europe where she could teach and testify; assigning us to Solihull; "accidentally" learning about the Griswolde line—and I can't help but wonder if, when it all came together, that Heavenly Father was not delighted with what He had done.

This much Lynn and I both know: this has been a powerful witness to us—one of so many others—that God is our loving Heavenly Father. He knows our thoughts and motives and desires. He sees all things and knows what is best for us and will bring us great happiness. And He delights in blessing us and all of His children. These blessings have become a strengthening and confirming witness to us of these things, and we thank Him for them. We can say without reservation that God truly does delight to honor His children.

Notes

Epigraph. Heber C. Kimball, in *Journal of Discourses,* 26 vols. (Liverpool: Latter-day Saints' Book Depot, 1854–86), 4:222.

1. *Random House Webster's Unabridged Dictionary* (New York: Random House Reference, 2010), s.v. "delight."

Signatures of Appreciation

I have come to believe that there are times when the Lord is deeply pleased with our efforts to serve Him or be more like Him, or when we work our way successfully through a difficult challenge. I also believe that He wants us to know of His appreciation, and so He sends us a blessing in the form of one of His divine signatures.

Here is another example of a woman of faith who never lost sight of the covenants she had made with the Lord. Though not as dramatic as the story of Amanda Barnes Smith or Drusilla Dorris Hendricks, it is nevertheless a good example of how the Lord delights to honor those who serve Him in faith and righteousness.

Ellen Breakell Neibaur and a Pair of Shoes

Ellen Breakell lived in Preston, England. She and her husband, Alexander Neibaur, were some of the first converts in England when Heber C. Kimball came in 1837. As the call came for the Saints to immigrate to America, the Neibaurs responded and came with the first company, arriving in Nauvoo in 1841.*

---

* This account was included in *Hearing the Voice of the Lord: Principles and Patterns of*

After they arrived in Nauvoo that fall, Brother Neibaur set up a dental practice. When the Church was enduring a new wave of persecution in 1845 and Brigham Young called on the Saints to prepare to leave the following spring and head west, the Neibaurs responded again. They sold all they had to finance an "outfit"—wagon, livestock, food, and equipment—to go west. They were finally driven out of Nauvoo by the mobs in September 1846.

They went to Winter Quarters and stayed there for more than a year while the first pioneer companies went west. The next spring, 1848, the Neibaurs once again sold everything they had in order to continue west. This left no money for trail-worthy boots or shoes, so Ellen crossed the plains with her feet wrapped in rags.

They arrived in the Salt Lake Valley in the fall of 1848. Conditions in the Valley were very difficult and for the next eight years there was still little money for anything other than necessities. Not until 1856 did Ellen save enough money to send off to a mail-order house for a pair of high-button shoes, and she knit herself a pair of stockings. One can only imagine what a joy it must have been for her—and women will probably appreciate that more than us men.

October Conference 1856

Though it is not specified exactly when the shoes arrived, it was not long before the October general conference of that year. That proved to be a momentous conference. On Sunday, October 5, Brigham Young stood up and announced that they had just learned there were two more handcart companies out on the plains and that the Saints had

---

Personal Revelation (Salt Lake City: Deseret Book, 2007), 116–18. After the first printing was released, I received a letter from a descendant of Ellen Breakell Neibaur. Her family records showed some slightly different details regarding the Neibaurs's coming to America. The corrections were made in the next printing. The account here is the corrected one.

to go rescue them. Brigham called for wagons, teams, food, blankets, and clothing, *including shoes,* from the Saints to be sent with the rescue wagons. In an inspiring example of covenant and sacrifice, Ellen gave her new pair of shoes and the stockings to the rescue effort.

What a wonderful story of faith and covenant keeping. After all those years of going without, Ellen sent off her shoes with the rescuers. Here, in her granddaughter's words, is what followed:

> Customarily, the Saints in the Valley lined the streets to welcome the weary companies as they entered Salt Lake. You can imagine as Ellen stood on the street that day to greet the beleaguered handcart pioneers, was she watching faces, or was she watching *feet* to see whose footsteps she had lightened? Much to her surprise, when she recognized her shoes, she also realized that the woman wearing those shoes was a dear friend of hers from England who had joined the Church after Ellen had left her native country. Through her sacrifice, she had unknowingly helped to rescue the life of her dear friend.[1]

Talk about a "coincidence"! There were close to a thousand people being rescued that winter, and yet somehow in the distribution of the supplies and clothing, Ellen's shoes ended up on the feet of her dear friend. Surely there were two women who wept that day in gratitude for this delightful blessing from the Lord. And surely Ellen understood that this was Heavenly Father's way of saying to her, "Thank you, my dear daughter. Thank you for being what you are."

Notes

1. In Theda Bassett, *Grandpa Neibaur Was a Pioneer,* and additional oral family history sources.

*Christ walked the path every mortal is called
to walk so that he would know how to succor
and strengthen us in our most difficult times. He
knows the deepest and most personal burdens we
carry. He knows the most public and poignant
pains we bear. He descended below all such grief
in order that he might lift us above it. There is
no anguish or sorrow or sadness in life that he has
not suffered in our behalf and borne away upon
his own valiant and compassionate shoulders.*

JEFFREY R. HOLLAND

Chapter Ten

"Come unto Me, All Ye That . . . Are Heavy Laden"

An Invitation to All

We have been looking at God's attributes and character traits. We have stressed the relationship between having a correct understanding of these attributes and strong faith. We have seen how different perceptions of God can weaken faith and leave individuals more vulnerable when the tests of life come. In the previous three chapters we have been exploring the fuller and richer knowledge of God that is taught in the scriptures, both in the Bible and modern scripture.

Let us continue now by examining one of the most well-known and beloved of all scriptures about the love of the Savior and how He helps us in times of need.

> Come unto me, all ye that labour and are heavy laden, and I will give you rest. Take my yoke upon you, and learn of me; for I am meek and lowly in heart: and ye shall find rest unto your souls. For my yoke is easy, and my burden is light. (Matthew 11:28–30)

The more I study and ponder His words, the more significance I find in them. There are wonderful insights to be found in virtually every phrase.

"Come unto Me"

The first thing we note from the opening phrase, "Come unto me," is that this passage is written in the first person. It is Jesus Himself speaking. He doesn't talk about coming to God, or coming to greater faith. It is a personal invitation: "Come unto me." Though put in the imperative form, the word "come" is less a command than an invitation. The tone is gentle. It is not like "Come here, Bill!" but more like "Come. I invite you to join me." It is an entreaty and an appeal to come to Him and accept what He is offering.

The next phrase tells us to whom that invitation is addressed: "Come unto me, *all ye that labour and are heavy laden.*" The word "all" makes this a sweeping inclusion. When we discussed the paradox of life, we noted that not all difficulties come from tragedy. Some challenges come in times of peace and plenty. There is one thing we know for sure about life, though, and that is that anything of worth requires labor. So this invitation is not just to those who are carrying burdens, struggling with misfortune, or suffering loss. It is to all those who labor. A person who sits in front of a computer screen all day may not physically perspire, but the principle given to Adam still applies. Man is to earn his bread by the "sweat of his brow." And whatever form it may come in, generally life itself is a labor.

I would venture a guess that as you read those words of the Savior, many of you were nodding to yourselves, saying, "Yes, that's me. Life *is* a labor. The load I carry is heavy. Sometimes it is almost more than I can bear." Difficulty and challenge are like ever-present music playing in the background of our lives. Sometimes it presses in loudly upon our consciousness. Other times it's only faintly heard. But it's always there.

So to whom was Jesus speaking when He said, "Come unto me"? He was speaking to you and me; to our neighbors across the street or in the upstairs apartment; to kings and paupers, beggars and tycoons. The invitation is to the strong and the weak, the sound and the handicapped, the old and the young, the happy and the sad. "Come unto me, *all ye* that labor and are heavy laden."

A Promise

Next comes a promise. To those who are burdened and labor much, He says, "I will give you rest." He repeats that promise in verse 29.

Rest from what? That is not a simple question to answer. When we have worked hard, there is great satisfaction in putting down the pick and shovel, turning off the computer, or stripping off the surgical gloves and mask, and quitting our labor for a time. Could that be what Jesus meant? That we won't have to work anymore? Fruits and flowers will start spontaneously bursting out all over in our lives? I don't think so.

The concept of rest is used many times in the scriptures with its common meaning: to cease work or other activities and take time to rejuvenate ourselves. But often in the scriptures, "rest" is given a deeper and more specific meaning. This seems to be how Jesus is using it here. Note that when Christ spoke of "rest" the second time in this passage, He added the phrase, "unto your souls."

We are told by the Lord that "the spirit and the body are the soul of man" (D&C 88:15). We know how to rest the body. We even know how to rest the mind. But how do we rest the spirit? I'm not sure I fully understand the significance of that idea, but here are a few passages that have expanded my way of thinking about rest.

- "Behold I say unto you, that if ye will harden your hearts *ye shall not enter into the rest of the Lord*" (Alma 12:36).
- "Teach them to never be weary of good works, but to be meek and lowly in heart; *for such shall find rest to their souls*" (Alma 37:34).
- "Then shall it come to pass, that the spirits of those who are righteous are received into a state of happiness, which is called paradise, *a state of rest, a state of peace, where they shall rest from all their troubles and from all care, and sorrow*" (Alma 40:12).
- "We have a labor to perform whilst in this tabernacle of clay, that we may conquer the enemy of all righteousness, and *rest our souls in the kingdom of God*" (Moroni 9:6).
- "Be patient in tribulation until I come; and, behold, I come quickly, and my reward is with me, and *they who have sought me early shall find rest to their souls*" (D&C 54:10).

I like to think that the rest promised by Jesus is much more than laying aside the hammer or the trowel to take a break. As welcome as that respite is, this is something much deeper and more permanent than that, and it is directly linked to how we live our lives.

"Take My Yoke"

The next phrase in our scriptural passage contains another directive—actually two more directives: "*Take my yoke* upon you, and *learn of me.*"

For the Savior to use the metaphor of a yoke is fascinating and worthy of further exploration. The dictionary defines a yoke in several ways. It is "a device for joining together a pair of draft animals, esp., oxen." It is also "a frame fitting the neck and shoulders of a person, for carrying a pair of buckets or the like." The dictionary also says that a yoke is "an emblem or symbol of oppression, subjection, or servitude, etc."[1] There are other kinds of labor in life beside physical work, and typically, these can be much more difficult to shoulder than simply earning our daily bread.

One more insight into those few simple words. The Savior said, "take *my* yoke upon you." Here's yet a fourth definition of the word "yoke": "To join, couple, link, or unite."[2] I don't believe Jesus was saying that He is passing out individual yokes to all those in need. He is offering His yoke. He is offering to stand in the harness with us, help pull the load alongside us. He is offering the opportunity for us to be joined, coupled, linked, or united with Him. In the case of oxen or other draft animals, when two animals are yoked together, they can pull more than double the amount that they can pull separately. In other words, the yoke not only makes it easier for each individual animal to pull the load, it also helps them pull more.

This concept may seem bothersome at first. Many of us already feel yoked to our problems, to our addictions, to our weaknesses, to our adversities. Our first reaction may be, "The last thing I need is another yoke of any kind." But *Christ's* yoke? That is another matter indeed. That is an offer of assistance and relief.

One last note of interest about yokes, especially those made for oxen. Yokes are not mass produced. Each yoke is made for a specific pair of animals. The yoke has to fit the neck and shoulders just right or it will chafe the animals and reduce their ability to pull. Oxen are not the same size, weight, and height. If the yoke is not made to accommodate that difference, then the larger ox may drag the smaller one to some extent, or throw him off balance.

I love that concept. When I come to the Savior with my burdens, my problems, and my challenges, He doesn't hand me an off-the-shelf, one-size-fits-all yoke. He knows me intimately. He loves me infinitely. Therefore, the help that He offers me will be perfectly fitted to *my* needs, *my* abilities, and *my* circumstances. How profound are those words: "Take *my* yoke upon you."

"Learn of Me"

That injunction is coupled with another: "And learn of me." What does that mean? What does learning of Him have to do with carrying our burdens? It is very simple. Here, too, the phrase "learn of me" can be interpreted in two ways.

The first implies we learn *about* Him. That is why we have taken so much time to study the nature of God and His Beloved Son. If we do not know that they have all power to bless us, have all knowledge about us, love us perfectly, and are patient and long-suffering with our weaknesses and failings, then why would we want to be yoked with them?

The second interpretation is that He is suggesting that we are to learn *from* Him. To learn of Jesus we must be taught by Him. We must receive what He wants us to know. He tells us how to do it. It is an interesting invitation. First, "Come unto me." Second, "Take my yoke upon you." Third, "Learn of me." *Come. Take. Learn.* Here is an interesting related concept.

In the scriptures, pride is often described as being stiffnecked. Think about that. In the presence of royalty, it is traditional for a person to bow his or her head to acknowledge the other person's higher office or station. Since the neck controls the movement of the head, to be stiffnecked means that we refuse to submit to or acknowledge God's higher station and authority.

A condition closely related to stiffneckedness is hardheartedness. Why? Because if we are too proud to bow our heads in submission to God, it is because our hearts are hardened against Him. When we are stiffnecked and hardhearted, we cannot be taught by the Lord. In the Book of Mormon, one prophet directly tied being stiffnecked to *learning*: "And there are many among us who have many revelations, for they are not all stiffnecked. And as many as are not stiffnecked and have faith, *have communion* with the Holy Spirit" (Jarom 1:4). Moroni taught a similar concept: "Because of meekness and lowliness of heart cometh the visitation of the Holy Ghost" (Moroni 8:26).

In chapter five, we listed more than a dozen questions that come when tragedy or adversity strikes. When we are troubled, we seek for understanding. We want to know why these things are happening. I believe that the Lord is not at all troubled by such questions. His answer is, "Come. Learn of me, and your questions will be answered." A similar promise was extended to Martin Harris a month before the Church was organized: "Learn of me, and listen to my words; walk in the meekness of my Spirit, and *you shall have peace in me*" (D&C 19:23).

Before we can learn of Him, we have to humble ourselves, come unto Him, and be willing to take His yoke upon us. *Come, take, and learn.* That is surely simple enough.

"Meek and Lowly"

Let us move on to the next phrase in our scripture: "For I am meek and lowly of heart." Look at that phrase carefully. He does not ask *us* to be meek and lowly of heart, though He does that elsewhere. Here He says, "Learn of me, for *I am* meek and lowly of heart."

Note the use of the word "for" in that sentence. *For* is a preposition that can be used in many different ways. Sometimes it is used in the sense of *because,* e.g., "I felt I had to pay my debts for it was the right thing to do." I think that is how the word *for* is used in this passage. Look what happens when we substitute *because* here: "Take my yoke upon you and learn of me *because* I am meek and lowly of heart."

What does His being meek and lowly of heart have to do with

His invitation to come unto Him and take His yoke upon us? I believe that the use of that little word "for" has great significance for us, more than we see at first glance. To explore that idea further, let us first look at a lesson taught to Joseph Smith in Liberty Jail. Then I would like to share an experience I had that taught me why Christ's meekness and lowliness of heart allows us to learn from Him and have our burdens lifted.

In the spring of 1839, Joseph Smith was languishing under the most deplorable of conditions in Liberty Jail. His people had just endured the horrors of Haun's Mill and the fall of Far West. They were driven out of Missouri in the dead of winter, leaving footprints in the snow from bare, bleeding, and cracked feet.[3] His own family was among the fleeing refugees. Emma had to cross the Mississippi River on ice, with two children in her arms and two more clinging to her skirts. And all the while Joseph sat in jail, powerless to do anything to help them. Talk about being heavy laden. Is it any wonder that he cried out, "O God, where art thou?" (D&C 121:1).

It is in the Lord's answer to that cry that we gain a marvelous insight about the Savior and His meekness and lowliness of heart. After telling Joseph that even if he should be cast into the hands of murderers and have a sentence of death passed upon him, that even if the heavens were to gather blackness and the very jaws of hell should gape open its mouth at him, he should know that "all these things shall give thee experience, and shall be for thy good." Then followed a question that has stunning implications for each of us: "The Son of Man *hath descended below them all.* Art thou greater than he?" (D&C 122:6–8; see also D&C 88:6).

Few of us will ever carry a burden equal to the burden Joseph Smith carried, but even Joseph couldn't say to the Lord, "You don't understand what I am facing. You don't know how hard this is. If You did, my burden would be taken away." What a humbling concept.

There is nothing that we can bring to Christ that He has not personally experienced. There is no sickness, no suffering, no adversity, no loneliness, no pain but that He has descended below it. And because of that, we can learn things from Him and the Father that we can learn from no other source.

Kristi

One of the most treasured experiences I had while serving as a bishop occurred with a young woman named Kristi Merrell. Even now, more than twenty years after I first met Kristi, I still remember things I learned from Jesus and about Jesus as I worked with her. I share Kristi's story here with the permission of Keith and Carole Merrell, Kristi's parents. I express my sincere appreciation to them. The Merrells told me that one of the promises Kristi received in a priesthood blessing from her uncle was that she would be a blessing to people that she did not know. It is their hope that including her story here may be a partial fulfillment of that promise.

When I was called as a bishop in Bountiful, Utah, my wife and I had not been in the ward for very long, maybe little more than a year. We were getting to know who people were, but we really didn't know them very well yet.

I had been bishop for only a few months when I got a call from the Merrells asking if I could come up to the University of Utah Hospital in Salt Lake City and give a blessing to their daughter, Kristi. I said I would be happy to do so, but as I hung up the phone, I felt a little stab of guilt. I hadn't even heard that Kristi was in the hospital, and I had no idea what her problem was.

When I arrived at the hospital, the front desk directed me to a room in an upper wing of the building. As I got off the elevator, I saw a sign indicating this was the Cystic Fibrosis Center. I didn't give it much thought as I went in. I had no idea what cystic fibrosis was, nor did I make any connection with the disease to Kristi. When I walked into the room, however, a shock awaited me. Kristi, who was about twenty at the time, was sitting up in her bed with her family gathered around her. Her mother was standing over her and pounding up and down her back with her cupped hands. Kristi held a paper cup and was coughing up a bloody mucus into it. On the hospital tray beside her, three more cups were lined up, already filled with the same mucus.

I learned later that cystic fibrosis is a hereditary disease that causes a fibrous mucus to form in the lungs. Regular thumping on the back helps break up the congestion so the individual can breathe more easily.

That was my introduction to Kristi. Over the next three years I was privileged to come to know her very well. We spent many hours talking together and many blessings were given. She was amazing. She never saw her illness as something that should hold her back. I learned that she had gone to high school with an I.V. in her arm. She attended college, sometimes on oxygen and I.V. meds. When she was particularly ill, her mother would go to school for her so she wouldn't fall behind in her studies. She earned a bachelor of science degree in math and graduated *magna cum laude*.

Equally amazing to me was that she was always cheerful and happy. I never saw one iota of self-pity or resentment about this "burden" that had been laid upon her, or the "labor" it took for her to get through every day. She had great faith that this was part of her test in life and that if she remained faithful, eventually the Lord would heal her. Her family strongly believed this as well. This was an act of faith because the average life expectancy back then for those with CF was only about twenty years of age, and Kristi was already there. (With advances in medicine, life expectancy is now about thirty-five years.)

Kristi longed to live a normal life. It was not to be. She wanted to be a wife and mother. That was not to be either. One day, she asked if it would be possible for her to be endowed in the temple, even though she was single and not yet embarked on a career, a requirement suggested in the Church Handbook for those not getting married or going on a mission. Happily, the stake president concurred with my recommendation that an exception be made for Kristi. My wife and I were privileged to be with her and her family when she received her endowment.

As the months passed, it became clear that Kristi's strength and vitality were decreasing. As things looked more and more bleak, Kristi decided one day to go to the temple to see if she could find some answers. At that time, the Bountiful Utah Temple had not yet opened, so our temple was the Salt Lake Temple. Unfortunately, when she had these feelings, the Salt Lake Temple was closed. Knowing how much she wanted this, her father talked with a friend who was the temple recorder at that time. Her mother describes what happened:

He [the recorder] arranged for Kristi to go in at a time when she would be alone. She spent a little over an hour in the celestial room alone, praying. The question came into her mind: "What is it that you desire the most?" Her first thought was to be healed, but as she sat and prayed, she realized that her strongest desire was to live again with Heavenly Father and Jesus Christ.

When she came out of the celestial room and explained this to us, we both felt that her understanding was that she would still be healed of the disease. But her spirit must have understood what that experience meant—that she was placing her will in the hands of God—but her mortal mind, as well as ours, still felt that a healing would occur. We felt this way up to the moment she died.

Kristi Merrell finally laid aside her disease-ridden mortal body on September 14, 1992, just a few weeks before her twenty-third birthday. It was a time of great mourning in our ward. She had been greatly beloved and her example of courage and faith had inspired many.

As I thought about Kristi and her life, both before and after her death, I always felt somewhat guilty. My health was good. I was allowed to run and play and never have to give a second thought to what the scriptures call "the breath of life" (Genesis 2:7). I served a mission, married and had a family. Yet Kristi's life seemed so much purer and more righteous than mine. Why was she born with such a handicap?

I can remember thinking one day that if I were Kristi, when I got up to the judgment seat, I would be strongly tempted to step forward and say, "My life wasn't fair. What did I do that I should have been denied these righteous blessings? What did I do that earned me a life of handicap and pain and suffering?"

Our Pains, Sicknesses, and Infirmities

Somewhere during that time, thinking about Kristi prepared me to be taught by the Savior. I was reading in the Book of Mormon and came across a passage in Alma I must have read several times before, but that I had not noticed.

Alma says of Christ, "And behold, he shall be born of Mary" (Alma 7:10). That is a quick reminder of an important point. Jesus was the Son of God, but He was also the son of Mary. He was born a mortal. He too came into a fallen world. As a baby He was totally dependent on others for His care. He had to eat and drink each day. Even though He had once been a God, now He had to sleep at night. He got hungry and tired. If He hit his thumb in the carpenter shop, it hurt and His thumbnail turned black. In a word, He was one of us. Then Alma says:

> And he shall go forth, suffering pains and afflictions and temptations of every kind; and this that the word might be fulfilled which saith *he will take upon him the pains and the sicknesses of his people.* And he will take upon him death, that he may loose the bands of death which bind his people; and *he will take upon him their infirmities,* that his bowels may be filled with mercy, according to the flesh, *that he may know according to the flesh how to succor his people according to their infirmities.* (Alma 7:11–12)

We know that Christ took upon Himself the sins and transgressions of mankind so as to make it possible for us to return to live with God. Who can comprehend the extent and intensity of the suffering that it took to satisfy justice?

But if at the same time, Jesus *also* took upon Himself the pains, sicknesses, and infirmities of all mankind as well—that is an astonishing concept. Not only did He make infinite payment for all the wrongs and injustices on earth, but He also gained infinite empathy for each of us.

Somehow, in a way that is unfathomable to us, He knows exactly what Kristi endured with cystic fibrosis. He knows what it is like to suffer with terminal cancer. He knows the loneliness of depression. He understands the feelings of utter hopelessness that can come with some mental illnesses or from being sexually abused as a child. He knows the hardships that come from being permanently disabled. In short, there is no burden, no sorrow, no suffering that He hasn't already experienced. And because of that, there is nothing we can take to Him that brings a response of, "I'm so sorry, but I don't understand what you're going through."

To succor means to give help or relief to someone. Here is what Elder Neal A. Maxwell had to say about this passage:

> Jesus' daily mortal experiences and His ministry, to be sure, acquainted Him by observation with a sample of human sicknesses, grief, pains, sorrows, and infirmities. . . . But the agonies of the Atonement were infinite and first-hand! Since not all human sorrow and pain is connected to sin, the full intensiveness of the Atonement involved bearing our pains, infirmities, and sicknesses, as well as our sins.[4]

Think again of what Joseph was taught in Liberty Jail: "The Son of Man hath descended below them all." Elder Maxwell also observed:

> Can we, even in the depths of disease, tell Him anything at all about suffering? In ways we cannot comprehend, our sicknesses and infirmities were borne by Him even before they were borne by us. . . . We have never been, nor will we be, in depths such as He has known. Thus His atonement made perfect His empathy and His mercy and His capacity to succor us.[5]

Finally, I understood. In the balance of right and wrong, fair and unfair, just and unjust, Kristi had been shorted in this life. But at some point, in ways that we do not understand, all will be made right. I cannot picture Kristi ever demanding to know why life wasn't fair for her, but it is my firm belief that she will someday kneel at the judgment seat and say to her Father and her Savior, "It is enough. I have been more than repaid for all that I endured."

Before she died, Kristi left her written testimony with her family.

It is sweet and filled with a faith and understanding well beyond her years. But particularly note what she says near the end of it.

> I am thankful for Jesus Christ and his atonement so that I can return to live with my Heavenly Father. It makes a lot of difference when I pray to know that Christ experienced all of our physical, mental, and spiritual suffering. He knows and understands what we are experiencing here.

She may not have used the exact wording from Matthew 11, but Kristi Merrell had learned something from Jesus. She took His yoke upon herself and learned about Him and from Him. And that was a major source of the courage and humility with which she faced her personal burdens. Gaining that understanding from Kristi's experience has been one of the great blessings in my life.

Can you see how there is a direct relationship between Christ's meekness and lowliness of heart and His ability to lift our burdens? Abinadi said of the Savior, "Even so he shall be led, crucified, and slain, the flesh becoming subject even unto death, *the will of the Son being swallowed up in the will of the Father*" (Mosiah 15:7). It was His humility and submissiveness that led Him to Gethsemane and the cross, where He suffered infinitely and descended below all things. This is the direct source of His power and ability to ease our burdens and lighten our loads.

The Lord concluded this marvelous passage with these words: "For my yoke is easy, and my burden is light" (Matthew 11:30). We shall examine the significance of those two phrases in the next chapter.

Notes

Epigraph. Jeffrey R. Holland, *Christ and the New Covenant: The Messianic Message of the Book of Mormon* (Salt Lake City: Deseret Book, 1997), 223–24.

1. *Random House Webster's Unabridged Dictionary* (New York: Random House Reference, 2010), s.v. "yoke."

2. Ibid.

3. See Martha Pane Jones Thomas, in Richard Neitzel Holzapfel and Jeni Broberg Holzapfel, *Women of Nauvoo* (Salt Lake City: Bookcraft, 1992), 11.

4. Neal A. Maxwell, *"Not My Will, But Thine"* (Salt Lake City: Bookcraft, 1988), 54.

5. Neal A. Maxwell, *Even As I Am* (Salt Lake City: Deseret Book, 1982), 116–17.

The Touch of the Master's Hand

I n the chapter on perceptions of God, I quoted briefly a statement made by a woman who had been sexually abused as a young girl. I noted that though she believed in God, she felt beyond the reach of His love. In her words, "I believe He was holding out His hand, but I felt terribly unworthy to respond."[1]

In her efforts to escape from or cope with her terrible feelings of guilt and shame, she turned to a same-gender relationship and became addicted to alcohol and drugs. For years she struggled. Eventually she made her way back, aided by a loving and wise bishop. But this did not suddenly make everything easy. There were still setbacks and slip-ups. There were times when it seemed hopeless and she felt helpless. In her own words, here is how she describes an experience she had in one of those darker times.

Jesus Christ seeks to comfort us and show us His love. Before this earth life we walked with Him and talked with Him. Now a thick veil stands in the way. It is difficult to reach to hands that eyes cannot see and listen to voices that ears cannot hear. It can seem an unbearable challenge to stop seeking wholeness and comfort from homosexual relationships, enduring the pain and loneliness of spiritual stretching until Christ's love can be felt as he encircles each one of us "in the arms of [His] love" (D&C 6:20). . . .

Some people struggling with same-sex attraction fear they will have to spend the rest of their lives alone, without a close relationship with someone. But what "alone" feels like in the midst of the struggle is not what it feels like later. The love of Christ at first may seem little more than emptiness, but that's because sin or confusion or resentment or guilt or false feelings of unworthiness or all of those things stand in the way.

I used to think homosexual relationships brought pure love. Now I realize that pure love is not obtained by pursuing passions. It is gained by keeping passions within the guide-lines set by the Lord. As Alma said, "Bridle all your passions, that ye may be filled with love"—the pure love of Christ (Alma 38:12).

I am not alone. I now have a close, personal relationship with the Lord Jesus Christ. And I prefer a close relationship with the Savior over a homosexual relationship. It is impos-sible to maintain both. As Elder Neal A. Maxwell has said, "Whatever we embrace instead of Christ will keep us from be-ing embraced by Him!" (Address given to Church Educational System area directors, Salt Lake City, 1 Oct. 1992).

I bear testimony that Christ's redeeming love is truly re-deeming. Several months ago I became discouraged and over-whelmed. I reread my life story for the umpteenth time and came to the poem I had written [in one of her darker hours]:

Dear God, it's black again.
Two solid months of darkness.
Two solid days of light marked Christ's arrival.

I guess He isn't coming.
Have faith, you say?
But faith does not hold my hand.
Or stroke my hair and tell me I'm OK.

I did not get any further than that. Something, or someone, stroked my hair. I was overcome with the Spirit, physically as well as spiritually. I realized in a powerful, new way that I was okay, that the Savior was there for me. I wish I could express how real it was—somehow convey in words the incredible feeling of peace and comfort and love undefiled.[2]

Notes

1. Erin Eldridge, *Born That Way? A True Story of Overcoming Same-Sex Attraction with Insights for Friends, Families, and Leaders* (Salt Lake City: Deseret Book, 1994), 14.
2. Ibid., 84–85.

The thermostat on the furnace of affliction will not have been set too high for us—though clearly we may think so at the time. Our God is a refining God who has been tempering soul-steel for a very long time. He knows when the right edge has been put upon our excellence and also when there is more in us than we have yet given.

NEAL A. MAXWELL

CHAPTER ELEVEN

"My Yoke Is Easy, and My Burden Is Light"

Easy and Light

There is a saying that has become very popular in recent years. It is usually stated in the first person, as though it was a quote from the Master. It is seen on wall plaques, in picture frames on fireplace mantles, in plaques set on desks, printed on bookmarks, and as a caption beneath a picture of the Savior. It is not scriptural, though it has a scriptural "feel" to it. It is this:

"I never said it would be easy; I only said it would be worth it."

It is a lovely thought, and each time I read it, it causes me to ponder again what it means to be a disciple of the Master. But lovely as it is, in one sense it is incorrect, because Jesus *did* at one point say that it would be easy.

In chapter ten, we began an analysis of the Savior's invitation and promise as found in the Gospel of Matthew.

> Come unto me, all ye that labour and are heavy laden, and I will give you rest. Take my yoke upon you, and learn of me; for I am meek and lowly in heart: and ye shall find rest

unto your souls. For my yoke is easy, and my burden is light. (Matthew 11:28–30)

There it is, in the final sentence: "My yoke is *easy.*"

When you think about it, that statement seems contradictory. The very image of a yoke doesn't fit with the concept of ease. For example, a wooden yoke for a pair of oxen can weigh as much as one hundred and fifty pounds. Yokes are associated with hard work, heavy loads, and difficult burdens. So how can the Lord say that His yoke is easy? That brings us to the rest of the sentence, "My burden is light." That seems equally contradictory. Burdens are not light, they're heavy. That's what the word means.

So what are we to learn from that statement? If we "yoke up" with Christ, as He suggests, then how will that make life easier or lighter for us?

The word "easy" has two primary meanings: something can be easy in the sense that it is simple and uncomplicated. Or something can be easy because it doesn't require a lot of hard work or effort.

Note that here, too, Jesus used the personal possessive pronoun in both cases: "*my* yoke" and "*my* burden." That may be part of our answer. We know that when we commit ourselves to "come unto Christ" we are committing ourselves to shouldering—an interesting word considering that yokes are placed upon the shoulders—a new set of obligations, a different kind of lifestyle, a different list of responsibilities. We covenant to take His name upon us, to keep His commandments, and to always remember Him (see D&C 20:77). Is that what He means by His burden and His yoke? It seems that those would certainly be a part of it.

So let us examine what the Father and the Son have done to make the lives easier and the burdens lighter for those who choose to be His disciples.

The Doctrine of Christ

Let us first look at how the Savior makes things easier for us in the sense of being simple and uncomplicated. When you think about what an incredible gift eternal life will be, it would not be surprising if the requirements for achieving it would be incredibly complex. Think of what it takes for a person to become a physician—years of schooling, internships, residency, specialty training, and so on. So something as infinite as eternal life would seem to require a highly complicated and difficult set of requirements.

But actually, all that He asks is that we do five things. These will be enough to bring us back into the presence of God:

- Faith in Jesus Christ
- Repentance
- Baptism in the proper way and by the proper authority
- Receiving the gift of the Holy Ghost
- Enduring to the end

Those five requirements can be listed in a few lines on a page. How's that for simplicity? These five things are what are called "the doctrine of Christ," "my doctrine," or "my gospel." They are found throughout the scriptures so that we cannot miss their significance.

Suggestion for Further Study

The doctrine of Christ is taught throughout the scriptures with varying detail and emphasis. For those who wish to examine this doctrine in greater detail, see Acts 2:38; 2 Nephi 31–32; 3 Nephi 11:30–40; D&C 20:37; 39:6; Moses 6:49–62; Article of Faith 4.

You may be thinking, "Well, yes, it is simple to list those five things, but *living* the gospel, the application of these five principles and ordinances in our daily lives, is a highly complex and challenging task." Of course, it is. We must learn to increase and strengthen our faith. We must continually repent when we fall short. We must strive to keep our covenants, including those we make in the ordinances of the temple. It is a lifetime of striving to be righteous, to be faithful disciples, to stay faithful in times of adversity. But we are talking about simplicity of concept right now, and this is remarkably simple. Note Alma's word to his son, Helaman:

> By *small and simple things* are great things brought to pass; and small means in many instances doth confound the wise. And the Lord God doth work by means to bring about his great and eternal purposes; and *by very small means the Lord doth confound the wise and bringeth about the salvation of many souls. . . .* O my son, do not let us be slothful because of the *easiness* of the way. (Alma 37:6–7, 46)

With that said, let us now examine how the Lord makes living the gospel, in all of its complexities and challenges, easier. We shall discuss things that He has given to us to ease our way and lighten our burdens.

The Ultimate Gift

We have said several times now that God's desire for His children is for them to eventually receive a fulness of joy. This requires that we not only return to live *with* Him, but that we become *like* Him. This is the greatest thing He could offer us:

- "If thou wilt do good, yea, and hold out faithful to the end, *thou shalt be saved in the kingdom of God*, which is the *greatest* of all the gifts of God; for *there is no gift greater than the gift of salvation*" (D&C 6:13).

- "If you keep my commandments and endure to the end *you shall have eternal life,* which gift is *the greatest of all the gifts of God*" (D&C 14:7).

But in addition to the gift of eternal life, the Father put forth a plan to make it possible. It is variously called the plan of salvation, the plan of redemption, and the plan of happiness (see, for example Alma 42:5, 8, 11). Bringing that plan about for His children is His "work" and His "glory" (see Moses 1:39). President Joseph F. Smith said: "We sang together . . . when the plan of our existence upon this earth and redemption were mapped out. . . . We . . . were vitally concerned in the carrying out of these great plans and purposes."[1]

I like the phrase "mapped out." The gospel is the map that God has given us to help us find our way back home.

The Ultimate Help

"For God so loved the world, that he gave his only begotten Son, that whosoever believeth in him should not perish, but have everlasting life" (John 3:16). The Father set up His plan to give His children the ultimate gift. Then He sent down His Only Begotten and Beloved Son to make it all happen. He knew it would be impossible for us to do it on our own. He knew we would need succoring, inspiration, guidance, strength, enlightenment, comfort, and courage if we were going to make our way back. So He sent us His Son. That is why Jesus can extend such a powerful invitation: "Come unto me. Learn of me. Take my yoke upon you."

Volumes could be written about the help that comes from the Savior that makes His yoke easy and His burden light. I would like to cite some of the Savior's descriptions of Himself, all of which begin with the words "I am." This is only a partial list, but consider how each title conveys the idea of help in our mortal journey.

- "I am the light and the life of the world" (3 Nephi 9:18).
- "I am the same which spake, and the world was made, and all things came by me" (D&C 38:3).
- "I am the Son of the living God" (D&C 68:6).
- "I am the Spirit of truth" (D&C 93:26).
- "I am your advocate with the Father" (D&C 110:4).
- "I am the bread of life: he that cometh to me shall never hunger; and he that believeth on me shall never thirst" (John 6:35).
- "I am the door: by me if any man enter in, he shall be saved" (John 10:9).
- "I am the good shepherd: the good shepherd giveth his life for the sheep" (John 10:11).
- "I am the resurrection, and the life" (John 11:25).
- "I am the way, the truth, and the life" (John 14:6).

Those various titles denote power, knowledge, truth, patience, caring, sustenance, order, strength, peace, comfort, life, nurturing, direction, and protection. That is why He can promise that He will give us rest.

The Grace of God and Christ

The LDS Bible Dictionary has this to say about the concept of grace:

> The main idea of the word is divine means of *help or strength,* given through the bounteous mercy and love of Jesus Christ. . . . This *grace is an enabling power* that allows men

and women to lay hold on eternal life and exaltation after they have expended their own best efforts.[2]

The Greek word that is translated as "grace" means a gift. Here is another significant help given to us by God to help us when the load grows too heavy and the burdens become too overwhelming. The promises of that enabling power and divine strength and help are numerous in the scriptures. Though we have cited some of them before, we note a few again here:

- "The everlasting God, the Lord, the Creator of the ends of the earth, . . . *giveth power to the faint;* and to them that have no might *he increaseth strength.* . . . They that wait upon the Lord shall *renew their strength;* they shall mount up with wings as eagles; *they shall run, and not be weary; and they shall walk, and not faint*" (Isaiah 40:28–29, 31).

- "And *if men come unto me* I will show unto them their weakness. I give unto men weakness that they may be humble; and *my grace is sufficient for all men that humble themselves before me;* for if they humble themselves before me, and have faith in me, *then will I make weak things become strong unto them*" (Ether 12:27; see also v. 37).

- "And he said unto me [after Paul had prayed to have the 'thorn in the flesh' removed], My grace is sufficient for thee: *for my strength is made perfect in weakness.* Most gladly therefore will *I rather glory in my infirmities, that the power of Christ may rest upon me*" (2 Corinthians 12:9).

- "Yea, come unto Christ, and be perfected *in him,* and deny yourselves of all ungodliness; and if ye shall deny yourselves of all ungodliness, and love God with all your might, mind and strength, *then is his grace sufficient for you, that by his grace ye may be perfect in Christ*" (Moroni 10:32).

- "I can do all things through Christ which strengtheneth me" (Philippians 4:13).

The Gift of the Holy Ghost

Here is a rather discouraging statement from King Benjamin:

I cannot tell you all the things whereby ye may commit sin; for there are divers ways and means, even so many that I cannot number them. But this much I can tell you, that if ye do not watch yourselves, and your *thoughts,* and your *words,* and your *deeds,* and observe the commandments of God, and continue in the faith of what ye have heard concerning the coming of our Lord, even unto the end of your lives, ye must perish. And now, O man, remember, and perish not. (Mosiah 4:29–30)

As we have stated, the requirements of the gospel are simple, but living it is not. In fact, life is so complex and difficult that it is impossible to prepare a set of guidelines or a rulebook to cover every possible contingency with which we have to deal. The scriptures provide principles and guidelines, but even then we need help in seeing how the scriptures help us deal with some problems. Only a god has the wisdom and knowledge to know what to do in every situation. And that is exactly what the Father and the Son offer us. They gave us the gift of the Holy Ghost, one of the godhead, to be our personal companion and guide. This gift must surely rank in importance right up there with the gift of salvation and the gift of God's Only Begotten Son.

We know from the scriptures that the Holy Ghost fulfills the following functions, among others: He enlightens, instructs, warns, comforts, directs, guides, edifies, increases our capacity to do something, confirms, encourages, solves, answers, testifies, gives us the gifts of the Spirit, gives us the fruits of the Spirit (see Galatians 5:22–25), helps us discern between good and evil and right and wrong, brings flashes of pure intelligence, increases understanding and wisdom, brings a burning of the bosom or a stupor of thought, comforts us in sorrow, brings us peace, and is the source of all testimony. As Elder Bruce R. McConkie put it, "These are by no means all of the gifts. In the fullest sense, they are infinite in number and endless in their manifestations."[3]

How often do we remember to thank God for this incredible gift that can lift and lighten our burdens and make the yoke of life so much easier?

These are some of the great and marvelous gifts we have received from the hand of the Lord that are designed to make our lives easier and our burdens lighter. There are other examples of help that may not be as grand and glorious but that bless us nevertheless. We shall look at those next.

Notes

Epigraph. Neal A. Maxwell, *All These Things Shall Give Thee Experience* (Salt Lake City: Deseret Book, 1979), 46.

1. Joseph F. Smith, *Gospel Doctrine* (Salt Lake City: Deseret Book, 1939), 93.
2. LDS Bible Dictionary, s.v. "grace."
3. Bruce R. McConkie, *Mormon Doctrine,* 2d ed. (Salt Lake City: Bookcraft, 1966), 314.

Blessings That Come
without Asking

As we have recounted the many stories of divine aid and tender mercies, we have seen that in most cases, they come in response to individuals searching for the truth, looking for answers to problems, dealing with a particular crisis, or experiencing some other kind of need.

Sometimes they have come as an expression of the Lord's appreciation for a particular act of service or sacrifice. Such was the case with Ellen Breakell Neibaur and her shoes. Occasionally, however, we find examples where tender mercies are given and divine signatures sent when there seems to have been nothing specific that triggered them. They come unbidden, but still remind us of God's bounteous goodness and mercy. Here is one of those stories.

Adoption

When my wife and I were living in Bountiful, Utah, there was a family in our ward that we came to admire and appreciate. Larry and Sue Rigby had a great family and were strong, contributing members of our ward.

When Sue's youngest of four children was two, she began to

have "overwhelming, very intense" feelings that they should try to adopt a child from Korea. This was not a new feeling; in fact, she had expressed this same idea to her mother some five years previous. The Rigbys made contact with an agency in Idaho, who worked with Korean Social Services to bring orphaned children to the United States through adoption. They applied to adopt two children, a boy and a girl, and waited. Finally the application was approved, and Larry and Sue flew to Korea. There they were shown a four-month-old boy and a one-day-old baby girl.

After doing all of the required paperwork, the Rigbys were told that it would take a few months for the legal work to be completed in the Korean courts and that the two children had to stay in Korea until it was finished. Disappointed, they returned home. Two months later, Sue returned to pick up the children. But Korea was then under martial law, and Sue had a very stressful time getting the children home.

By the time Lynn and I moved into the ward, Jon and Sarah (their two Korean-born children) were happy, well-adjusted teens in the Rigby home. A few years later, Jon announced that he had received a mission call to serve in Italy. Here then is Jon's story as told by his mother.

Going to the Temple

I have never really written this experience down, but I still vividly remember the feelings I had almost eleven years ago like it was yesterday, and I think of it often.

Jon was leaving to go on his mission to Italy. He was to report to the MTC in Provo on Wednesday. We had been to the Bountiful Temple several times with Jon, but I had the strongest feeling that he needed to go to the Salt Lake Temple at least one time before he went to the MTC. He was really going through a tough time and at times during the week before he was scheduled to leave, he wondered if he was even going to be able to leave on his mission. So on the Tuesday morning before he left, I said, "We are going to the Salt Lake Temple."

At the last minute, Larry couldn't go with us, which meant that Jon would be alone as we dressed and prepared for the endowment session. But I still felt we should go. We rushed out the door so we could be to the 10:00 A.M. (I think) session, which was the only time we could go that day. Our schedule was such that if we missed that session, we wouldn't be able to wait for the next one.

We skidded into the doors of the temple about twenty minutes before the session was to start, and we each went our separate ways. I told Jon that if he needed help to just ask for it and to hurry! It took me only a few minutes to get ready and then I waited for Jon in the first room. After about five minutes with no sign of Jon, I began to worry and wonder if something had happened. Had he decided he didn't feel like he could go to a session? Or had someone made him feel stupid? Maybe he didn't know what to do or where to go. I was so worried about whether he was going to make it to the session. With only about five minutes left before it was time to start, I looked back and saw Jon walk through the doors into the room. I smiled and waved to him but—nothing! It was so strange.

Finally, he smiled and nodded, but not to me. He was looking at the woman sitting next to me. Then he sat down on the right side of a man across from us, which left just one seat on the aisle empty. I wondered what in the world had happened and why Jon didn't turn and at least make eye contact with me. I felt a great pit in my stomach.

Then, just as they were about to shut the doors, the real Jon Rigby walked in with that familiar smile on his face. I heard the woman next to me audibly gasp. Jon waved and smiled, this time to me, and sat down in the empty aisle seat on the other side of the man. The man glanced at him, then turned and stared. He looked to his right at the other boy, then back to his left at Jon, then finally at the woman sitting next to me. He had a very surprised look on his face!

I whispered to the woman next to me and asked her what was going on. I learned that she and her husband, the man sitting between the two boys, had adopted their son from the same agency where we had adopted Jon, only their son had been unable to get out of the Philippines until he turned two or three. I knew that the man from the adoption agency was taking children into and out of both Korea and the Philippines. Everyone had always told us that Jon looked more Filipino than Korean, and bells began to go off in my head! As it turned out, their son was entering the mission home the next morning also and would be serving a mission in Texas! How strange!

How strange that we would be in the temple on the same session as this family. How strange that Jon would end up seated so close to another Asian who looked enough like him to fool even their mothers, who kept noting how similar the boys were, in mannerisms, build, and features!

For some reason, I felt a great peace come to my heart, the heart that had been so worried about Jon and his mission. I felt that these two could be twins and that they had been given the blessing of meeting each other on this earth if only for this short time.

We may never know for sure if these two really are twin brothers or not. We have not seen the other family since that time in the celestial room where we spoke for a few minutes. It really doesn't matter to me, for I will never forget the overwhelming feelings I had in my heart that Heavenly Father knew me so well. He knew I would recognize this as a very special experience and be grateful for it. I know that the Lord is aware of us, that He loves us and that He has a plan and a time frame for all things.

A few days after our experience in the temple, Jon was able to meet the other boy at the MTC. They had their picture taken together, and Jon sent it home to us with the words jokingly written on the back, "I have found my brother." Perhaps so, but even if not, it was a very sacred experience for us both.

I have pondered this experience over the years and have considered the following as tender mercies or divine signatures as opposed to coincidences:

- The fact that we even made the session.
- The fact that we were in the same session as the other family.
- The fact that I sat right next to the other boy's mother.
- The fact that the other boy's father sat between the two boys.
- The fact that we both got our children through the same adoption agency.
- The fact that the boys appeared to be identical twins, enough so that we could barely tell them apart.

- The fact that the boys were the same age and going into the MTC on the same day.
- The fact that the boys could easily have come from the same place even though one came out of Korea and the other was from the Philippines.

On that day, I was reminded once again that the Lord is in charge. From that time on, I have had a peace and knowledge in my heart that has never wavered, confirming to me that Jon was brought to us for a very special reason and that it was all part of a great plan. I am thankful that I have been part of that plan.

In the first place, he hath created you, and granted unto you your lives, for which ye are indebted unto him. And secondly, he doth require that ye should do as he hath commanded you; for which if ye do, he doth immediately bless you; and therefore he hath paid you. And ye are still indebted unto him, and are, and will be, forever and ever; therefore, of what have ye to boast?

MOSIAH 2:23–24

CHAPTER TWELVE

"He Doth Immediately Bless You"

Continuing on with our list of ways the Lord makes our yoke easy and our burden light, we turn now to some things that are simple, everyday kinds of things, but which still greatly help us along the way.

Tender Mercies and Divine Signatures

I hope by this point in the book we have amply illustrated how much the Lord desires to bless us. He delights in honoring those who serve Him faithfully and He does so in some remarkable and even miraculous ways. I have chosen to describe these special kinds of blessings as divine signatures. We have now shared many different examples of such gifts.

Why do I include them here in a list of ways that the Father and the Son make life easier for us? Just ask Amanda Barnes Smith, Harvey Cluff, Drusilla Hendricks, LeGrand Black, the man who makes his living driving trucks, the merchant marine, Erin Eldridge, Yvonne Kerr, Francis Webster, Ellen Breakell Neibaur, a Jewish father and daughter, a young man from Albania, Margarete Hellwig and her daughter, or Lynn Lund. They can tell you.

Immediately

Here is one last insight in how the Lord makes our way easier and helps us carry the burdens of life. Sometimes when we get down and start feeling sorry for ourselves—what my mission president called a bad case of the "poor me's"—it is easy to emphasize the difficulty of living the gospel. However, there is another way to look at it.

While I was bishop, I was reading in Alma 34 about when Amulek was teaching the poorer people of the Zoramites and pleading with them to soften their hearts. He told them this was the day of their salvation, if they would but act. He said, "If ye will repent and harden not your hearts, *immediately* shall the great plan of redemption be brought about unto you" (Alma 34:31). The word *immediately* caught my attention, but then I went on, not giving it much thought.

A week or two later one of the members of my ward came in to see me. This was a man who had been offended deeply when he was a teenager. He had been misbehaving in class to the point where his teacher literally picked him up by the belt and threw him out the front door of the chapel. The teacher told him never to come back, and he hadn't. But he was a good man. He was a good husband and father. He helped out on service projects, often came to church with his family, and had no discernable bad habits that I knew of.

As he sat down, I could tell he was nervous, but after some preliminary chitchat, he told me that his daughter had just announced her engagement and planned to be married in about six months. This daughter was the apple of his eye, and after hemming and hawing, he finally asked what it would take for him to qualify for a temple recommend. We discussed that briefly. I confirmed that there were no problems with immorality or the Word of Wisdom. He said he had a testimony of Joseph Smith and could sustain the current Church leaders. He said he would commit to coming to church regularly. But when I reminded him that another requirement was that he be a full tithe payer, his head dropped. "I am willing to start, bishop," he said, "but I haven't paid tithing since I was a boy. How much would I have to pay?"

The question took me aback. I think he was asking how long he would have to pay it to be worthy, but another thought came into my mind. And with it, I remembered Amulek's use of the word *immediately.* I marveled as a flood of understanding came to me at that moment. I decided this was a good teaching moment, and so remaining very sober, I began to ask him other questions. Our conversation went something like this:

ME: Tell me about how many years it has been since you graduated from college and have been fully employed as an adult.

HIM (startled, then after a moment): Uh . . . about thirty years.

ME: I know you can't answer this exactly, but could you estimate what your average annual salary would have been during that time? (I knew he had worked for the same company for a long time, so I hoped this wouldn't be too difficult to do.)

HIM (brow wrinkling): Hmm, I'm not sure. Maybe fifty or sixty thousand dollars a year.

ME: Let's use fifty since it is easier to do the math. So during those thirty years, you would have owed an average of five thousand per year in tithing, had you been paying it, correct?

HIM (confused and a little wary): I suppose so.

ME (writing on a pad): So five thousand dollars times thirty years means that you owe approximately one hundred and fifty thousand dollars in back tithing.

There was no response from him. He just stared at me.

ME (musing, pretending not to notice): If we were to add compound interest to that, then . . .

I stopped, then with a suddenly husky voice because of the lesson

I was being taught at that moment, I said, "Brother Bill, if we were being strictly fair by human standards, you would owe somewhere in the neighborhood of two hundred thousand dollars in back tithing."

His eyes were wide, not sure if I was serious or not. Then I took out my scriptures and we read together what Amulek said to the Zoramites.

When we finished, I said, "Aren't we grateful that the Lord is not absolutely 'fair' as we use the term? Otherwise, He might have to say, Since you turned away from me for thirty years, give me thirty years of faithful obedience, then we'll talk about a temple recommend."

I told him that he had six months before the marriage. If he began faithfully paying his tithing, attending church, and doing all else that was required for temple worthiness, I told him that I would be honored to be the one to extend that privilege to him. Which he did, and which I did.

Thirty years for thirty years? That's the hard way. To immediately bless a person when they turn to the Lord, that gives a deeper meaning to the words "easy" and "light."

I love the parable of the prodigal son (see Luke 15:11–32) because it is another powerful example of this principle. No court in the land would support that rebellious son if he claimed that his father "owed" him once he decided to return home. Fortunately, the boy wasn't asking for that. He had truly had a change of heart. He would be grateful if he could even be one of the servants in his father's household. That certainly beat slopping the hogs.

But then comes this powerful statement: "And he arose, and came to his father. *But when he was yet a great way off,* his father saw him, and had compassion, and *ran,* and fell on his neck, and kissed him" (Luke 15:20). How did the father see his son while "he was yet a great way off"? There were no cell phones or fax machines back then. No telegrams. No texting. There's no indication that a letter was sent saying, "Dad, I'm coming home, if that's all right." The father had to be watching for his son. And when he finally saw him, he ran to meet him. He didn't wait until he came all the way back.

In my mind, there is no more beautiful lesson in all of scripture about the grace and mercy and love of the Father than this story. We make the way hard for ourselves by our foolishness or stubborn rebellion, but when we decide to turn back, the Father makes it "easy" for us to return to the fold and He will immediately begin to bless us.

The Tithing Principle

Here is another example of how the Lord eases our way as we strive to be obedient to His will. I call this the "tithing principle."

The scriptures make it clear that all things on this earth belong to God. He created the world and therefore, as He says, "all things therein are mine" (D&C 104:14). He has chosen to share His "personal property" in all of its richness and abundance with His children. One of the greatest of all human failings is the tendency to claim ownership for that which actually belongs to God. We purchase a car or discover a vein of gold or raise a bumper crop of wheat or invent a new technology, and say, "This is mine." That God tolerates our selfish and shortsighted view is, in and of itself, a marvelous demonstration of His long-suffering grace.

In return for this limitless gift, God asks that we return one-tenth of our increase. We call that a tithe. What an incredible deal that is. If some wealthy benefactor gave us a million dollars on the condition that we would someday return even half of it back to him, we would consider this to be astonishing generosity. Even if he asked that we pay back nine hundred thousand of it, we would still be richly blessed.

God, however, asks only for one-tenth, a penny out of a dime, a dime out of a dollar. If we do that, He turns around and blesses us even more as He opens the "windows of heaven" (see Malachi 3:8–12). Here are other examples of the tithing principle:

- There are seven days in each week, but we are asked to set aside only one as His day and stop our normal activities. That is not even fifteen percent of the total week.
- A week has 168 hours. We are asked to spend only three of those hours attending formal worship services. We are asked to serve Him in other ways and to always remember Him, but as far as formal worship together as a congregation, He asks for less than two percent of our total time.
- In a twenty-four-hour day, if we spend even half an hour in scripture reading, prayer, and pondering about spiritual things (an investment of less than three percent), we will receive enormous spiritual returns.
- Physical fitness experts say that forty-five minutes of vigorous exercise five or six times a week is sufficient to maintain our bodies in good physical shape. That's less than 1/24th of our time.
- One can plant a single bushel of wheat and reap a hundred or more in return.

The examples of this principle go on and on. Of course God requires something of us in return for some of these blessings, but in most cases we don't have to return even a tenth of our goods. There is no tithing required for sunshine and rain, wildflowers and birdsongs.

To Summarize

We are here on earth to prove ourselves and to be tested. We live in a fallen world so that the conditions required for such testing are present. That means we will all experience adversity, trials, hardships, setbacks, tribulation, pain, suffering, sickness, and death. That is the paradox we face.

But in their great mercy and love for us, the Father and the Son have given us much to lighten our burden and ease the loads we must pull—a plan to help us find our way, a Savior to make it possible, the gift of the Holy Ghost, tender mercies, and divine signatures. With those in mind, let us close with the scripture that we started with in chapter ten:

> Come unto me, all ye that labour and are heavy laden, and I will give you rest. Take my yoke upon you, and learn of me; for I am meek and lowly in heart: and ye shall find rest unto your souls. For my yoke is easy, and my burden is light. (Matthew 11:28–30)

Deliverance from Danger

A colleague of mine in the Seventy once said that there was probably a whole legion of angels assigned full-time to watch over and protect missionaries. The Doctrine and Covenants doesn't talk about there being legions, but it does confirm that angels do watch over those in missionary service. The Lord said, "I will go before your face. I will be on your right hand and on your left, and my Spirit shall be in your hearts, and mine angels round about you, to bear you up" (D&C 84:88).

In my service with the Seventy, I learned again and again how true that was. Not all missionaries are protected from all harm. Occasionally, a full-time missionary dies while in service, through accident, sickness, or sometimes violence. Those are heartbreaking losses for the families, for the mission, and for the Church. But thankfully those are rare exceptions. However, the reports of premonitions, warnings, or feelings of uneasiness that protect missionaries and take them away from danger are numerous. I suspect for every one of those that are reported, there are several others where the missionaries weren't even aware of the Lord's protecting hand.

During World War II, especially in Nazi Germany, the situation deteriorated so rapidly that many missionaries were caught in the war zone. In this case a more direct and evident intervention was needed.

War Clouds

Adolf Hitler came to power in Nazi Germany in 1933 and immediately began preparing Germany for war. Once the war machine was fully ready, Hitler began his move to dominate Europe. Austria was annexed to Germany in 1938, and in March of 1939, Germany was allowed to take Czechoslovakia as well. Europe held its collective breath and prepared for war.

In April 1939, the First Presidency of the Church assigned Elder Joseph Fielding Smith of the Quorum of the Twelve "to make an inspection tour" of the European missions and hold a mission presidents' conference with the eight European mission presidents. Accompanied by his wife, Jessie Evans Smith, Elder Smith began touring the missions as the tensions between the countries continued to rise.

By August 24, the Smiths had finished their tour of Scandinavia and reentered Germany. That afternoon, M. Douglas Wood, president of the Swedish and West German Mission, received a telegram from the First Presidency in Salt Lake telling him "to be prepared to move upon immediate notice." The following day Thomas E. McKay, president of the Swiss and East German Mission, contacted Elder Smith and said that he was moving his missionaries to Denmark immediately.

Recognizing how serious the situation was, the Smiths took a train to the mission headquarters in Frankfurt. Everything there was in near chaos. That afternoon they received another cablegram from the First Presidency stating that all missionaries were to leave Germany immediately and go to either Denmark or Holland and await further orders. The Smiths went straight to the train station and bought tickets for Holland. They arrived in The Hague on

Saturday, August 26. Shortly after their arrival at the mission office, they learned through a phone call that they had been the last two members of the Church to get out of Germany. They also learned that a group of elders from Germany were at the border and were not going to be allowed into Holland.[1]

What follows are excerpts of the story by John Robert Kest of what happened to those missionaries who were stopped at the border and refused entry into Holland.

There was tension in the air that 26th day of August, 1939. . . . By early evening the telephone was ringing every hour or so. . . .

Sometime after 10:30 P.M., President Murdock received a call from President Wood in Germany informing him that a number of missionaries were arriving in Holland by way of Oldenzaal, a tiny village on the eastern border of Holland, not more than seven kilometers from the German border city of Bentheim. A number of elders from Germany, he said, were to arrive sometime the following day. As a matter of fact, the six elders comprising the group at Bentheim crossed the border into Holland late on the night of the 26th but were hurried back to Germany after having emphatically been refused entry to Holland. This, President Murdock learned as a result of a phone call received much later that same evening.

Because of these phone calls and the help the elders at Bentheim obviously stood in need of, Elder Smith and President Murdock decided I was to go to Oldenzaal with sufficient funds to conduct the brethren from that point to the mission home. It was assumed, of course, that we would have no trouble transporting the elders across the border as we thought they had been refused entry because of lack of funds and not having had through tickets to England in their possession. I would be able to guarantee the government officials their passage to England, and would be carrying enough money to assure these same cautious officers the young men would in no way be a burden to the Dutch government while in Holland. . . .

The next morning, Elder Kest arose at 5:30 and caught a train to Oldenzaal. He continues:

There were innumerable delays. The train trip, which could usually be made in two hours, took well over four, and it was after 11 A.M. when the train finally arrived in Oldenzaal. The station master there, . . . proved very helpful. "Yes," he said, "a number of young American missionaries were sent back to Germany late last night and have not crossed back into Oldenzaal since." This was upsetting news, for we had fully expected the brethren to be waiting at Oldenzaal, needing only money and an assurance of transportation to England in order for the Dutch authorities to consent to their passage to The Hague. . . . Already a good twelve hours had elapsed since they had been returned to Germany: something must be *very wrong* indeed.

Attempting to call Bentheim in order to learn the whereabouts of the elders proved of little value and after three hours I gave up the job as hopeless. Telephone connections with Germany had been cut off. . . .

I phoned President Murdock in The Hague along about 2:30 P.M. and told him that it had not been possible to contact the elders, all attempts at phoning them had proved fruitless; it was impossible to contact Bentheim by phone. The station master told me the young men had been almost without funds and had nothing except cameras to declare at the Dutch border. It was obvious that they had no tickets in their possession and probably scarcely enough money adequately to take care of their needs. Therefore, the fact that they were obliged to return to Bentheim began to assume even more serious proportions. President Murdock had said the elders must be helped at any cost. "Do your best and use your judgment as to what should be done, Brother Kest." . . .

Elder Kest then explains that because the decision to go to Oldenzaal had been made in such haste, and because they expected to find the missionaries in Holland, a visa had not been acquired for Elder Kest. He could not enter Germany without a visa. For an hour he called various government offices, but he was told it was impossible to get a visa.

> After thoroughly discussing the matter with the station master and finding that under no circumstances would they allow the brethren to enter Holland, it became apparent that I must go into Germany, visa or no visa.
>
> President Murdock had given me something over 300 guilders; it was thought this amount would take care of any eventuality which might arise. It took almost this entire amount to purchase tickets from Oldenzaal to Copenhagen, Denmark. . . . It seems ten tickets were purchased, for it was a speculation how many brethren were stranded in Bentheim. The ten tickets used up nearly all the funds and I hoped there would be sufficient transportation to take care of the elders' needs.
>
> The 2:30 train sped on toward Bentheim. Why the Dutch authorities allowed me to board that train, never asking for a visa, is a mystery; it was most irregular. Sitting tense

and excited on the hard seats, the thought reoccurred again and again: "Is this the right thing to do?" Here I was speeding into Germany without a visa, under circumstances that were hardly promising, hoping somehow the brethren might still be there. The train stopped; we had arrived.

A moment later there was a sharp clicking of heels. German Blackshirts stepped quickly through the car, their eyes cold as steel, taking in at a glance the occupants of each car. Handing the leader my passport, the inevitable question was shot at me: "Why is no visa stamped on the proper page?" This thought suddenly flashed through my mind: "Brother Kest, you have always enjoyed acting. If you have ever acted a part well, do it now!" I explained in exasperatingly slow and deliberately incoherent English that at present I was living in Holland, had heard that some of my friends were in Bentheim and knowing that railroad and train transportation was being curtailed, wanted to visit them while possible. Suspicion shone from the cold eyes of the officers. I rambled on, deliberately, on utterly pointless tangents, hoping all the while they would have great difficulty understanding me; which they did. . . .

It was fortunate that the German officer in charge spoke rather poor English. As I went on, talking disjointedly, tossing in a Dutch or German phrase here and there, the effect I wished to produce took hold of the men. They must have concluded that here was a simple, foolish American trying to see some friends for no good reason.

Inside the little cubicle in the station where they had taken me for questioning, they searched me thoroughly. What would they do to the precious tickets which I had in my suit coat pocket? This thought was paramount. In my possession was a folder in which were M.I.A. lessons written in English which we were translating into Dutch to be used the coming winter season. These they read over thoroughly, finally deciding they were harmless. They confiscated binder, papers, passport, *all* the money on my person and started going through each pocket in both coat and vest. I took the ten tickets out of my pocket and placed them on the table before me. *No one seemed to see the tickets.* The officer in charge gave me a receipt for the money, binder, papers and all my personal effects, and said, "You have forty minutes to catch the return train to Holland. After that time we cannot guarantee your safety."

Taking the tickets from the table I stuffed them in my pocket. *Not an eye flickered. I had the strong impression that the action had been entirely unobserved.* Hurriedly I left the station, my knees weak, my palms sweating. Few people on the street seemed to know where any American boys were staying, but finally someone directed me to the Hotel Kaiserhoff. There the elders were, trying to determine what course they should follow, as they were almost out of money and could no longer afford a hotel bill.

After quiet introductions and firm handshaking, my message was quickly delivered. Giving the tickets to Brother Ellis Rasmussen, who seemed to be in charge of the group, I told them quickly that these tickets from Holland might, with luck, insure their passage to Copenhagen. "You must leave immediately, brethren, and try to make connections into Denmark, as all railroad transportation is being cut off at an alarming rate!" The elders needed no urging, and in less than five minutes were ready, having very little luggage with them.

Quickly kneeling down, we held a prayer circle and asked our Father that we might be safely conducted to our respective destinations. As the seven of us knelt in fervent prayer, we all felt a closeness and unity experienced very infrequently in life. We were truly united and prayed with power and faith, believing our request would be granted, for we realized the desperate nature of our situation.

After prayer we rushed to the station where Elder Rasmussen and his group finally managed to catch a train . . . to Copenhagen—one of the last out of Germany carrying civilians.

After the brethren had left, and we waved each other good-bye, I hurried back to the office of the Blackshirts only a few yards away, where my passport and effects were being held. The station master gave me my money and papers immediately, but a Blackshirt guard stuck my passport in his wide cuff and marched insolently before me as the passengers boarded the train for Holland. The whistle of the train was blowing, and I noted the clock indicated only three minutes until departure time. What was going to happen? Finally the Blackshirt strutted over and with a sneer handed me my passport, muttering some deprecatory remark under his breath. He pushed me to the ticket window where I was obliged to buy a German ticket to Oldenzaal even though my Dutch ticket assured passage to Bentheim and return. It was necessary to run in order to catch the train—the wheels had just begun to turn. I sank into the seat, grateful for the brethren's escape and my own now certain and safe return. . . .

The following Friday, September 1, war was declared.[2]

Chile Santiago West Mission

Not all of the dangers that missionaries face are caused by man. Protection is also needed from the forces of nature. Here are two more stories of how the Lord watches over His missionaries, even in times of great natural disaster.

Chile, February 27, 2010

At 3:34 A.M., local time, an earthquake measuring an 8.8 magnitude on the Richter scale, one of the strongest earthquakes in recorded history, struck the nation of Chile. It triggered tsunami warnings in fifty-three countries and did damage as far away as the east coast of Japan. The final official death toll was 521. Chile is in an earthquake zone and has strict building codes or the loss would have been much higher.

The earthquake was so strong that it moved the entire city of Concepcion ten feet to the west, according to global positioning satellites. Scientists also estimate it moved the earth's axis by 8 centimeters (3.15 inches), and shortened the length of our day by 1.26 microseconds.[3]

Chile has more than half a million members of the Church and several missions in the country. Concern for the members and the missionaries immediately surfaced as the world woke up to the news of what had just happened in Chile. The capital of Santiago was hit pretty hard and sustained some damage, but the hardest hit was Concepción, about 270 miles south of the capital.

My wife and I have a grandson, Elder Nathan Stoddard, who was serving in the Chile Santiago West Mission when the earthquake struck. In our home, as in many others that day, we spent long hours huddled in front of the television as we tried to learn what was going on. Later in the day, the Missionary Department called our daughter and son-in-law to say that all the missionaries in Chile were safe. The day after the quake, the mission president asked missionaries to stay in their apartments or nearby and authorized them to e-mail their families. Here are excerpts from Nathan's e-mail dated March 1, 2010.

Like an 80-MPH Trailer Ride on Washboardy Road!

Saturday morning at 3:34 AM, we woke up to find our whole world dancing. It was pretty insane. I can still remember very vividly the sound and the feeling. The closest I can come to describing it would be riding in the trailer on a very washboardy (bumpy) road at like 80 miles an hour. When things start shaking, it starts out really slowly, and there is like a deep low rumbling sound. Then—at least in the bigger ones—the whole world starts dancing. In the first big one, I was on the top bunk of our highly sturdy beds (they are metal so they won't fall, they just shake a ton). When it started shaking everything just became instinctive and I did everything on instinct. It was almost as if someone else was moving me, and I was just a robot. I jumped down from my bed and went to my desk to find my keys to the door. When I found them somehow, they flew out of my hand. (I found them later next to the trash can.) I quickly realized that I wasn't going to find them, so the window was our next option. Almost all the windows in Chile are barred, but ours is one of the very few that is unbarred because we live behind another house.

Fortunately [!!!], like a month and a half ago Elder Ikeda had dreamed that there was going to be an earthquake, so I had put my headlamp and flashlight in a very easy place to get to, just in case. So we left out the window with the lights.

Once outside, it kept shaking for a little bit more (it lasted almost 3 minutes in total). Our neighbors have a swimming pool, and in the swimming pool it was a tsunami. The waves were huge, that just showed us how strong it really was. In Concepción it was 8.8 on the Richter scale, and it was between 7 and 8 where we are. . . .

After things stopped shaking, the missionaries went around to their neighbors to see if anyone was hurt. There was some minor damage, but nothing serious. The people, of course, were all frightened and greatly upset. As word came in from the south, the nation began to grasp just how great a disaster this had been. Aftershocks were also frequent and hard. Later that day, as things settled down somewhat, Nathan and his companion decided to visit members and investigators to see how they were doing.

Nathan then continues:

It has been a terrible thing in the south, but it has been good for missionaries. For example, last night we went to visit a contact we had, and she came out of her house crying. She didn't know anything about her family in the south, and they live really close to the epicenter. So we entered into her house, started to talk to her, and asked if she would like us to pray. As we got down on our knees to say a prayer with her, her phone rang. It was her niece from the south calling to say that they were all alive, even though they were without water, food, shelter, etc. So our contact felt very comforted to know that they were all okay. Then we said a prayer, and it was totally awesome! We then gave her a Book of Mormon and explained about the earthquake that had happened after Jesus' death. Then we left her with 3 Nephi 11 to read, and she was so grateful. As we were leaving, her husband and son showed up and she explained to them everything that had happened and kept saying how we had come, and that it couldn't have been in a more precise moment. So that was just one of the many miracles that has happened as a result of this.

Chile Santiago East Mission

The hardest hit areas of Chile were south of Santiago, and most of that area is in the boundaries of the Santiago East Mission, presided over by President Larry Laycock and his wife, Lisa. Here is their story, taken from an e-mail sent by Sister Laycock to friends and family and published in the *LDS Church News* a day or two after the earthquake.

Promptings in the Night

When we were set apart for this calling, Elder [Richard G.] Scott of the [Council] of the Twelve Apostles taught us many important lessons. He spoke from personal experience when he was a mission president in Argentina. One message that he shared with us is this: "At times, during your mission, you will be awakened in the middle of the night or the early morning hours with thoughts of specific things you should do for certain missionaries. Do not ignore these thoughts. They are promptings from the Holy Ghost who will communicate with you in the stillness of the night or the peace of the early morning hours. He will speak to you then because that is when you are still enough to hear." Elder Scott further instructed us to keep a notebook beside our bed so that we could record these precious promptings. He said that by the next morning, we would be likely to forget the promptings if we didn't write them down.

Sister Laycock told how they had followed that counsel many times and received precious promptings. Then she said:

Nearly two and one half weeks [before the earthquake], I was awakened at around 4 A.M. by just such a prompting. I did not hear a voice, but the thought was as clear as if it had been in the form of spoken words: "There is going to be an earthquake. Prepare your missionaries." I sat up in bed and immediately remembered Elder Scott's counsel. That morning I told Larry what had happened. He immediately set to work organizing our missionaries to prepare for an earthquake.

In talking with our office missionaries to arrange for them to put together a list of everything we would need to prepare . . . in both Spanish and English . . . we discovered that the Lord had also let two of our office missionaries know of the possibility of an earthquake (in the form of dreams) and the need to prepare our mission. We set a goal and arranged our schedule so that we could visit every apartment in the mission to check for safety and to review with our missionaries what to do in case of an earthquake. What a wonderful experience we have had as we have met with them and shared scriptures with them about being spiritually and physically prepared. ". . . If ye are prepared ye shall not fear" (D&C 38:30). We instructed every missionary to have a "go-bag" (36-hour kit). We reviewed our emergency action plan with them of where to go and what to do if they had phone service and in case they did not. We gave everyone a paper with all instructions in English and Spanish, and we reminded them that "this life is the time . . . to prepare to meet God" (Alma 34:32). We shared with them our thoughts and feelings about the need for spiritual and physical safety. Some of them became frightened and asked us if we knew something they didn't know. We smiled and repeated, " . . . If ye are prepared ye shall not fear." We didn't want to unduly alarm them, but we did want to impress upon them the need to be prepared. . . . Then we knelt with them in their apartment and dedicated each apartment, asking for a blessing of safety and security to be upon every apartment.

She doesn't say how many missionaries they had in the mission, but if the promptings came only two and half weeks before the quake struck, it was good that they did not delay starting the preparations.

As the earthquake became more violent, the mission home groaned and wailed. The power died, so the whole city was black. The windows made a hideous screeching sound, and flying objects banged against swaying walls. The printer/fax machine, books, bookends, and [a] fifty-pound television burst from the entertainment center and crashed to the floor. Cabinets emptied, drawers flew open, the refrigerator moved, water sloshed out of the toilets, the floor jolted up and down as we ran across it trying to hold onto the walls to keep from falling down, and the piano toppled over like a small toy. As we made our way to the backyard, I remember thinking, "God is all-powerful. He is our only refuge from this horrible mess." I prayed and prayed for Him to still the earth. When we reached the backyard, we watched in terror. By the light of the moon we could see the swimming pool water form giant waves and crash out onto the rocks. House and car alarms screamed into the night . . . some from being crushed by falling debris and others I guess from the bizarre movement of the earth. I am not sure if the intense rumbling sounds came from the earth itself or from everything else that was shaking so violently. Finally, it stopped. When the calm came, we had to sit down because our legs were weak and unstable. My legs stayed wobbly all day and night yesterday.

Here is a wonderful example of how a strong testimony and deep faith in God can see us through even the most horrible circumstances. Note how as the Laycocks ran into their backyard, Sister Laycock's thoughts turned to God's attributes: "God is all-powerful. He is our only refuge from this horrible mess."

Elder Kest expressed a similar confidence that God would be with him in this task of finding the missionaries. In a closing paragraph, Sister Laycock bore her testimony to those who were reading her e-mail. Her words are a wonderful example of someone whose testimony of God included a knowledge of His attributes and perfections. This was the bedrock she turned to when caught in one of the strongest earthquakes in recorded history:

When the earthquake came, we were prepared. . . . We were blessed with peace in the midst of chaos. We learned an important lesson: our preparation helped us to avoid panic and fear, but the Lord, *in His wisdom,* allowed us to experience enough discomfort to know that *He has all power.* He is in charge. *We are nothing without Him. We are dependent upon Him for every breath we take.* Only He can save us from death and destruction. He is the way, the truth, and the life. He is our perfect example. If we follow Him, we will be saved through obedience to the laws and ordinances of His Gospel.[4]

Once again we are reminded of the words of Helaman:

And now, my sons, remember, remember that it is upon the rock of our Redeemer, who is Christ, the Son of God,

that ye must build your foundation; that when the devil shall
send forth his mighty winds, yea, his shafts in the whirlwind,
yea, when all his hail and his mighty storm shall beat upon
you, it shall have no power over you to drag you down to
the gulf of misery and endless wo, because of the rock upon
which ye are built, which is a sure foundation, a foundation
whereon if men build they cannot fall (Helaman 5:12).

Notes

1. See Joseph Fielding Smith, Jr., and John J. Stewart, *The Life of Joseph Fielding Smith* (Salt Lake City: Bookcraft, 1972), 269–77.

2. John Robert Kest, "Border Incident: Inside Holland," *Improvement Era* (December 1943): 793–97; emphasis in original.

3. See Wikipedia.com, s.v. "2010 Chile Earthquake," accessed July 21, 2010.

4. Lisa Laycock, in *Church News*, 3 March 2010. See www.ldschurchnews.com/articles/58894/Report-on-earthquake-from-Chile-Santiago-East-Mission.html.

Some individuals . . . may discount or dismiss in their personal lives the availability of the tender mercies of the Lord, believing that "I certainly am not one who has been or ever will be chosen." We may falsely think that such blessings and gifts are reserved for other people who appear to be more righteous or who serve in visible Church callings. I testify that the tender mercies of the Lord are available to all of us and that the Redeemer of Israel is eager to bestow such gifts upon us. . . . Each of us can have eyes to see clearly and ears to hear distinctly the tender mercies of the Lord as they strengthen and assist us in these latter days.

DAVID A. BEDNAR

CHAPTER THIRTEEN

What Can I Do to Have More Faith and a Stronger Testimony?

What We Have Learned So Far

We began this book with the first lines of a Primary song:

Heavenly Father, are you really there?
And do you hear and answer ev'ry child's prayer?[1]

It is a question that even the faithful sometimes ask. It is a yearning, a pleading cry for reassurance, for confirmation and affirmation.

We live in difficult times. We live in a world where the paradox of life is ever present. Joy is tempered by sorrow; sickness limits health; evil battles good; virtue is often drowned out by vice. Life is hard. Like the relentless grinding of the threshing sled, it wears us down, wrings us out, drains us dry. The particularly perilous times in which we live only complicate our passage through this "vale of sorrow" (Alma 37:45) and the lone and dreary world.

We have said that the antidote for all of this is to strengthen our faith and deepen our testimony. No question. This is the cure for doubt. This is the answer to confusion. This is the bedrock that allows us to build so that we can weather the raging storms of life.

But while it is true, it is still too general. The question is *how?*

This is especially important for those who are struggling. If we are not careful, we can give what seem to be circular answers. For example, "If we are consumed by doubt, where do we find the faith to sweep away doubt?" To a person who isn't even sure God is there, we have to be careful that we don't say something like, "If you don't have a testimony, then what you need is a stronger testimony." That is not only unhelpful, it can be downright maddening.

What we want to do is come through these difficult times and keep our balance. To do that, we must have strong faith and a deep testimony. And that is our question:

How do we strengthen faith and deepen testimony, especially in times of trial?

What about repentance? Humility? Inspiration? Prayer? Scripture study? Considering how many things there are in the gospel that we could talk about, this may seem like an oversimplification.

A lesson from American history has application here. After winning the Revolutionary War, the thirteen colonies set about creating a new country, which proved to be almost more difficult than conquering the British. Two men were especially influential throughout that time, especially in the drafting of a new constitution—George Washington and Benjamin Franklin. Thomas Jefferson, commenting on why this was so, said they "'laid their shoulders to the great points, knowing that the little ones would follow of themselves.'"[2]

I believe the same principle holds true here. All of those other things are important, but I strongly believe that if we concentrate on strengthening and fortifying individual faith, it will automatically lead to deeper and more committed testimonies. And if a person has strong faith and a deep testimony, then those other things will come along quite naturally.

"Dispute Not Because Ye See Not"

As we begin a discussion on faith, let's first look at a key passage taught by Moroni. Speaking of the Jaredites, he said, "They did not believe, because *they saw . . . not*" (Ether 12:5). In other words, they refused to believe in what the prophets were saying because they had no evidence or proof that they could see for themselves. Then Moroni continues, "I would show unto the world that faith is things which are hoped for and not seen; wherefore, *dispute not because ye see not, for ye receive no witness* until after the trial of your faith" (Ether 12:6).

Let's put that in other words. Moroni warns his readers not to get caught in the same trap as the Jaredites. Faith is to believe in, or hope for, things that are not experienced with the normal senses, i.e., for which we have no tangible proof. We can't see or hear God. You can't hold faith in your hands. Repentance is not something you can buy off a shelf, and so on.

Then he warns us against "disputing" (not believing, arguing against, or rejecting) that something is true because we don't have that hard evidence. Then comes this critical comment, "For ye receive no *witness* until after the trial of your faith" (Ether 12:6). What is that witness, and why is it a trial of faith? As we seek to answer that, let us consider what the word "witness" implies. Here are some synonyms: evidence, proof, assurance, testimony, confirmation.

Some people are willing to believe in God if the following process would happen: Once they are told of a doctrine, principle, or concept, they are offered proof that it is true. Then, and only then, will they believe and act on that belief. Moroni says that just the opposite is required. We are given a doctrine, principle, or concept and then we are asked to act based on a hope that it is true. If we do act, then and only then, do we receive the witness or confirmation that it's true.

This is what we mean when we say we must *exercise* our faith.

It's very different from pumping iron, but just like physical exercise strengthens muscles, exercising our faith strengthens our faith as well. Notice that the exercise consists of hearing, hoping that it is true, then acting on that hope. Once we've done that, then the witness or confirmation comes. This is also what is meant by the phrase "strengthening faith" and what the scriptures refer to as "learning . . . by faith" (D&C 88:118).

An Example of the Trial of Faith

In Erin Eldridge, whom we have quoted earlier in this book, we have a wonderful example of how this process works in real life. What makes her story especially valuable is how far away from the Lord she was when she decided to start the process of exercising her faith.

Because Erin was horribly mistreated by a man when she was twelve years old, she turned to a life that was totally counter to all that she had been taught. She wanted to reach out to God but, based on her experience, she wasn't sure she could trust any "man," including her Heavenly Father. Yes, everyone told her that God was loving, but she had no evidence, no witness for herself that this was true.

However, she had been taught the gospel as a child. As she sank deeper and deeper into despair, she kept thinking back to those teachings. This brought a glimmer of hope that what she once knew was true. Alma taught that even "a particle of faith" (i.e., even the tiniest hope that something unseen might be true) is enough to start the process. "Yea, even if ye can no more than desire to believe," such desire is sufficient to initiate change (Alma 32:27). Well, Erin desired to believe.

At one point in this journey, Erin reached rock bottom. Here in her own words is what happened:

In desperation, I took the gun I used for protection from beneath my bed. I pulled back the hammer and placed the tip of the barrel at the back of my mouth. I rested my finger on the trigger. My entire life did not pass before my eyes, just the agony of the moment and the recent past. . . . I figured that if I was going to hell, I should just get it over with.

Try as I might, I could not pull the trigger. It was neither cowardice nor bravery that stopped me. It was an impression that came into my mind—the impression that a bullet would not stop the turmoil. I needed to fight the battle on this frontier.

Though she does not say it, and may not have even recognized it as such, we see the hand of the Lord in that impression that came into her mind. Surely that was from Him. What she said next is a wonderful insight into the process of faith.

With that impression came a little ammunition—hope. From somewhere came the reassurance that life would not always be so horrific.[3]

Things didn't miraculously change that night. There were other times when she took out the pistol again. But she fought off the darkness. For all the bleakness in her life, she let that tiny glimmer of hope work in her. She went to her bishop. She started to take action. She broke off her same-gender relationship. She stopped drinking. Her actions were not because she had proof that this was going to work. It was an act of faith because it was based on hope. She slipped, fell, tried harder. It happened again. She nearly gave up, but now her hope was stronger. Little by little she clawed her way upward, and as she did so, she began to feel herself changing. She found strength, and her feelings toward God began to soften.

Though feelings are not the kind of hard evidence that you can see and handle, they are nevertheless real. And Erin's feelings were the first confirmations from her trial of faith. Though she still had a long way to go, this was working for her. Eventually, she put aside the other lifestyle completely. She came back into full activity, received a temple recommend. Her testimony was getting stronger and stronger. Why? Because she was learning by faith, and testimony follows faith as surely as night follows day. She began receiving answers to her prayers, another form of evidence that God was really there for her.

Then one night, despair and discouragement washed over her, almost overwhelming her. She felt like she was drowning again. She took out her journal and began to read. She found a line she had written years before where in her loneliness she said that she wished there was someone to stroke her hair so she would know that she was loved. And at that very moment, she felt someone stroking her hair. Talk about a witness! She had passed the trial of her faith and the confirmation came. She had real, tangible evidence that God was out there, that He knew her, and that He felt her inner pain.

Faith and Divine Signatures

Why have I included so many examples and stories (which I refer to as divine signatures) in this book? Because every one of them provides an example of how the Lord gives us a personal witness to strengthen our faith. Each one shows how we can receive confirmation of our faith. This is true even of those people who weren't in the Church when they had the experience. They didn't know a lot about the gospel, or have the gift of the Holy Ghost with them, but they were searching. They had turned their gaze heavenward, *hoping* that there was something out there of value for them. Like Alma said, they desired to believe. More important, they acted on that belief, and immediately things began to happen.

We have seen that these tender mercies do something else. They not only confirm that God is there, but they also teach us about His attributes and character. What did Sister Hellwig and her daughter learn that day when the ship they had been on was torpedoed and thousands drowned? They learned that God knew them. He knew where they were and that they were in danger. Joseph Smith said that having a correct idea of God's attributes is one of the requirements of faith. So by definition, that experience strengthened their faith, which in turn deepened their testimony.

When Yvonne Kerr challenged God to help her know whether she should join the Church or not, she asked that He bring two missionaries to her right then, right there on the deserted streets of Edinburgh. She thought she had God over a barrel with that one. A moment later, a bus appeared (on Sunday, by the way, when normal bus service was suspended), and she received an immediate and sure confirmation that God was there, that He understood her hesitance, and that He wanted her to join the Church.

Warned of a coming earthquake, the missionaries in Chile came to know in a powerful way that God was watching over them.

When LeGrand Black told Genadijus Motiejunas that he had taught both of the two sister missionaries who had contacted him, Genadijus immediately saw that as confirmation that the hand of the Lord was in the project to translate the Book of Mormon into Lithuanian.

And so it is with every example we've shared.

The tender mercies of the Lord are sometimes given in such a way that they become divine signatures. They are an important way God uses to help us strengthen our faith and deepen our testimony. President Gordon B. Hinckley once said this about true conversion (which, when you think about it, is but another manifestation of one's faith):

We should be concerned with the spiritual dimension of our people and the enlargement of this dimension. . . .

When there throbs in the heart of an individual Latter-day Saint a great and vital testimony of the truth of this work, he [meaning, of course, men and women] will be found doing his duty in the Church.[4]

Faith is one of the "great points" in the Church. If we focus on that and learn how to exercise faith, it will become stronger and stronger. Then we don't have to worry as much about prayer, scripture study, repentance, and other gospel principles. These things naturally follow when faith begins to grow. As President Hinckley said, a truly converted person will be found "doing his duty."[5]

An Actual Knowledge That My Life Is Pleasing to God

The third requirement for having strong faith, according to Joseph Smith, is to have "*actual knowledge* that the course of life which he is pursuing is according to his [God's] will."[6]

Here is the next challenge. Even if we come to know and understand God's attributes, our faith can be weakened if we are not living as God has directed. We are not talking about perfection here, but there must be a desire and a sincere effort to put our lives in harmony with God. But this is a frequent stumbling block for us. Just as I learned that night when my baby daughter was struggling with the croup, if you know that your life is not pleasing to God, it becomes a serious hindrance to faith. It reduces the ability to see and feel the Lord's love and influence in our lives.

This is why repentance is so critical in the plan. It is not some gloomy, dour principle we must drag ourselves through in order to gain favor with the Lord. It is how we change so that we can know our lives are pleasing to the Lord. It is a liberating principle. We

actually desire to become more like God, and repentance greatly ac-
celerates the process of learning by faith. In fact, repentance is one of
the most important ways that we "exercise" our faith.

Repentance allows the love of the Lord to permeate our lives,
to lead, guide, and direct us into greater happiness, to help us make
course corrections so that we stay on the strait and narrow path. And
as that happens, our motivation to be obedient is driven more and
more by love and gratitude, rather than fear of the Lord.

But we must remember that Satan understands these principles
too. He knows that a correct idea of God's nature is critical to faith,
so one of his major strategic initiatives is to spread confusion about
the nature of God. He tries mightily to mislead us about what God is
really like. He may be especially pleased when someone rejects God
entirely, but if he can get others to believe that God is distant and
unapproachable, or harsh and punitive, or uninvolved in our lives, or
like a grandfather deity who just wants us to be happy, then he lessens
our faith. And that leaves us more vulnerable to his temptations.

The same is true with the third principle of faith. Satan understands that if we are unsure about our standing with God, our faith
is weakened. Have you noticed how often things go wrong on the
night you decide to go to the temple? Or how many reasons we can
find for not volunteering to help a neighbor in need or serve at the
welfare farm? Or the good excuses we come up with for not reading
our scriptures or saying our prayers? Many missionaries will tell you
that once they decided to send in their papers, or once they got their
call, all kinds of setbacks and problems arose, even to the point where
they seriously considered not going.

Well, of course. Get that missionary out in the field serving the
Lord full time and the next thing you know, his faith will grow and
so will his testimony. These kinds of activities make us feel good
about ourselves because we know they please God. So that's where

Satan draws a line in the sand and tries to stop us from crossing it. These things will add to our knowledge that we are doing what is pleasing to God, and thus our faith will be enhanced.

Focusing on the basics is fundamental to strengthening our faith. And we have to determine to do so even when we don't feel like it, even if we aren't sure that it will make any difference. We pray even if we don't feel like praying. We read and study the scriptures even when it feels like we're getting nothing out of it. We hold family home evening even if some nights are total disasters. We attend church even when it seems there is nothing there for us, or when we feel empty, guilty, or alienated from those around us.

Brigham Young understood this concept well when he gave this counsel:

> When we neglect any one of these duties, the enemy says, "I have made so much ground." If the Devil can induce an Elder to drink a little, he is not satisfied with this triumph, but says to him, "Your wife and children know it, don't pray tonight." The Elder says to his family, "I feel tired tonight, we won't have prayers." The enemy says, "I have gained another point." You indulge still further, and you will find other excuses. Your head is not right, your heart is not right, your conscience is not right, and you retire again without praying. By and by, you begin to doubt something the Lord has revealed to us, and it is not long before such a one is led away captive of the Devil.[7]

When our lives are congruent with the Lord's will, we are empowered spiritually. Remember what Joseph Smith was taught in Liberty Jail? If we let "virtue garnish [our] thoughts unceasingly; *then shall [our] confidence wax strong* in the presence of God" (D&C 121:45). That is what we want as we seek to strengthen our faith. We want our confidence to be strong in God's presence. We don't want to shrink away because we are filled with shame. We want the kind of faith that caused Amanda Barnes Smith to immediately ask God for help in a time of extreme need. She did so in full confidence that He would answer because by then she had given up her home, she had been ostracized by her family, and she had been hated and persecuted for His name's sake. *And so she knew her life was pleasing to her Heavenly Father!*

I believe this is what Paul meant when he said, "Let us therefore *come boldly* unto the throne of grace, that we may obtain mercy, and find grace to help in time of need" (Hebrews 4:16). That kind of confidence, that kind of boldness comes from having actual knowledge we are living as God would have us live, doing what God would have us do.

Here is another reason why these tender mercies and divine signatures are so important to us. They not only teach us about God's nature, which strengthens our faith, but they are also a confirming witness that God is pleased with us—sometimes even delighted with us. On that night when I realized that the Lord had taken a hand in my life and protected me from a possible accident on Vine Street, I can remember thinking to myself, "You're not anything special. Why would He do this for you?" And I decided that while I was not doing anything remarkable with my life at that time, God must be at least somewhat pleased with me.

Learning by Faith

Let us close with one last thought about how we can strengthen our faith and deepen our testimony.

We are admonished by the Lord to "seek learning, even by study *and also by faith*" (D&C 88:118). Most of us have a clear idea of how to learn by study, but how do we learn by faith? First of all, I firmly believe that this is essentially the same as "exercising" our faith, as we have discussed. But in the process of exercising our faith there are some fundamental things we must do. Nephi is a good example of how this is done. Laman and Lemuel are a clear example of how it is not done. Let's compare the two.[8] (All references are from 1 Nephi.)

Nephi	Laman and Lemuel
"Having *great desires* to know of the mysteries of God" (2:16).	"We *cannot understand the words* which our father hath spoken" (15:7).
"*I did cry* unto the Lord" (2:16).	"*We have not* [inquired of the Lord]; for the Lord maketh no such thing known unto us" (15:9).
"He did visit me, and did *soften my heart*" (2:16).	"If ye will harden not your hearts, and *ask me in faith, believing* that ye shall receive, with *diligence in keeping my commandments,* surely these things shall be made known unto you" (15:11).
"*I did believe* all the words that had been spoken by my father" (2:16).	"They *did not believe* that I could build a ship; *neither would they believe* that I was instructed of the Lord" (17:18).
"I will *go and do*" (3:7).	"Thou hast declared unto us hard things, *more than we are able to bear*" (16:1).

Desiring, believing, asking, seeking, acting—these are the key elements in learning by faith. And these are the key elements in strengthening faith and deepening testimony. When we do these things, then the Lord confirms our efforts with knowledge and comfort and power. Then we can have our own tender mercies and divine signatures.

A Caution

The stories we have read are so remarkable, so sweet, and so tender, that they may create in each of us a desire to have our own tender mercies and divine signatures. That is good in a way. But we have to be careful that we don't set our hearts on receiving such things for ourselves. That is what the Jaredites wanted. They wanted confirmation before they would exercise faith.

The way to receive your own divine signatures and blessings from the Lord is to follow the process. Let us quickly review again the scriptures that talk about the Lord's blessing for His children. You will see that there is a pattern in all of them:

- "The eyes of the Lord are *over the righteous,* and his ears are open unto their prayers" (1 Peter 3:12).
- "I, Nephi, will show unto you that the tender mercies of the Lord *are over all those whom he hath chosen, because of their faith*" (1 Nephi 1:20).
- "He loveth *those who will have him to be their God*" (1 Nephi 17:40).
- "I would desire that ye should consider on the blessed and happy state *of those that keep the commandments of God*" (Mosiah 2:41).
- "Be glad in the Lord, and rejoice, *ye righteous*: and shout for joy, *all ye that are upright in heart*" (Psalm 32:11).

- "I, the Lord, am merciful and gracious unto *those who fear me,* and delight to honor *those who serve me in righteousness and in truth unto the end*" (D&C 76:5).

These blessings and confirming experiences come *after* the trial of our faith, not before. As the Lord said when he warned against seeking signs, "Behold, faith cometh not by signs, but *signs* [the witness, evidence, confirmation, proof, and assurance] *follow those that believe. Yea, signs come by faith*" (D&C 63:9–10).

When we learn for ourselves that these things are true, then we will no longer have to ask, "Heavenly Father, are you really there?" We will know that He is.

In Conclusion

Here is what we have tried to establish in our study together:

1. If we are to successfully endure to the end, we must have strong faith and a deep, enduring testimony.
2. To strengthen our faith and deepen our testimony, we must know for ourselves, with a surety, that

    - God is our Heavenly Father, and we are His literal children.
    - He and His Beloved Son want us to be happy and to eventually come to a fulness of joy.
    - They know us intimately and love us infinitely.
    - They want to bless us and actually take great joy in doing so.

3. When we strive to be obedient, walking in the paths that He has shown, then the Father and the Son bless us beyond measure. Many of these blessings come in the form of divine signatures and tender mercies.

"As it is written, Eye hath not seen, nor ear heard, neither have entered into the heart of man, the things which God hath prepared for them that love him" (1 Corinthians 2:9).

Notes

Epigraph. David A. Bednar, "The Tender Mercies of the Lord," *Ensign,* May 2005, 100–102.

1. Janice Kapp Perry, "A Child's Prayer," in *Children's Songbook* (Salt Lake City: The Church of Jesus Christ of Latter-day Saints, 1989), 12. Used by permission.

2. Thomas Jefferson, in Thomas Jefferson Randolph, ed., *Memoirs, Correspondence, and Private Papers of Thomas Jefferson, Late President of the United States,* 4 vols. (London: Henry Colburn and Richard Bentley, 1829), 1:50.

3. Erin Eldridge, *Born That Way? A True Story of Overcoming Same-Sex Attraction with Insights for Friends, Families, and Leaders* (Salt Lake City: Deseret Book, 1994), 14.

4. Gordon B. Hinckley, in "News of the Church," *Ensign,* May 1984, 99.

5. Ibid.

6. Joseph Smith, *Lectures on Faith* (Salt Lake City: Deseret Book, 1985), 38.

7. Brigham Young, *Discourses of Brigham Young* (Salt Lake City: Deseret Book, 1954), 81.

8. Adapted from Gerald N. Lund, *Hearing the Voice of the Lord: Principles and Patterns of Personal Revelation* (Salt Lake City: Deseret Book, 2007), 276–77.

"I Will Go and Do"—
Learning by Faith

While touring the Switzerland Geneva Mission in December 2003, my wife and I had an interesting experience. It is another example of how we learn by faith and how the witness comes after the trial of our faith.

The mission president at the time was President Stephen D. Nadauld, who had served as a member of the Second Quorum of the Seventy from 1991 to 1996. His wife, Margaret Dyreng Nadauld, had served as general president of the Young Women organization from 1997 to 2002. They were called to serve in the Geneva mission in July 2003. We knew the Nadaulds well because for a time they lived in our ward in Bountiful, and I served as their bishop. My wife had also given two of their boys piano lessons. So we were pleased when we were assigned to tour their mission with them.

The Switzerland Geneva Mission at that time included the French-speaking part of Switzerland, a sizeable chunk of eastern France, and the little country of Luxembourg. Lynn and I flew into Strasbourg, France, arriving around 8:00 P.M. We were met by President and Sister Nadauld. We then drove to Nancy, France, where our first zone conference would be held the next day.

As we were driving along, renewing old times, President Nadauld's mobile phone rang. As he talked I could tell he was receiving some kind of a report from a missionary. After a few minutes, he thanked the elder, but before hanging up, he asked this question: "Any little miracles this week, Elder?" There was a long pause as he listened, then he commended the elder, thanked him again, and hung up. President Nadauld then told me that he had his zone leaders call in each week, half on one night, half on another, to give the president a verbal report on the week.

His question to the elder intrigued me, and I started to ask him what he meant by "little miracles," but before I could do so, the phone rang again. It was another zone leader calling in his report. As they finished, the same question was asked: "Any little miracles?" Again there was silence as the president listened. Again he commended the elder and thanked him. That happened twice more in quick succession.

Finally, the last report was finished and it was quiet again in the car. So I said, "President, tell me about these 'little miracles' you keep asking them about." He laughed and then explained. He told me that a few weeks before he had had the thought come to him that missionaries wasted a lot of time on cancelled or missed appointments. Usually it took a lot of time for the missionaries to travel to appointments, either walking or by taking public transportation, and even when they confirmed the appointment, sometimes they would arrive at the investigator's home and find no one there. Discouraged, they would turn around and come back.

He then gave them this advice. "Elders and sisters, when an appointment falls through, it is natural to feel like you've had a failure and be disheartened about the waste of your time. But remember, the Lord knows where you are. There may be another reason for you being there. So any time an appointment falls through, I want you to immediately look around and find someone to talk to. You can do this either by finding someone on the street or by knocking on doors."

He said that as the missionaries started to do as they had been counseled, they started reporting in what they called their "little miracles." So now, President Nadauld made it a practice to ask for a report on such experiences as part of the zone leader's weekly reports.

By now I was really curious and asked him to share some examples of what his missionaries had experienced. He shared four such stories, at least some of which had just been reported to him that night.

"Are You the Ones I'm Supposed to Talk To?"

Two missionaries went to an apartment building for an appointment. It was about ten in the morning when they knocked on the door, but no one answered. They stepped back in the main hall, and, remembering the president's counsel, they started to talk about how they could find someone else to talk to. Just then the elevator doors opened, and a very large man got out. He was barefoot and wearing trousers and a tank-top type of T-shirt.

The moment he saw the missionaries, he started toward them. That immediately made them nervous for they had never seen the man before, and he was obviously coming at them. Then the man said, "So are you the ones I'm supposed to talk to?" They asked what he meant. He explained that he worked midnight shifts. He had come home that morning as usual and went to bed. But suddenly he woke up out of a dead sleep and had a strong feeling that he needed to get dressed and go downstairs because there was someone there he needed to talk to.

"You Are Wearing Those Name Tags"

Two other missionaries came out of a large apartment building after their appointment had fallen through. They immediately started looking around for someone to talk to. They saw a man crossing the square some distance away. They started toward him, hoping to intersect him. However, as they approached him, the man slowed his step, peering at them closely.

"Ah," he said. "I notice that you are wearing those name tags."

Surprised, they said yes, then explained that they were Mormon missionaries and had a message to share about Jesus Christ.

The man seemed pleased. "I thought so," he said. "I've seen you or others like you around town before, and I always had a feeling that you had something to do with religion. I'd like to hear your message because I've been searching for religion in my life for the last little while."

"He May Not Be Interested, but I Am"

Two sister missionaries got on a train. They chose a seat beside a man who was sitting alone. Like good missionaries should, they struck up a conversation with him. They told him who they were and what they were doing in France and then initiated a little gospel discussion.

The man was polite, but after a few minutes he said, "I'm sorry. I am not interested in religion." Then he got up and moved to a different seat.

Disappointed, the sisters sat back. Just then one of them felt a tap on her shoulder. She turned around, and the man sitting directly behind them leaned forward. "I couldn't help but overhear your conversation. That other fellow may not be interested in your message, but I am. Would you be willing to speak with me?"

A Stupor of Thought

In a large city, two elders came back out onto one of the main streets after their investigators turned out to be no-shows. They looked around, but there was no one close by whom they could talk to. So the senior companion decided that they would look in their daily planner to see if there was someone they knew who lived in the area whom they could visit.

He sat down on a low wall and began to look through his book. He described what happened next as an absolute stupor of thought. He read through one page, but when he got to the bottom he realized that he could remember nothing of what he had read. Puzzled, he started again. The same thing happened. And again. Completely baffled, he looked at his companion, who by now was getting a little impatient.

"What are we going to do, Elder?" his companion asked.

"I don't know, Elder," he replied. "It's like my whole brain has shut down." So he started once again to go through his book.

Just then a young man approached them on a bicycle. As they looked up, to their surprise he stopped beside them. "Do you have a message for me?" he asked.

Totally taken aback, the senior companion said, "Well, yes. Yes, we do. But how did you know that?"

The man explained that he had been riding his bicycle in the opposite direction on the other side of the busy street. Suddenly he heard a distinct voice in his head saying, "Turn around. Cross the street. There is someone over there who has a message for you."

Faith Is a Principle of Action

I know the follow-up question to each of those stories is "So, did they get baptized?" I'm sorry to say that I don't know. These reports were of initial contacts, not final, post-conversion reports. But for our purpose here, it doesn't matter if they were baptized or not. Part of a missionary's purpose is fulfilled when he or she talks to people. The scriptural phrase the scriptures uses is "open your mouth" (D&C 30:5; 30:11).

The LDS Bible Dictionary states that "faith is a principle of action."[1] Nephi is often cited as the epitome of acting on faith because of his famous statement to his father: "I, Nephi, said unto my father: I *will go and do* the things which the Lord hath commanded, for I know that the Lord giveth no commandments unto the children of men, save he shall prepare a way for them that they may accomplish the thing which he commandeth them" (1 Nephi 3:7).

That is what these missionaries did. They heard their president give them a challenge, and they believed that if they were obedient, it would work. And it did! It is a classic example of learning by faith. They heard a concept taught. They wanted to believe it would work—in other words, they hoped it was true. Then they acted in faith on that hope. And they immediately began receiving confirmations that it was a true principle.

President and Sister Nadauld had a strong mission with obedient missionaries, but I'm fairly certain that there were a few missionaries who, when they heard President Nadauld teach them that principle, reacted with something like this: "That's a nice idea, but . . . well, you know how the president is. Always so positive and upbeat. That would never work for me. Those kinds of things don't happen to me." And thus they missed out on the kinds of little miracles that were available and waiting. And they missed out on the opportunity to strengthen their faith and deepen their testimony.

Incidentally, I was so impressed with what President Nadauld had taught, I started sharing the principle and those four examples in other mission tours. In every single case, within one day's time, the mission president was receiving phone calls from missionaries saying, "President, you'll never believe this, but we did what Elder Lund taught us, and guess what happened?" Then they'd share their own success experience.

Remember what we are trying to teach here. There is a way for any individual to receive confirmation of God's reality—that He is really there and that He does indeed answer a child's prayer.

And as we have also shown, we will need that kind of testimony for the days that lie ahead.

Notes

1. LDS Bible Dictionary, s.v. "faith."

Blessings Prepared
Long Years in Advance

In the early days of translating the Book of Mormon, Joseph Smith was persuaded by Martin Harris to let him take 116 pages of the finished translation manuscript. It was lost through Martin's carelessness, and Joseph was sharply rebuked by the Lord. Though he never spoke specifically about it, as far as I am aware, surely one of the most humbling lessons Joseph ever experienced came from that loss.

And yet, the Lord had inspired Nephi to write a more sacred record of his people and Mormon to include that with the record (see 1 Nephi 9:5; Words of Mormon 1:2–7). What that meant was that the Lord had known about Joseph's mistake more than 2,000 years before and had made preparations to cover for that mistake (see D&C 10). How humiliating that must have been for Joseph!

God knows all things from the beginning (see 1 Nephi 9:6). For Him there is no past, present, and future for "all things are present before mine eyes" (D&C 38:2). In Joseph's case, He prepared things more than two millennia in advance to counter one of Satan's cunning plans. He also taught a young, still-learning prophet some valuable lessons at the same time. There are other cases where we find

God's foreknowledge operating in a way that can influence events far into the future.

"I Don't Believe in Miracles"

I should like to close this book on divine signatures with just such an example. This particular story has personal significance for our family, as I will explain later, but I share it here because it is a crowning example of God's great love for His children, and how He sends divine signatures to bless them, strengthen their faith, and deepen their testimony.

This story involved a couple who were living in Colorado at the time the events unfolded. It is told by the wife, Linda, who experienced it most directly.

August 22, 1997, was a life-changing day for us as a couple and for our family. I say life-changing because all (and I really do believe all) big decisions that we now make for ourselves and our family are made in some part with Mike's biking accident in the back of our minds.

On that day, Mike was involved in a bicycle accident with a fully loaded cement truck. The cement truck won. Riding a road bike is a passion that Mike has had for years. He has his favorite places to ride, and he was on one of those that day. A cement truck approached Mike from behind while he was pedaling up a slight grade and attempted to pass him on a "no pass" curve. When another car approached from the opposite direction, the cement truck quickly returned to its lane and the stabilizing trailer attached to the rear of the truck ran over Mike. He was slammed so hard to the ground that it split his bicycle helmet in two.

Those who found him on the road and the emergency

teams did not think he would make it to the hospital alive. The rear wheel of the trailer went right across the back of Mike's body, leaving the imprint of the tire tread embedded all the way up his back. From there, our long journey began. Mike had multiple broken bones in his arm, ribs, shoulders, neck, and back. He had a severe TBI (Traumatic Brain Injury), and though he had been wearing a helmet, the damage was still great enough that underlying problems were causing havoc with his blood pressure and organs.

He was placed in an induced coma and remained in the critical care unit for three weeks. The first few days were really rough. I overheard comments by the medical staff when they came on shift, saying that they were surprised that Mike was still with us. One doctor suggested we quit trying so hard to stabilize him. (I made sure that doctor never returned to Mike's room.)

After his stay in CCU and an additional two-weeks' stay on another floor, he was moved to a rehab hospital where he would stay as an in-patient for two months, then spend ten hours a day as an out-patient for another two months.

Many miracles and experiences took place during this time. Many took place right before our eyes as we made our way through this difficult time. We learned that *some miracles had taken place so many years before that we would never have known about them if we had not been put in this situation.* One in particular, which occurred during a consultation session, was an amazing miracle for us.

During Mike's recovery, we would have regular conferences with doctors, nurses, caseworkers, and insurance representatives. I attended most of these on my own, but this one happened much later so Mike was able to attend. The meeting that day was to decide which path we should take to treat his multiple bodily injuries and the damage to the brain. The discussion went well. But as we came to the end of the meeting, the lead doctor asked everyone to leave but Mike and me. The insurance people wanted to stay, but the doctor firmly informed them that he wanted to speak to just the two of us.

This man was a wonderful doctor. He specialized in the brain, focusing specifically on TBIs. He always had Mike's best interest in mind. Once we were alone, he started out with this surprising statement: "Before we begin, I need to tell you something. I don't believe in God, and I don't believe in miracles." What an opening statement! To us, that was what had gotten us to the point where we were on that day, with Mike alive and talking about rehabilitation. We knew we had a loving Heavenly Father who had never left our sides and given us many miracles.

"You Have Seen a Miracle in Your Life"

After that introduction, he then proceeded to walk to the screens where Mike's X-rays, MRIs, and CAT scans (I can't remember which) had been displayed during the conference. He said he wanted to show us something. It was like he had a surprise for us and couldn't wait to show us.

He showed us an X-ray of a skull. "Here is an X-ray of the brain," he began. "You can see the different parts of the brain." He pointed to a spot at the base of the skull just above the spinal cord. "This is the cerebellum. It processes input from other areas of the brain and the spinal cord. In other words, this is the part of the brain that controls motor functions for the body."

Then he removed that X-ray and put another one up, also of a skull. "Do you notice anything different about this one?" he asked.

It took me a moment, but then I pointed. "There doesn't seem to be a cerebellum on this one," I said.

"That's right," he said, pleased. "There is no cerebellum." Then he turned to Mike. "This is the X-ray of your head, Mike." He tapped the X-ray. "And this is where your cerebellum should be. But it is not. You don't have one."

He continued, "If I had not personally seen you myself, heard you speak and watched your mobility, and I had been given this film to view, I would have diagnosed you as being in a vegetative state without any mobility." He then peppered Mike with questions. Had he enjoyed an active childhood? Did he have problems with mobility? His balance? Then he caught himself as he remembered that Mike's accident had occurred while he was on one of his twenty-mile bike rides.

Very sober now, he told us that was why he had asked everyone else to leave the room. He didn't want this information in any way to influence the decisions being made for Mike's care. He explained that when he saw the films, he was amazed and stunned. We all knew that when Mike had been slammed down onto the pavement, one of the wheels of the 2,000-pound stabilizing trailer had run up Mike's back and directly over the base of his skull. The doctor said that force would very likely have crushed the cerebellum and left him with severe physical and perhaps mental handicaps.

He said that the only thing he could figure out to explain any of it was that while Mike was in the womb, the cerebellum had never developed. But the brain, being the wonderful organ it is, had taken upon itself to reroute things so that the functions of the cerebellum were assumed by other areas. He then said that in all his years as a neurologist and brain surgeon, he had never seen anything like it before.

We were in awe. We sat there for a few moments in silence. Then the doctor leaned forward and said, "Let me say again what I said earlier. I still don't believe in God, and I still don't believe in miracles, but I think we've seen one today. So when you go home, you kneel beside your bed, and you thank whatever God you believe in for what has happened, because you have seen a miracle in your life."

After many months in the rehab hospital and many more of physical therapy, life eventually returned to normal (whatever normal is). With time, Mike was able to go back to work. He became physically stronger and eventually started taking his favorite bike rides again.

We still talk about the accident and how everything fell into place. There were many little things, like our pager (no cell phones then) that was accidently dropped in water but miraculously still worked. That pager was my lifeline to my children at home and school during Mike's hospitalization. Or like the ER nurse being LDS and finding Mike's temple recommend in his wallet and alerting the Church to our needs. Or having just the right medical personnel show up who had the answer that no one else could figure out.

In a priesthood blessing, Mike was told that "all would be okay," and from that point on, I knew it would. It was a rough road, but I knew that in the end we would be okay. We both know that our Heavenly Father was forever mindful of us and our family. We recognized it then, and we recognize it even more now. When things aren't going as planned, we have learned to have faith, do the best we can, and then try to enjoy the journey as much as possible and see what is at the end of the tunnel.

This story has particular significance for our family because this miracle happened to Michael R. Lund and his wife, Linda. Michael is my youngest brother.

Mike is employed as a civilian attorney for the Air Force at Hill Air Force Base near Ogden, Utah. He also served as an attorney in the Air Force Judge Advocate General's Corps and continues to serve in that capacity as a reservist in the Air Force.

While Lynn and I were in Europe, Mike and Linda were transferred to Germany to work with the military for three years during the Iraq War and we were able to spend a week touring Holland and parts of Germany together. While in Germany, Mike was called as a branch president and then as a member of the stake presidency.

When the 2002 Winter Olympics came to Salt Lake City, Mike's oldest daughter secretly filled out an application for Mike to be considered as one of the torch carriers for the Olympics. She told his story as part of the application. To the family's joy and surprise, Mike was selected. He carried the torch in one of the last relay laps before the torch moved into the Salt Lake Valley and on to the Olympic stadium.

Today, Mike and Linda live in Mountain Green, Utah.

As it is written, Eye hath not seen, nor ear heard, neither have entered into the heart of man, the things which God hath prepared for them that love him.

1 Corinthians 2:9

Epilogue

Divine Signatures

This book is about the God we worship. It is about our Heavenly Father and His Beloved Son, Jesus Christ. It is about their nature and their attributes. Its primary premise is that the better we know and understand their perfections, their attributes, and their true nature, the stronger we will be as we face the paradox of life and endure the perilous times in which we live.

The Father and the Son want us to know them! And they want us to understand that *their* knowledge of *us*—our hopes, dreams, concerns, problems, sorrows, and fears—is perfect and intimate and their love for us is perfect and infinite. Knowing this truth is critical to our spiritual survival in these times.

And because God is our Heavenly Father, He not only is willing to bless us, He wants to bless us! Just as we take great joy in bringing happiness to our children, so it is with our Eternal Father. In the Doctrine and Covenants it even says that He "delights" to honor and bless us (D&C 76:5). I love that concept. I love to picture my Heavenly Father as delighted with aspects of our relationship.

Throughout this book I have shared dozens of true-life examples of divine signatures to illustrate how widespread and common they are in the lives of those who are trying to live good and decent lives.

Perhaps it is fitting to conclude the book with one more story of a truly remarkable divine signature.

An Unplanned Detour

I finished writing this book near the end of June, 2010. At that point, I had concluded the book with the story of my youngest brother's remarkable experience following a bike accident. That seemed like a powerful way to end the book. But around the first of August, as my wife and I were preparing for a vacation to Montana, I received some feedback suggesting that a short epilogue might bring more closure to the book. I liked the idea and thought about it over the next few days, but nothing very exciting came to mind. I decided I wouldn't worry about it until I returned.

Our driving route into northern Montana took us north along Interstate-15 through Utah and Idaho and into Montana. By coincidence, one of our daughters and her family left that same day for another part of Montana for their vacation. We were not traveling together, but would be covering much of the same route. About half an hour after we crossed into Montana, my phone rang. It was our daughter, asking how far along we were. I told her we were just passing the Clark Canyon Reservoir, which is about twenty miles south of Dillon, Montana. She said that they were about an hour behind us.

As she was about to hang up, she had a thought. "Have you ever stopped at the Lewis and Clark monument on the west side of the lake?" I had to admit that I knew of no such monument, though I have long been enthralled with the Lewis and Clark story. "It's worth a stop if you have time," she said. "The exit is right there at the dam."

As I hung up, I realized we were only a few hundred yards from the dam. The exit sign was right in front of me. I braked hard and made the turn. Sure enough, as we crossed the dam, we could see the monument on a hilltop about half a mile away. We drove up to the site, and, glad for a brief break from a long ride, we got out. We were not prepared for what awaited us.

The Corps of Discovery

On April 30, 1803, the United States finalized the Louisiana Purchase, a huge swath of land belonging to France. The purchase encompassed more than 800,000 square miles. With a price of fifteen million dollars, the United States doubled its territory for a cost of about three cents an acre.

On May 21, 1804, the Corps of Discovery, lead by Merriwether Lewis and William Clark, set out from St. Louis. By October, they had only traveled about a thousand miles upriver and decided to winter at Fort Mandan (near Bismarck, North Dakota) among the Mandan and Hidatsa Sioux. While there, the two captains learned that the Rocky Mountains were still another thousand miles ahead of them, and that, contrary to commonly held beliefs, there was no place where they could easily portage their boats across the mountains and continue on to the Pacific Ocean, which was their charge.

However, they were told that the Shoshone Indians roamed a wide area around the Upper Missouri and they had many horses. Perhaps they could be persuaded to help them portage their baggage across the mountains. However, the Shoshones had never seen white men before and could easily prove to be hostile. The exploring party would be vastly outnumbered. And how could they even communicate with them? Sign language was not suited for such delicate negotiations.

While at Fort Mandan, a French trapper by the name of Charbonneau introduced himself and offered a solution. He had two wives who were both Shoshone women. Now in their teens, they had been captured five years earlier by a Hidatsa war party. For payment, Charbonneau offered to provide translation for the party with the help of the women. Lewis and Clark agreed, but told Charbonneau they could take only one of the women. The Frenchman chose the younger of the two. She was fifteen at the time and six months pregnant. Her name was Sacagawea,* which means "Bird Woman."

The next spring, the Corps got underway again. Charbonneau and his young wife were with the company, Sacagawea carrying a newborn son strapped to a cradle board on her back. The way westward was difficult and slow. It was near the end of July when they reached the point where three rivers came together to form the Missouri (near modern Three Forks, Montana). Sacagawea announced that this was the very place where she had been captured five years earlier. The captains were elated. They were in Shoshone territory at last and there was still time to cross the mountains before winter.

To everyone's growing dismay, however, many days passed without sign of any other human beings. Finally, in mid-August, as the Continental Divide loomed closer and closer, they realized that they were just weeks away from snow in the high elevations. This was a crisis. The group was totally exhausted and running out of food. They had to find a way through the mountains, and they needed help to do it. The success of the entire endeavor was in jeopardy.[1]

Finally, the company decided that Lewis would take three men with him and press ahead on foot until he made contact with the Shoshones. Clark would follow as quickly as possible. On the fourth day out, shortly after crossing the Continental Divide, Lewis's party stumbled upon three Shoshone women gathering berries. One young

---

* The explorers pronounced the name *Sacajawea*, and it is often written that way, but this more closely represents the Shoshone pronunciation.

girl fled in panic, but the other two—an old woman and a child—bowed their heads, perhaps expecting to be killed or captured. Lewis treated them kindly and, signing that they were friends, gave them gifts.

That was wise. The young girl had evidently sounded an alarm because a short time later, about sixty armed Shoshone braves came thundering towards the four white men. In an act of great courage, Lewis laid down his rifle and told his companions to do the same. He again made signs that they came in peace. When the old woman told the braves that the strangers had treated her kindly, the chief relaxed. After giving the chief some gifts, the company were taken to the village a short distance away.

That night, struggling to communicate through sign language, Lewis asked the chief, whose name was Cameahwait, if he would return with him to meet the rest of the party. He said they needed help in bringing their baggage over the mountains. The Shoshones had no guns and were at the mercy of other tribes, so Lewis promised them that in return for their help, future trade would be opened up, including firearms. The chief agreed to help, but some of his braves were afraid Lewis was in league with the Hidatsa and would lead them into a trap. It took all of Lewis's power of persuasion to prevail, but finally about two dozen Shoshones cautiously started back with the four explorers.

As they descended the east side of the pass toward the rendezvous site, Lewis searched the land ahead for any sign of Clark. There was nothing. The Indians, nervously watching for any possible ambush, grew visibly more suspicious as time wore on. The situation, already highly volatile, was unraveling quickly. What if Clark had gotten lost and was still several days away? Would the suspicious Indians turn on the four explorers? Lewis put on a brave face, assuring the Indians that his people were coming, but his anxiety was rising fast. That night as they bedded down, Lewis wondered what the morrow would bring.

The next morning, a shout went up. Downriver a short distance, Clark appeared with Charbonneau and Sacagawea. The rest of the party was not far behind. As Lewis introduced Clark to Chief Cameahwait, something unusual happened. A young Shoshone girl who had accompanied the group of braves, cried out and ran toward Sacagawea. The two women threw themselves into each other's arms and began chattering away in great joy and excitement. It turned out that this young woman was Sacagawea's childhood friend and had been with her the day the Hidatsa had taken her captive. She had barely escaped herself. The Shoshone warriors were greatly relieved. Here was one of their own. The white men had spoken the truth.

After initial greetings, Lewis called everyone together. It was time to get down to business. This was why Sacagawea and Charbonneau had come. Communication, though, proved to be cumbersome. Lewis, who spoke only English, told one of his men who spoke French what to say. He would then repeat it to Charbonneau in French, which the trapper would translate into Hidatsa for Sacagawea, who would translate it into Shoshone.

As the translation got underway, something truly astonishing happened. In the joy of meeting her girlhood friend, Sacagawea had not paid much attention to the others of her tribe. But now, as Lewis began negotiations with Cameahwait, Sacagawea peered more closely at the chief. She was sure she knew this man. Then with a cry of exultation, she leaped to her feet and ran to embrace him, tears streaming down her cheeks. Incredibly, Cameahwait was *her older brother!*

In that moment, the crisis was over. Potential enemies turned into friends. These white men had brought back the chief's sister. A debt was owed. Horses would be forthcoming. A guide over the mountains would be furnished. The expedition would continue on to the Pacific, and the course of history for the United States of America would be forever changed.

It says much about the emotions of that day that on the maps they made, Lewis and Clark labeled the place where all of this happened as "Fortunate Camp."

The Invisible Hand of God

Today the site of the camp where the reunion with Cameahwait and Sacagawea took place is under the waters of the Clark Canyon Reservoir. The monument we visited that day marks the site and recounts the events which took place there. As my wife and I read the brief accounts on the markers, we were amazed. I knew that Sacagawea had found her brother, but I didn't know any of the detail of how it came about or its significance for the Corps of Discovery.

As we finished taking pictures, returned to the car, and continued on our journey, my thoughts would not keep still. If my daughter had called even thirty seconds later, we would have been past the exit. The next exit is eleven miles up the road. Would we have taken the time to turn around and come back all that way? Not likely. This was a rather simple, quiet, but nevertheless sweet, tender mercy of our own.

Here was a divine signature! And not only one, but several. In addition to learning about the monument in time to make a detour to visit it, I considered the following:

- Sacagawea's reunion with her brother at this critical moment firmly established the relationship between the expedition and the Shoshones and the Corps of Discovery. In 1802, the western boundary of the United States was the Mississippi River. The British had already crossed the continent through Canada and were rapidly setting up trading posts all across the Great Northwest. Russian explorers had discovered Alaska and had established a presence there. Spain still claimed much of what is now the American Southwest, and the French owned the center part of the continent. President Thomas Jefferson had the vision to see that a United States hemmed in by European powers would be greatly limited in its ability to become a great nation.

- The Lord's intervention very likely saved the lives of many, if not all, of the exploring party. It was late in the season and they were out of food and unable to go any farther. Even if they had decided to turn back, they likely would have perished before they could return to civilization.

- And what of Sacagawea? Here was a young Indian maiden, barely ten years old when she was captured, taken hundreds of miles away to live among the hated enemy of her people. Viewed as a piece of chattel, she was won by Charbonneau in a wager with the Hidatsa who had captured her. At fifteen, she was the wife of a white man and carrying his child. What were the chances that she would ever see her people again? Then along came a group of white men headed up the Missouri River in need of someone who spoke Shoshone.

Good Luck or the Hand of Divine Providence?

George Washington said this later in his life: "No people can be bound to acknowledge and adore *the invisible hand which conducts the affairs of men* more than the people of the United States. Every step, by which they have advanced to the character of an independent nation, seems to have been distinguished by *some token of providential agency.*"[2]

Upon our return home from our vacation, I continued my research on this particular part of the Lewis and Clark expedition. I soon noticed a pattern in what the historians and scholars had to say. Note the following:

> The explorers hoped to meet friendly Indians who would provide horses and information to guide the party through the region. *Luckily,* in mid-August, they met a band of Shoshone Indians whose chief was Sacagawea's brother.[3]

> Lewis' *luck* improved *phenomenally* when Clark finally arrived. . . . As if Sacagawea's acceptance by the tribe wasn't *opportune enough,* she recognized the leader of the band. . . . These *strokes of luck* [settled the situation].[4]

> August 13, 1805, was an exceptionally full and *fateful day.* . . . It really started off with a *chance meeting* with an old Shoshone woman. . . . The day was crowded with *some of the most momentous* events of the entire expedition.[5]

> [There were] several *strokes of luck* including Sacagawea's recognition of her brother and Clark's *nick-of-time arrival.*[6]

It is not fashionable nowadays for historians to talk about divine influence or providential intervention in the affairs of men. In fact, it seems that they often go to great lengths to avoid even hinting at any divine influence. Yet this remarkable set of circumstances and the timing of events leaves them grasping for adequate words to describe them. I don't object to the use of words like "luck," "chance," "opportune," "fate," or "nick-of-time" to describe these amazing events, but I personally believe there is a simpler explanation.

Earlier, we mentioned a scripture wherein the Lord said that He "delights" to honor and bless His children (D&C 76:5). When we consider the multiple layers of blessings and divine signatures which occurred here, I cannot help but think that the Lord was particularly gratified with what His hand had wrought that day.

Heavenly Father? Are You Really There?

I have said that divine signatures have had a profound influence in my life. I have shared examples—some sweet and simple, some incredible and miraculous—which illustrate the great love our Heavenly Father and His Beloved Son have for us. There at Clark Canyon Reservoir, my own testimony of my Heavenly Father and His Son were deepened and renewed and refreshed once again. And I am grateful for it.

There is an answer to those heart-wrenching and poignant questions expressed in the song sung by Primary children around the world:

Yes! I am really here!
Yes! I do hear and answer prayers.
And no, heaven is not so far away that I cannot reach you.

Notes

1. See Steven E. Ambrose, *Lewis and Clark: Voyage of Discovery* (Washington, D.C.: National Geographic Society, c2002), 114. Lewis made it clear that in his mind, the whole endeavor was on the verge of complete failure at that point.

2. George Washington, cited in W. Cleon Skousen, *The Five Thousand Year Leap* (Washington, D.C.: National Center for Constitutional Studies, 1981), 76.

3. *World Book: Millennium 2000*, s.v., "Lewis and Clark Expedition," 12:223.

4. Montana State website, http://lewisandclark.state.mt.us/sites.asp?IDNumber=15.

5. Discovering Lewis and Clark, http://lewis-clark.org/content/content-article .asp?ArticleID=1785.

6. Montana's GoldWest Country, http://goldwest.visitmt.com/specialfeatures/ lewisandclark/campfortunate.htm.

Index

of Paul, 108–10; Neal A. Maxwell
on, 218; of faith, 262–64
Truck driver, repentance of, 135–37
Turning point(s): missionary work and,
31–32; understanding Jesus Christ
as, 32–34; for Jewish convert, 34–
37; for Church of Evans member,
37–40

Vengeance, 129–30

War. *See* World War II
War with Mexico, 116–20
Washington, George, 260, 296–97
Weaknesses, 100–103
Webster, Ann Elizabeth Parsons, 90
Webster, Francis, 90–91
Whitney, Helen Mar, 107

Whitney, Horace K., 107
Whitney, Orson F., 82
Wilhelm Gustloff, 58–60
Williams, Thomas, 119
Willie, James, 88–90
Willie Handcart Company, 83–92
Will of God, 12–14, 266–69
Wood, M. Douglas, 243
The Work and the Glory, 136–37
World War II, 58–60, 244–49

Yoke, 202–4, 219–20
Young, Brigham: on trials, 3, 76; sends
aid for handcart companies, 86,
196–97; Mormon Battalion and,
117; on faithful women, 120; on
neglecting basic duties, 268